Rally 'round the Flag

RECENT TITLES IN

OXFORD STUDIES IN CULTURE AND POLITICS
Clifford Bob and James M. Jasper, General Editors

Gains and Losses
How Protestors Win and Lose
James M. Jasper, Luke Elliott-Negri,
Isaac Jabola-Carolus,
Marc Kagan, Jessica Mahlbacher, Manès
Weisskircher, and Anna Zhelnina

The Silk Road
Connecting Histories and Futures
Tim Winter

Unconventional Combat
Intersectional Action in the Veterans'
Peace Movement
Michael A. Messner

Discursive Turns and Critical Junctures
Debating Citizenship after the Charlie
Hebdo Attacks
Donatella della Porta, Pietro Castelli
Gattinara, Konstantinos Eleftheriadis,
and Andrea Felicetti

Democracy Reloaded
Inside Spain's Political Laboratory from
15-M to Podemos
Cristina Flesher Fominaya

Public Characters
The Politics of Reputation
and Blame
James M. Jasper, Michael P. Young,
and Elke Zuern

Empire's Legacy
Roots of a Far-Right Affinity in
Contemporary France
John W. P. Veugelers

Situational Breakdowns
Understanding Protest Violence and
Other Surprising Outcomes
Anne Nassauer

Democratic Practice
Origins of the Iberian Divide in Political
Inclusion
Robert M. Fishman

Contentious Rituals
Parading the Nation in Northern Ireland
Jonathan S. Blake

Contradictions of Democracy
Vigilantism and Rights in Post-Apartheid
South Africa
Nicholas Rush Smith

Plausible Legality
Legal Culture and Political Imperative in
the Global War on Terror
Rebecca Sanders

Legacies and Memories in Movements
Justice and Democracy in Southern Europe
Donatella della Porta, Massimiliano
Andretta, Tiago Fernandes,
Eduardo Romanos, and Markos
Vogiatzoglou

Taking Root
Human Rights and Public Opinion in the
Global South
James Ron, Shannon Golden,
David Crow, and Archana Pandya

Curated Stories
The Uses and Misuses of Storytelling
Sujatha Fernandes

The Human Right to Dominate
Nicola Perugini and Neve Gordon

Some Men
Feminist Allies and the Movement to End
Violence against Women
Michael A. Messner, Max A. Greenberg,
and Tal Peretz

Rally 'round the Flag

*The Search for National Honor and
Respect in Times of Crisis*

YUVAL FEINSTEIN

OXFORD
UNIVERSITY PRESS

Oxford University Press is a department of the University of Oxford. It furthers
the University's objective of excellence in research, scholarship, and education
by publishing worldwide. Oxford is a registered trade mark of Oxford University
Press in the UK and certain other countries.

Published in the United States of America by Oxford University Press
198 Madison Avenue, New York, NY 10016, United States of America.

Library of Congress Control Number: 2022935965
ISBN 978–0–19–762971–0

DOI: 10.1093/oso/9780197629710.001.0001

1 3 5 7 9 8 6 4 2

Printed by Integrated Books International, United States of America

Contents

Preface   vii
Acknowledgments   ix

INTRODUCTION

1. The Puzzling Rally-round-the-Flag Phenomenon   3

PART I. THEORY

2. The Rally Phenomenon in Light of Competing Approaches to Public Opinion   23

3. Why Do People *Really* Rally? Context, Actors, Meaning, and Emotions   38

PART II. INVESTIGATION

4. A Plan for Solving the Rally Puzzle   73

5. Saving the Nation's Face: Rallies in Militarized Conflicts   83

6. Standing Up Proudly: Rallies in the Aftermath of Attacks on the Nation   121

7. On the Verge of a Rally: Borderline Cases   136

8. Chivalrous Struggles: Rallies for Saving the Free World   145

9. War That Feels Good: The Role of Emotions in the Emergence of Rally Periods   163

CONCLUSION

10. Moving Forward: Directions for Future Research on the Rally-round-the-Flag Phenomenon   191

Appendix   197
Notes   217
References   241
Index   259

Contents

Preface

This book is about the emergence of rally-round-the-flag periods in the United States in response to military actions and security crises. However, the book was born out of an experience related to a war between Israel and Palestinian armed organizations. In late December 2008, Israel initiated a large military operation against Palestinian armed forces in Gaza, which had launched rockets on Israel. I was born and raised in Israel, but at the time I was living in the United States and attending graduate school in the Sociology Department at the University of California, Los Angeles. One afternoon, while riding my bike to campus, I passed by the tall federal building on Wilshire Boulevard and noticed two groups of protesters, one on each side of the road, waving flags and signs. One group waved Israeli flags and held signs supporting the Israel Defense Forces and the military operation. The other group waved Palestinian flags and held signs calling for both an end to the attack on Gaza and the liberation of Palestine. For a brief moment, I found myself experiencing an affection for the people rallying in support of Israel and feeling somewhat disturbed by the seemingly anti-Israel sentiment of the other protest. These feelings, ephemeral as they were, caught me very much by surprise. Years of service in the Israeli military, including in the West Bank, had forged my antipathy toward war and my criticism of the Israeli maltreatment of the Palestinian people. My subsequent studies at the Sociology Department at the University of Haifa had given me words to express these feelings and beliefs and had helped me turn these emerging thoughts into serious intellectual questions. The strong dissonance between my intellectual views and my affective reaction to the protests, which occurred thousands of miles away from the conflict zone and my homeland, was a defining moment in the formation of my research agenda. My quest to decipher the role that national identity and emotions play in rallying people behind military actions and the leaders who order them arose from that personal experience.

Acknowledgments

Several institutions and many people have assisted me in the various stages of research and writing that led to this book. Uri Ben-Eliezer was my first academic mentor at the University of Haifa and has remained a dear colleague and friend. I am grateful beyond words for the encouragement and emotional and intellectual support Uri has kindly provided for many years. In my doctoral studies at UCLA, Andreas Wimmer became my second mentor and my dissertation advisor. I will always be indebted to Andreas for his mentorship and support, which were vital for the development of this book. I would also like to thank UCLA professors Rogers Brubaker, Michel Mann, David O. Sears, and the late Robert D. Mare, all of whom contributed tremendously to the initial stages of my research on the rally-round-the-flag phenomenon. My graduate school colleagues have been an essential source of intellectual stimulation and comfort. This book benefited directly from the wisdom and knowledge of Marie Berry, Philippe Duhart, Eric Hamiton, Wesley Hiers, and Zeynep Ozgen.

I wrote most of this book as a faculty member in the Sociology Department at the University of Haifa. I am grateful to my colleagues in the Department for their friendship. I was also fortunate to have the assistance of several graduate students at the University of Haifa: Elinor Atari, Linoy Groisman, Yaara Pur, Gal Yadlin, and Anan Zaher. I completed the book during my time as a visiting scholar at the Weatherhead Center for International Affairs and as a visiting associate professor in the Sociology Department at Harvard University. I am especially grateful to Michèle Lamont for her kindness and the wisdom she shared with me during my time at Harvard.

I would like to thank Jennifer Eggerling-Boeck for editing the text of this book, Sivan Trachtenberg-Mills for helping with the cover design, Leonie Huddy for sharing the TNSS data I analyze in Chapter 9, and a librarian at the Oral History Center in Columbia University whose name I have regrettably forgotten but whose kindness was unforgettable. I am also grateful to four anonymous reviewers who provided helpful comments on a draft of this book, James Cook and Emily Mackenzie Benitez at the Oxford University Press for helping me turn a book manuscript into a book, and James Jasper and Clifford Bob, who edit the Oxford Studies in Culture and Politics series. The University of Haifa provided generous financial support for the publication of this book.

I have presented parts of the book in several academic forums and received helpful feedback, for which I am thankful. I reserve special thanks for Bart Bonikowski, my friend and research partner, whose writing on nationalism inspires me and who supported me at critical junctures in the process of writing the book.

Last but certainly not least, I am grateful for the love and support of my family: my parents and siblings, my lovely wife Lotem and her parents and siblings, and my wonderful daughters Idan, Gal, and Tom.

INTRODUCTION

1

The Puzzling Rally-round-the-Flag Phenomenon

The phrase "rally-round-the-flag" has been an American cultural idiom since the Civil War, when George Fredrick Root used the expression in his 1862 pro-unionist poem, *Battle Cry of Freedom*. Since the early 1970s the idiom has also appeared in studies of public opinion as a scientific concept denoting "a surge of patriotism and public approval for [the president's] administration and its policies during an international crisis" (Baker and Oneal 2001: 661). Most of the literature on public opinion in the United States has identified rally-round-the-flag periods based on a spike in presidential job-approval ratings. Such spikes have occurred several times in the past 75 years, for example, during the Cuban Missile Crisis in 1962, President Kennedy's job-approval rating rose from 62 percent to 74 percent; following the invasion of Panama in December 1989, President George H. W. Bush's job-approval rating increased from 71 percent to 80 percent; at the beginning of the first Gulf War in 1991, 86 percent of Americans approved of President Bush's performance as president, an increase of 28 percentage points from his prior approval rating; following the September 11 attacks and the invasion of Afghanistan in October 2001, President George W. Bush's approval rating increased from 57 percent to 90 percent; and at the onset of the Iraq War in March 2003, three-quarters of the American public supported the war and an estimated 71 percent approved of the way President Bush was handling his job, an increase of 13 percentage points from his earlier approval rating.[1]

In brief, a rally-round-the-flag effect emerges when, in response to a major conflict that entails direct US involvement—specifically, in response to a military operation or security crisis—many citizens who previously opposed a sitting president or were indifferent become supporters (Edwards and Swenson 1997; Groeling and Baum 2008: 1028), thus elevating presidential approval ratings from the range prevalent during "normal" times (30–60 percent for most presidents) to the range evident during rally periods (70–90 percent during most rallies). Following John Mueller's (1970,

Rally 'round the Flag. Yuval Feinstein, Oxford University Press. © Oxford University Press 2022.
DOI: 10.1093/oso/9780197629710.003.0001

1973) seminal study, which identified rally-round-the-flag periods in public support for sitting presidents in the United States, the bulk of the research about the rally phenomenon has focused on the United States. The phenomenon, however, is not unique to this country. Studies have also identified rally periods in other countries, including Britain (Lai and Reiter 2005; Lanoue and Headrick 1998; Norpoth 1987), Germany (Bytzek 2011), France (Georgarakis 2017), Russia (Hale 2018; Theiler 2018; Yudina 2015), and Israel (Feinstein 2018).

This book continues the geographic focus initiated by Mueller's work by examining US rallies, especially those that occurred after 1950 (the era when polling firms began to regularly collect reliable data on presidential job-approval ratings). This examination of the rally phenomenon includes three complementary parts. First, after reviewing the prominent current arguments about political attitude formation during military conflicts (Chapter 2), I develop a novel theoretical framework that diverges from these arguments (Chapter 3). Next, I conduct an extensive comparative-historical investigation of public reactions to US military actions and security crises in the years 1950–2020, with the goal of identifying the unique conditions under which only a few of these events generated rallies (Chapters 4–8). Finally, I analyze data from surveys and opinion polls to detect the individual-level mechanisms that drive attitudinal change during rally periods (Chapter 9). While this book investigates the rally-round-the-flag effect in the United States, its core theoretical argument about the phenomenon, which highlights people's desire to protect the honor and prestige of their national group when these precious collective symbolic assets seem to be in decline or at risk, likely applies to other countries as well; in the concluding chapter (Chapter 10), I outline several ideas for extending and adapting the book's argument in research about rallies in other countries.

An Empirical Puzzle

The rally-round-the-flag effect constitutes a fascinating empirical puzzle. What causes public opinion in the United States, which is usually organized around partisan and ideological identities (Gries 2014; Jacobson 2010), to temporarily become harmonious and in some rally periods almost monolithic? What causes members of the public, a large portion of whom often express skepticism about or even mistrust of politicians, to set aside these attitudes and close ranks behind the government during rally periods?

The first studies of public opinion that mentioned the rally phenomenon (Mueller 1970, 1973; Polsby 1964; Waltz 1967) offered a simple explanation: in response to dramatic international events with direct US involvement,[2] patriotic citizens who wish to see their country succeed in the international arena close ranks behind the sitting president—John Mueller (1970: 22) once described the rally phenomenon as a "let's-get-behind-the-president" effect. However, the investigation for this book reveals that, in the focal period (which covers the administrations of thirteen US presidents, from Harry Truman to Donald Trump), while there were numerous major international conflicts that directly involved the United States, including many major war events and security crises, fewer than a dozen of these engendered rally-round-the-flag periods (see Appendix, Figures A1–A13).

Remarkably, more often than not, political attitudes in the United States in general, and attitudes about the sitting president in particular, remain relatively stable in the aftermath of extraordinary international events that entail US involvement. For example, in the spring of 1960, a US spy plane was shot down near Soviet air space, and a subsequent attempt by the US administration to cover up the event was exposed in a public speech given by the Soviet Union's leader Nikita Khrushchev, causing the United States major embarrassment in the international arena. Surprisingly, the available evidence suggests that the "U-2 Incident," which made the headlines of all major news outlets in the United States and became a pinnacle of the Cold War, had no noticeable (positive or negative) influence on the popularity of President Eisenhower.[3]

Perhaps even more surprising is the lack of a surge in support for President Reagan during the invasion of Grenada (October 25–29, 1983) or following the United States' victory in Grenada, even though the official rhetoric highlighted the geopolitical importance of this military operation by linking it to the larger US effort to block the expansion of Moscow's influence in the Western Hemisphere.[4] Further, victory was achieved quickly, and the conflict claimed relatively few US lives. Why didn't this successful military confrontation and its perceived international context give Reagan's job-approval rating a significant boost?[5]

The invasion of Grenada is one of several "negative" cases discussed in this book. Taken together, these cases suggest that the rally-round-the-flag effect does not emerge as an automatic, "Pavlovian" response of the US public to international competition or conflict.[6] Instead, the phenomenon emerges only under specific conditions. The goal of this book is, therefore, to explain precisely when, why, and how rally outcomes have emerged in the United States. This book applies a comparative method, investigating events that did and did not produce a rally-round-the-flag effect. This research framework, which I elaborate in Chapter 4 and apply in Chapters 5–8, moves away from the correlational or probabilistic arguments of past research on rallies, and toward conjunctural causal argument. In other words, rather than pointing to distinct conditions that made the emergence of a rally more *likely*, I seek to identify sets of conditions that, when co-present, were *sufficient* for the emergence of a rally. This unique research strategy leads to a conclusion that differs markedly from the initial explanation of the rally-round-the-flag phenomenon.

The Essence of the Argument

In short, this book shows that the rally-round-the-flag effect is a relatively rare phenomenon that has emerged only under a narrow set of conditions— specifically, conditions related to the characteristics of events, the historical circumstances, and the reactions of national leaders—that convinced the majority of Americans it was necessary to take military action to maintain or restore collective honor and gain the respect of other nations. This type of assessment and meaning-making evokes strong positive feelings about an expected or ongoing military engagement with a national enemy, which in turn motivates people to rally behind their commander-in-chief.

My explanation of the emergence of a rally-round-the-flag phenomenon in the United States (developed in detail in Chapter 3) has two layers. The first layer focuses on *individual-level mechanisms* that emerge during rally periods and motivate people who are usually critical of the president, are un- decided, or are generally uninterested in politics to shift to approving of the president's work. I contend that people rally behind a sitting president when three circumstances converge: (1) they feel that the nation should reclaim its honor and its respect from other nations; (2) they believe that the president's military tactics will make this possible; and (3) therefore they experience strong emotions that prompt them to rally behind the president (especially high levels of national pride, strong confidence in the capability of the United States to win wars, and hope that taking military action against America's enemies will lead to a better future). This set of arguments, which centers on concerns about the symbolic value of the nation and the emotions that are triggered by such concerns, differs markedly from competing arguments (reviewed in Chapter 2 and tested in Chapter 9) that attribute political attitudes during violent conflicts to the rational assessment of military policies or concerns about security threats.

The second layer of the explanation shifts the focus from individuals to events, specifying the *conditions and processes that propel people to believe that military action is required in order to claim national honor and prestige.* There are two preconditions that can catalyze a public demand to claim national honor and prestige through war: (1) a preexisting feeling of national humiliation due to a previous military defeat or diplomatic fiasco, or (2) a call from the United Nations to the United States to lead the free world in a struggle against a regime that violates the world order, which conveys a recognition of the moral leadership of the United States. However, neither precondition, by itself, is sufficient to generate a rally-round-the-flag effect. I argue that in the context of one of these preconditions, three factors jointly generate a rally: (1) *intense media coverage* of events that adopts a celebratory tone, which charges the event with a special symbolic meaning of testing what most members of the nation perceive to be the nation's core elements: the common qualities of members (e.g., courage and determination), solidarity among compatriots, their shared values, and its unique place in the world of nations; (2) *an enemy who puts up a fight* against the United States and thus becomes the target of a military attack through which the nation can demonstrate its special collective virtue; and (3) presidential *nation-affirming rhetoric*, which highlights the implications of a military confrontation with the enemy for the honor of the nation and the respect it receives from other nations.

My argument about the conditions that stimulate the emergence of rallies in US public opinion differs markedly from those in the extant literature. One line of previous arguments suggests that rallies follow directly from certain types of events, and thus overlooks the process through which an event becomes a rally point. A second line of argumentation highlights the role of "opinion leaders" (i.e., politicians and the media) who influence public opinion during rally periods, but fails to acknowledge that rallies are co-produced by the general public—the ordinary people who evaluate the messages they receive from public speakers. Further, in contrast to prior research on the rally-round-the-flag phenomenon, my argument about the emergence of rallies is non-probabilistic: rather than pointing to distinct conditions that make a rally more likely, I argue that several concurrent conditions are jointly sufficient for the emergence of a rally (Chapters 5–8 discuss several sets of jointly sufficient conditions).

Setting the Stage for Understanding the Emergence of a Rally

Defining and Measuring Rally-round-the-Flag

Following Mueller's original conceptualization, most studies define the rally-round-the-flag effect as a sharp increase in public satisfaction with the work of the head of the government (the president, or the prime minister in parliamentary democracies). A few studies have extended this definition to include an increase in confidence in national institutions, a spike in the number of citizens (in parliamentary democracies) who intend to vote for the ruling party in the next election (Lai and Reiter 2005), or growth in public trust in subnational governmental institutions (Hetherington and Nelson 2003; Parker 1995). The current study adopts the narrower and more common conceptualization and operationalization of rallies, which are limited to public approval for the head of state. The reason for this choice is practical: the only potential variable for which reliable data have been collected frequently over a long time span (and thus are suitable for detecting and measuring rally effects) is the public approval rating of the president.[7]

While in this book, the focal indicator of a rally-round-the-flag effect is a transition among members of the public from being unsatisfied with the president's work or being undecided to being satisfied with the president's work, a parallel occurrence is the transition of many people from being somewhat satisfied with the president's work to being very satisfied. This type of transition, which is most likely to occur within the president's own political camp, cannot be readily detected with conventional public opinion data in the United States because most opinion polls measure approval or disapproval of the president's work on a three-point scale: disapprove, approve, or have no opinion. More nuanced measures would allow researchers to detect people's transitions from relatively weak approval of the president's work to stronger approval; however, such measures were not consistently included in opinion polls during the period examined in this book.

Data limitations aside, there are good reasons to pay closer attention to the former type of attitude shift than the latter. Theoretically, increased satisfaction with the president among the president's political "base" is less puzzling than the transition of many people outside the president's constituency from being critical or undecided to being at least somewhat supportive. Moreover, shifts outside the constituency may have significant political implications (discussed later in this chapter) because they boost the president's overall job-approval rating. To summarize, for both theoretical and practical reasons, this book focuses on temporary shifts in which people who are usually critical of the president or hold no opinion about the president's work move toward approval. I understand this type of shift, when it occurs among many people at roughly the same time, as the defining characteristic of the rally-round-the-flag phenomenon.

Who Rallies?

A preliminary question in the search for an explanation for the rally phenomenon is "Who actually rallies?" People differ in their propensity to rally behind the president, and no rally has ever included the entire population. In general, people who do not hold strong attitudes in the first place are more likely to experience a shift in attitudes because these people may change their minds in response to changing circumstances. This general principle applies to rally processes: people who hold relatively weak negative views about the president and/or whose general attitude toward politics can be characterized as moderate apathy are the most likely to shift to supporting the president during rally periods. Therefore, while ardent supporters of the president certainly become even more enthusiastic during a rally-round-the-flag period, it is individuals who do not already support the president, but can experience a change of heart due to the rally effect, who actually produce rally outcomes (Groeling and Baum 2008: 1028; Baum 2002).

The extent to which political attitudes in general, and views about the sitting president in particular, are rigid or flexible and vary by context likely depends on certain characteristics of individuals that are linked to their membership in social categories such as class, race/ethnicity, gender, age, and level of education. One important characteristic that influences people's likelihood of being part of a rally is their level of political awareness (Perrin and Smolek 2009: 143). Shifts in political attitudes are especially unlikely for individuals with extremely low levels of political awareness (Zaller 1991), be-cause they are more likely than others to remain detached from politics and the public discourse during rally periods.

Rallying is also unlikely for individuals with very *high* levels of political awareness because they tend to have solid policy preferences and identify strongly with one of the political parties. Among those with high levels of political awareness, members of the president's party cannot become *new* supporters of the president, because they already support him. Ardent supporters of the opposition party are also unlikely to begin supporting the president (Edwards and Swenson 1997), whom they see as a bitter political rival. Moreover, having a strong partisan identity may systematically influence people's evaluations of any new information about the president and his policies: studies show that strong advocates of the opposition party are more likely than other citizens to skip, dismiss, or distort positive informa-tion about the president and his policies and are especially eager to embrace information that lends itself to a negative evaluation of the president and his policies (Jacobson 2010).[8]

To summarize, among the citizens who do not approve of the president before a rally, those most likely to shift to approval are individuals who nor-mally maintain at least some level of interest in politics but do not hold strong ideological and political identities. These people's views of the president are malleable and can shift (under rally-producing circumstances) from nega-tive or indifferent to supportive.

Stronger and Weaker Rallies

Rally periods vary in their magnitude: some have been stronger and lasted longer (e.g., the aftermath of the September 11 attacks), while others have been weaker and shorter (e.g., the aftermath of the *Mayaguez* incident in 1975, discussed in Chapter 5). While a full consideration of the variation in the intensity and duration of rally-round-the-flag effects is beyond the scope of this book (but see Baum 2002), four conditions that influence the magni-tude of rally effects merit a brief discussion.

The first condition is the objective characteristics of the rally-producing event. Not all conflicts with external actors (a country or other organization or group) have produced rally reactions in the United States—indeed, not even all violent conflicts have evoked rally reactions. Only massive attacks against American civilian targets and US military operations have produced rallies. Certainly, the intensity of the event is one factor that influences the strength and duration of a rally effect. For example, the scale of the horrific events of the September 11 attacks surely increased the magnitude of the public reaction.

The next two conditions are related to subjective interpretations of the situation. Media broadcasts that are focused on wars and security crises influence the magnitude of rally effects. Rally effects tend to be stronger if mass media channels shift to around-the-clock live broadcasting of the events or at least keep the events at the center of public attention, and if the content of the broadcast induces a feeling among the public such that, while they are alert to and worried about security threats, they also experience a sense of festivity and national pride about an ongoing or expected US military action (this issue is discussed in detail in Chapter 3).

Rally outcomes also tend to be stronger if the political elite (in particular, senators and members of Congress) closes ranks behind the views and policy presented to the public by the president, and tend to be weaker if oppositional voices challenge the president's interpretation and the wisdom of his policy. For example, (as discussed in Chapter 9) in the aftermath of the September 11 attacks the entire political elite rallied behind President Bush, and about 90 percent of Americans joined the subsequent rally behind Bush and the declared "war on terror"; in contrast, during the 2003 invasion of Iraq, about a quarter of US citizens (mostly Democratic voters) refrained from rallying behind Bush because some members of the opposition Democratic Party, and even a few Republicans, had criticized the motives and justification for the war (Baum and Potter 2008: 40).

The fourth condition that influences the size of a rally effect is the public's view of the president *before* the rally. Specifically, the extent and intensity of public opposition to a president during "non-rally" periods constrains the increase in popularity that a president enjoys during a rally period. The previous public view of the president affects the magnitude of rallies in two seemingly opposite ways. On one hand, a stronger rally may emerge if prior to the rally period a president and his policies were relatively unpopular, because there is significant room for improvement (i.e., there can be a sharp increase in public approval if the initial ratings were low; Baum 2002). On the other hand, certain factors that make a president unpopular on the eve of a rally process—for example, the president's personality, his past actions and policies, the state of the economy, and the geopolitical conditions—may limit the public approval ratings of the president, meaning that an extremely unpopular president may not be able to achieve a very high level of approval, even during rally periods. For example, before the Iran hostage crisis began, Jimmy Carter was a very unpopular president, so even though there was a rally period during the crisis, Carter's public approval ratings peaked at a relatively lower point (Carter's ratings before and during the Iran hostage crisis are discussed in Chapter 6).

Moreover, leaders who seek to rally the public multiple times may lose credibility, and this "audience cost" (Fearon 1994) may reduce the potential for a massive rally effect. This scenario may be especially likely if, in previous rally periods, leaders' policies failed to restore national honor and prestige; in this case, a later attempt by the leader to mobilize a rally may become a referendum on their leadership. For example, in Israel, the 2014 war with Hamas in Gaza evoked a massive rally behind Prime Minister Netanyahu (Feinstein 2018); however, a similar confrontation with Hamas in 2021 did not evoke a rally even though Netanyahu used a similar nationalist rhetoric and an overwhelming majority of Israelis supported taking military action against Hamas.[9]

In the United States in the period examined in this book, two presidents experienced more than one rally during their presidency. In the case of George H. W. Bush, the rally effect of the 1991 Gulf War was even stronger than the effect of the invasion of Panama in 1989 (perhaps because the latter event achieved its main goals and thus did not leave a bitter taste in the mouths of Americans). In contrast, during George W. Bush's presidency, the rally effect of the September 11 attacks was more substantial than a later rally in the aftermath of the Iraq invasion, but it is likely that this difference was due primarily to the unique characteristics of the events: a horrific terrorist attack of unprecedented scale on the United States generated a stronger rally effect than a controversial invasion of another country. At any rate, there is insufficient evidence to reach a conclusion about the impact of initial rallies on later rallies. Further, presidents who repeatedly *attempt* to mobilize public opinion by playing the nationalist card—whether or not they are successful—may reduce the potential for the emergence of a substantial rally behind their leadership (this might have been the case for the anti-terrorism rhetoric of Ronald Regan discussed in Chapter 7, but a thorough investigation of this possibility remains outside the scope of this book).

To summarize, the size and duration of a rally effect depend on the intensity of the rally-producing event, the media coverage of the event and subsequent developments, the reactions of the political elite, and the public's previous view of the president.[10] Although this book does not focus on the size and duration of rally effects, these factors are important to consider because understanding the emergence of a rally period requires understanding the conditions that are necessary for a sufficiently large number of Americans to transition to approval of the president so that the cumulative outcome of their transition is a rally-round-the-flag effect.

Crucially, however, even when all four conditions that jointly create the potential for a sizable rally effect in the United States—a significant international or military confrontation, extensive media coverage of an event, a relatively united political elite, and a large number of ordinary citizens who do not hold strong opinions about the president—are present, several additional conditions must arise for a rally-round-the-flag effect to emerge. In the period examined in this book, significant rally effects emerged when the *content* of media reports, the rhetoric of sitting presidents, and the portrayal of the actions of US enemies by public speakers and the media transformed confrontations with enemies into symbolic struggles for collective honor and respect. Further, in most cases in which rallies emerged, the efforts to charge events with such a profound meaning for the perceived collective worth were bolstered by a preexisting public feeling of collective humiliation caused by previous confrontations with enemies. Chapter 3 develops a more nuanced argument about the rally process in the United States, and Chapters 4–9 present empirical evidence for this argument.

Why Are Rallies Important? The Political Implications

A rally in public support for the government can have serious implications for policymaking, especially if that effect is substantial and lingering. During rally periods, relatively low levels of political polarization and an overall positive public mood may lead policymakers to take actions they would otherwise be reluctant to take, such as starting or escalating a war and restricting certain civil liberties.

Changes in public mood and opinion are more likely to influence policymaking in democratic countries than in countries with non-democratic regimes, because in democracies political parties and elected officials who seek re-election tend to be concerned about their overall popularity, as well as about public approval ratings for specific policies (Russett 1990).[11]

Therefore, rally-round-the-flag processes give governments more leeway to pursue their preferred policies. During some rallies, politicians may even implement policies without proper deliberation or sufficient supervision by Congress (or the parliament), because some members of opposition parties themselves are rallying around the flag, and those who are not rallying nonetheless feel compelled to show support for the government or at least refrain from criticizing the government in order to avoid appearing unpatriotic.

Further, the policies developed and implemented during rally periods may have especially dramatic consequences in the context of an ongoing or anticipated war. In times of war, rally-round-the-flag periods are characterized by widespread agreement that the country is fighting a just war and the government is handling the situation in a satisfactory way. During rally periods, support for aggressive war policies is not based on well-informed, rational-strategic assessments of the military policy and its potential outcomes. Instead, among decision-makers and ordinary citizens alike, a rally-round-the-flag reaction generates overconfidence about the chances of winning the war. High levels of confidence that "our side" will win represent what Kahneman and Renshon (2009) called "positive illusions" and Lawrence LeShan (1992) called the "mythical evaluation of reality." This type of confidence is not based on rational assessments of the power of the two (or more) opposing sides in a conflict, but on people's strong identification with the government and the military, which serve as symbols and guarantors of national sovereignty, and the projection of the assumed superiority of the nation onto these institutions. In addition, the experience of a positive mood creates an optimism bias in people's assessments of future outcomes and thus a stronger tendency toward risk-taking (Druckman and McDermott 2008: 300). An overconfidence about the chances of winning a war makes people both more likely to support military actions and more willing to tolerate war casualties, including a large number of casualties on "our" side (Gelpi, Feaver, and Reifler 2006).

In addition to sparking overconfidence, rally periods involve an increase in militancy, driven by the rage people feel because of the actions and intentions they attribute to the enemy. This rage makes the nation's members seek retaliation and at the same time overlook or dismiss the imminent hazards of military confrontation and their potential negative long-term consequences (Huddy, Feldman, and Cassese 2007).

To summarize, the public mood during rally periods in the United States—especially the righteous anger and overconfidence about the power of the nation—provides a tailwind for the passage of aggressive policies aimed at external enemies. Precisely how much weight national leaders give to public opinion when deciding on foreign and military policies is the topic of an ongoing scholarly debate that is largely outside the scope of this book. The notion that politicians make foreign-policy decisions based partly on their assessment of the policy's future impact on public opinion (Zaller 1994a: 250–51) is probably accurate, especially for leaders in democratic countries who seek re-election. However, equally true is the notion that making significant policy decisions is more likely when the public rallies around the flag and offers support for the policy and the leaders. In particular, the decision to send troops to risk their lives in a war (that is also economically costly) is easier to make when the public has the government's back or when leaders believe that the public will close ranks behind their war policy. The US intervention in the 1990–1991 Persian Gulf crisis is a useful example. There is fairly strong evidence that President Bush did not give much weight to public opinion when making his initial decision to intervene in the crisis (Zaller 1994a: 252–55). However, there is also compelling evidence that when the Bush administration decided to deploy a massive US military force to the Gulf, they kept an eye on domestic public opinion and sought to bolster public support (Zaller 1994: 258).

In addition to having a potential impact on the executive branch, a rally can have a serious impact on the political opposition in the legislative branch when legislators are asked to authorize the use of military force and approve a special war budget. During rally periods, concerns about electoral retribution may prompt the leaders of opposition parties to refrain from publicly criticizing the government or taking actions to restrict its power. This was the case in January 1991, when the US Congress voted to authorize President George H. W. Bush to use "all necessary means" to force Iraq to withdraw from Kuwait (Zaller 1994a: 260–70).

In addition to influencing foreign and military policies, the public mood during rally periods may spur the passage of problematic domestic policies that restrict civil liberties. In particular, at times, aggressive policies that are motivated by an uninhibited desire to retaliate against perceived enemies of the nation also encompass actions directed toward domestic minorities who are suspected of being disloyal to the country and potentially a fifth column (secret supporters of the enemy engaging in sabotage and/or espionage within the nation's borders) because they share an ethnic identity and/or religious affiliation with the enemy. Such policies were passed during World War

II, when the United States incarcerated Japanese Americans in concentration camps after the attack on Pearl Harbor, as well as after the September 11 attacks, in the form of actions taken against Muslims and Arabs. According to Louise Cainkar (2009: 119), after the September 11 attacks, the US government implemented policies directed at Arabs and Muslims living in the United States that permitted "mass arrests, secret and indefinite detentions, prolonged detention of 'material witnesses,' closed hearings and the use of secret evidence, government eavesdropping on attorney-client conversations, FBI home and work visits, wiretapping, seizures of property, removals of aliens with technical visa violations, freezing assets of charities, and mandatory special registration."

Many of these problematic policies were enacted under the umbrella of the Patriot Act, which was passed in October 2001, at the peak of the September 11 rally period. The fact that the Patriot Act, which expands government agencies' authority to infringe upon civil liberties for security purposes, was approved after only a relatively brief discussion and by an extremely large majority in the US House of Representatives and almost unanimously in the US Senate, is a telling example of how the public mood that emerges during a rally period removes some of the restrictions on the operation of the executive branch of the government, allowing it to implement policies that it would otherwise be reluctant or unable to pursue.

The Broader Issues

While the book focuses on a relatively infrequent phenomenon of public opinion in the United States (the rally-round-the-flag effect), the analysis of this phenomenon helps to establish several broader principles of public opinion (in the United States and elsewhere). First, while this book reinforces prior research by students of political rhetoric, media scholars, and some experts on public opinion that highlights the key role of politicians and the media in steering public opinion, and extends this work by illustrating the contribution of political leaders and the media to the rally-round-the-flag phenomenon, the investigation also shows that the public does not passively absorb the messages of so-called opinion leaders (Kertzer and Zeitzoff 2017). Rather, political attitudes are co-produced from below through an *interaction* between the rhetoric and symbols employed by leaders and the media and the attitudinal and affective dispositions of ordinary people, which are rooted in their identities, subjective memories, beliefs based on past events, and assessments of the current situation and potential future developments.

Second, the analysis contained in this book indicates that rational choice theory, which has been the preferred theoretical perspective of prominent scholars of public opinion in the United States (Gartner and Segura 2000; Larson 1996; Larson and Savych 2005; Eichenberg, Stoll, and Lebo 2006; and perhaps most surprisingly, many students of public opinion during wars: Eichenberg 2005; Voeten and Brewer 2006; Lorell et al. 1985; Russett 1990: 46), is an inadequate framework for explaining political attitudes (Druckman and McDermott 2008: 298; see Chapter 2 for a more detailed discussion). Notably, the explanation proposed herein for attitude formation during rally periods highlights the central role of emotions, reflecting an increasingly influential approach to political attitudes that highlights the role of affective reactions in attitude formation (Clore, Gasper, and Garvin 2000; Peters et al. 2006; Schwarz and Clore 2003; Slovic et al. 2007). It is particularly important to consider the role of affective reactions in public opinion about foreign affairs events and policy (the type of events and policies that take center stage in this book) because many Americans are not well informed about these policies and events and thus tend to rely on their gut feelings to develop an opinion (Gries 2014: 43). Further, the focus of my theorization of individual-level attitudinal shifts during rally periods is also inspired by studies on the role of emotions in social movement mobilization (Aminzade and McAdam 2001; Emirbayer and Goldberg 2005; Goodwin, Jasper, and Polletta 2004; Flam and King 2007; Jasper 1998), and by studies of emotions in violent ethnic conflicts, which show that emotions are the key mechanism driving individuals' attitudinal and behavioral shifts (toward greater militancy) during heated ethnic conflicts (Horowitz 1985: 140; Petersen 2002; Kaufman 2001; Tambiah 1996).

Third, the theoretical framework for the discussion links rally-producing emotions to national identities, and more specifically, to the way that, during rally processes, the public discourse uses certain aspects of a perceived collective national identity to make sense of events and policies and assess their impact on the national group. Mueller's (1970, 1973) original explanation of the rally-round-the-flag phenomenon—which highlighted the public's desire to see their national leader gain the upper hand in international conflicts—seems to assume that salient national identities play an essential role in rally processes. However, Mueller did not elaborate on precisely how national identities influence attitude formation during rally periods, except to assert that people tend to stand behind national leaders during conflicts. Many subsequent studies have continued to presume that rallies are simply consequences of people's deep-seated commitment to support their nation during conflicts with other nations; like Mueller, these studies have assumed a direct causal link between international conflicts and rallies at home. However, if the rally-round-the-flag phenomenon resulted from a straight-forward attitudinal tendency, every international conflict would generate a rally. That has not been the case in the United States, at least not in the period examined in this book. Indeed, relatively few international conflicts gener-ated significant rallies during this period. Therefore, this book develops a more nuanced analysis of when and how national identities help transform events into rally periods. By doing so, the book contributes to an ongoing de-bate about how national identities (as well as other types of identities, such as partisan, ideological, and religious identities) influence the formation of political attitudes.

Fourth, over the last few decades, the research pendulum in the field of nationalism studies has swung from the postwar interest in the eruptive, emotional, and sometimes "dark" side of nationalism—which exposes itself most clearly in wartime, in the activity of national liberation movements, and the actions of the ultranationalist far right in established nation-states—to a current focus on a widely diffused national sentiment (Billig 1995; Merriman and Jones 2017) and the transient (mostly benign) modes of national identification that emerge in various social contexts (Antonsich 2016; Brubaker 2006; Fox and Miller-Idriss 2008). While the growing in-terest in "everyday" nationalism has contributed tremendously to the schol-arly understanding of how diffused national identities endure (Bonikowski 2016: 431–35), the other side of nationalism's Janus face—that is, the capacity of national identities to cause irregular attitudinal and behavioral reactions to changing circumstances—is now often taken for granted and thus remains undertheorized.[12] This book contributes to a better understanding of the way nationalism operates as a motivational force in politics, specifically in periods of transition from "banal" to "hot" nationalism, which are charac-terized by intense emotions centered on the nation and its relationship with domestic or foreign others.

Outline of the Book

Part I of the book presents a theoretical discussion of the rally-round-the-flag effect. Chapter 2 examines the rally phenomenon in light of prominent theoretical approaches to public opinion in the United States. The chapter explains why each of these extant approaches falls short of explaining the rally phenomenon, but identifies several specific elements of these approaches as useful for the proposed explanation of rallies. Chapter 3 presents the theoretical framework used for the analysis of rallies in this book.

Part II of the book examines the emergence of rally-round-the-flag periods during wars and security crises after 1950. Chapter 4 outlines the analytical framework that is used in subsequent chapters to determine the necessary conditions for rally periods and the mechanisms that transform events into rally periods. Chapters 5–8 present a comparative examination of the US public reactions to a large set of wars and security crises. In particular, these chapters compare and contrast the events that triggered rally-round-the-flag reactions to those that had similar characteristics but nonetheless did not evoke rally reactions. Chapter 5 discusses the emergence of rallies during four military confrontations: the 1962 Cuban Missile Crisis, the 1975 *Mayaguez* incident, the 1989 invasion of Panama, and the 2003 invasion of Iraq. The analysis shows that the rally reactions to these military confrontations were driven by a desire to restore collective honor and gain the respect of other nations via military retaliation against despised enemies. Chapter 6 illustrates a similar mechanism (i.e., a desire to claim collective honor and prestige through retaliation) driving the public reactions to two major attacks against American civilian targets: the Iran hostage crisis and the September 11 attacks.

Chapter 7 further establishes the importance of key elements of the causal claim made in Chapters 5 and 6. This chapter focuses on several events that were on the verge of becoming rally points, but did not ultimately evoke rally reactions in the public because certain conditions that are necessary for the emergence of rally-round-the-flag effects were absent.

Chapter 8 discusses a distinct path to the emergence of a rally-round-the-flag effect that stems from the special position of the United States as a global superpower, focusing on the 1991 Gulf War as an example. The chapter shows how, under specific conditions, the American public rallied behind a president's goal of demonstrating the international leadership of the United

States by leading a coalition of armies in a joint operation against countries who were perceived as violating the world order.

Chapter 9 zooms in on the individual-level mechanisms that drive the development of a rally-round-the-flag effect by analyzing survey data collected during and between two rally periods: the months after the September 11 attacks, and the time during the 2003 invasion of Iraq. This chapter highlights the role of positive emotions centered on membership in the nation, which emerge during rally processes.

Chapter 10 concludes by proposing directions for future research on rallies in both the United States and other countries.

PART I
THEORY

2

The Rally Phenomenon
in Light of Competing Approaches
to Public Opinion

Numerous studies on public opinion in the United States have pointed to rally-round-the-flag periods as deviations from the usual pattern of political attitudes in the country, but very few have investigated the rally phenomenon in a systematic manner, perhaps because scholars were satisfied with the initial explanation proposed in the late 1960s and early 1970s—namely, that in response to dramatic international events with direct American involvement, patriotic citizens who wish to see their country succeed in the international arena close ranks behind the sitting president. However, the inadequacy of this preliminary account is clear—it does not explain why most dramatic international conflicts (including many armed conflicts) with direct US involvement did *not* generate significant rally outcomes.

Although relatively few studies have analyzed the rally-round-the-flag phenomenon as their focal outcome, the academic literature on public opinion in the United States and specifically studies of public opinion during wars highlight several mechanisms of attitude formation that may be responsible for the generation of rally reactions in the public during wars or security crises. This chapter contains a critical review of the explanations of the rally phenomenon that core approaches to public opinion in the United States offer either explicitly (when rallies are the topic of investigation) or implicitly (when an explanation for the rally phenomenon can be deduced from more general arguments about political attitude formation).

A Typology of Current Approaches

The dominant approaches to understanding public opinion in the United States during wars and security crises can be categorized based on two main

Rally 'round the Flag. Yuval Feinstein, Oxford University Press. © Oxford University Press 2022.
DOI: 10.1093/oso/9780197629710.003.0002

factors, motivation and agent, as shown in Table 2.1. The column headings show how theoretical arguments vary in their assumptions about the *motivation* that drives the formation of political attitudes. Arguments based on *rational choice* theory suggest that ordinary citizens are motivated to minimize costs and maximize benefits, and thus form attitudes via a rational assessment of the cost–benefit ratio of proposed or enacted policies. In comparison, arguments rooted in the *realism* paradigm from the field of international relations suggest that ordinary citizens always prioritize maintaining national security and other vital interests of the nation. While these two types of arguments are not necessarily incompatible, they lead to different expectations regarding how people decide whether they approve of a given military action and the president who ordered it, and, by extension, whether they rally behind the president's leadership.

The row headings in Table 2.1 show how the extant arguments about public opinion formation vary with respect to the *agent* that steers public opinion during wars and security crises. "Event-based explanations" (Groeling and Baum 2008) assume that during unsettled times, public opinion is influenced directly by the *nature of events.* In contrast, "opinion leadership" explanations (for a review, see Feldman, Huddy, and Marcus 2015) emphasize that the political elite and the media guide public opinion, especially opinions about foreign affairs—a topic about which ordinary citizens lack the knowledge and expertise to make an independent assessment (Lippmann 1922).

Categorizing theoretical arguments about public opinion during wars or security crises with respect to motivation and agency results in four types

Table 2.1 Summary of the Main Explanations of the Rally-round-the-Flag Phenomenon

Motivation Agent	Rational Choice	Security concerns
Events	*Rational public:* 1. Events as informational cues 2. Feasibility and cost of policy objectives are assessed.	*Security-concerned public:* 1. Events perceived as posing a security threat produce negative emotions. 2. Military initiatives are assessed based on their implications for security.
Opinion leaders	*Elite consensus:* Members of Congress serve as opinion leaders.	*Manipulation of threat:* President propagates security threats.

of arguments about the rally phenomenon. First, a *rational public* approach (upper-center cell in Table 2.1) suggests that ordinary citizens use available information about relevant events to rationally assesses the likelihood of success and the expected cost of military policies. This approach highlights a cost–benefit calculation, and therefore suggests that a rally-round-the-flag effect emerges in response to a war or security crisis when people think that "our" military policy is likely to succeed and that the cost (mostly measured in human lives, but sometimes also the financial cost) is low. Second, the *elite consensus* approach (lower-center cell) proposes that rally periods emerge when the political elite feed the public (whose members are assumed to be rational but differ in their ideological and political predilections) information that is biased in favor of the president and his foreign policy, and in light of this information, the public's support for the policy and the president increases.

Two somewhat less influential approaches to US public opinion about foreign and military affairs are inspired by the *realism* paradigm from international relations, which presumes that citizens prioritize national security. Here, too, some scholars draw a direct line between events and public reactions—the *security-concerned public* approach (upper-right cell) argues that events become rally points if they evoke in the public a feeling of security threat and/or if the public believes that the level of security has increased (or will increase) due to "our" response to a security-threatening event. Finally, the *manipulation of threat* approach (lower-right cell) focuses on how the political elite propagate security threats to mobilize popular support for actions that they claim address those security threats.

The following sections review these four approaches. For each approach, I explain why it falls short of fully explaining the rally-round-the-flag phenomenon. I then identify useful insights from the approach that can serve as building blocks for the theoretical framework developed in this book.

Rational Choice Approaches

Many studies have noted that the US public has reacted differently to various wars and security events. Some have explained this variation by employing the principles of rational choice theory, proposing that the public's reaction to a war or security crisis is based on a rational assessment of the actual or expected outcomes of US military actions and their costs to the American people.

The Rational Public Approach

Several of the scholars who have applied the rationalist framework have proposed that Americans support the president and his foreign military policy when they believe this policy is likely to succeed (e.g., the United States has won or is very likely to win the war) and that the cost, measured primarily in the number of American fatalities, is tolerable (Larson and Savych 2005; Larson 1996). However, most experts believe that the general public is not able to gather sufficient information to make a complete assessment of the costs and outcomes of military operations. Therefore, modified arguments have suggested that attitudes about policies and leaders are formed through *bounded* rationality: people make the best assessment possible within the constraints presented by incomplete information, time pressure, and the formidable nature of the cognitive task.

An especially influential line of argumentation proposes that the public assesses the success or failure of military operations based on the outcomes of major battles and casualty figures. In times of war, events such as winning a major battle become rally points because they signal to the public that the war is going well (Eichenberg, Stoll, and Lebo 2006; Eichenberg 2005; Voeten and Brewer 2006). Large numbers of American casualties, in contrast, have a negative effect on support for military operations because they signal to the public that the operation is not going well (Gartner and Segura 2000; Lorell et al. 1985; Russett 1990: 46).

Empirical studies, however, have found there is not a straightforward relationship between number of casualties and public support for war (Baum and Groeling 2010: 208–9; Berinsky 2009: chap.4; Gelpi, Feaver, and Reifler 2006, 2009; Kull and Clay 2001; Voeten and Brewer 2006). Importantly, at the beginning of wars, a large number of casualties might actually cause the public to be more hawkish and supportive of the use of military power (Schwarz 1994). These findings contradict a straightforward rational public argument; therefore, scholars have developed modified arguments about public support for or opposition to military actions in order to maintain a rationalist core assumption.

In one such modified approach, Gelpi, Feaver, and Reifler (2006) proposed a rationalist interpretation of their findings from an analysis of public opinion polls conducted during the invasion of Iraq in 2003, which showed that Americans were more tolerant of US casualties during the first few months of the war than during other phases. To explain why the public reacted differently to casualties during different phases of the war, Gelpi and his coauthors claimed that casualties have little effect on popular support "when the public appears to be confident of a U.S. victory. . . . But if the public's confidence is shaken, then casualties erode support" (Gelpi, Feaver, and Reifler 2006: 23; for similar arguments see Eichenberg 2005; Kull and Clay 2001; Voeten and Brewer 2006). Put simply, this argument suggests that a rally-round-the-flag effect that occurs at the beginning of a war is driven by a high level of confidence that the country will achieve victory, which makes the collective sacrifice bearable.

But what inspires this initial confidence in the government and its war effort? To what extent is this confidence based on a rational assessment? As Adam Berinsky (2007) noted, rationalist claims are problematic precisely because rally effects usually emerge in the initial phase of war, when the public has the least information about both the degree of success of the military engagement and its cost. Moreover, what causes members of the public, who often express general skepticism or even mistrust of politicians, to lay this incredulity aside during rally periods?[1] This question is especially puzzling for rally periods that followed major security catastrophes, such as the attack on Pearl Harbor or the September 11 attacks. The rationalist point of view would predict that such devastating attacks would cause a rational public to lose confidence in the officials who failed to protect the nation. Instead, the popularity of the sitting president skyrocketed in the aftermath of both events (Schildkraut 2002). While the rationalist perspective provides a helpful description of this high level of confidence in the capacity of national institutions to implement policies, *a comprehensive theory of the rally phenomenon must include an explanation for this boost in confidence.*

Attributing public confidence in the capacity to win wars to rational assessment is especially tempting in the case of the United States, which for decades has been much more powerful than its enemies. However, two historical facts must be considered. First, throughout the history of human warfare, both the more powerful participants and the weaker participants (which had no rational reason to expect to win the war) have been overconfident (Johnson 2004). This observation suggests that despite America's military might, overconfidence during war may be based on something other than a rational assessment of each nation's likelihood of military success. Second, and perhaps more importantly, in recent US history, several tenacious enemies (most notably the Viet Cong in the Vietnam War) have frustrated the United States despite the latter country's overwhelming advantage in firepower. A rational assessment of the chances of winning later wars would have considered the possibility of repeating this pattern. Therefore, a rational approach would expect initial confidence following the outbreak of a war *to be low* (but possibly to increase later if the cumulative evidence suggests that the United States is indeed winning the war).

A second modification of the rational public argument focuses on the varying levels of public support for different types of wars—irrespective of the casualties suffered or anticipated. This line of argument suggests that public support or opposition is based on an individual's rational evaluation of the distinct policy objectives of military actions. According to Jentleson (1992), military operations tend to receive high levels of public support when their declared goal is to restrain foreign aggressors because this policy objective is feasible and likely to be seen as legitimate in the international community. In contrast, the American public is not likely to support using military power to intervene in another country's internal political affairs because success is less feasible and because the international community views this type of war as a violation of the principle of state sovereignty (see also Eichenberg 2005; Gelpi, Feaver, and Reifler 2009: chap. 4; Jentleson and Britton 1998).[2]

While scholars have interpreted lower than average levels of support for wars of public intervention as the result of ordinary citizens considering these wars less feasible than wars against foreign aggressors, there is no direct evidence that people assess military operations based on their declared goals. Further, this approach conflates feasibility and the desirability of different war objectives. Put simply, the lukewarm support for intervention in another nation's internal affairs may not be the result of infeasibility, but rather may be the result of a majority of the public not believing that the goals of the war justify spilling American blood or spending American money.

The Elite Consensus Thesis

The rational public arguments described in the preceding section assume that the public reacts directly to the characteristics of events, the number of American casualties, or the objectives of official policies. However, this assumption has been challenged by scholars who argue that most of what members of the public know about events and policies is learned from the media. These researchers have highlighted the media's capacity to shape public opinion about wars in three ways: priming (using the military engagement as a yardstick for evaluating other issues, institutions, or political leaders); framing (discussing the events and the official policy within a certain interpretative framework); and agenda-setting (placing the war at the center of public attention and deliberation) (Groeling and Baum 2008; Iyengar and Simon 1994; Scheufele, Nisbet, and Ostman 2005). This approach conceives of people as "information processors" who assess events and governmental policies based on information they receive through the mass media (Taber 2003). However, while the media play an important role in public opinion formation in both rally periods and normal times (Chapter 3 contains a detailed discussion of the role of the media in rally periods), several scholars have attributed sudden shifts in public opinion not to the media itself, but to the political elite who utilize the power of the media to influence public opinion.

The *elite consensus* thesis, a highly influential argument about the rally phenomenon, asserts that ordinary US citizens form their trusted attitudes toward governmental policies based on the reactions of their congressional representatives (Larson 1996; Larson and Savych 2005). This argument suggests that public opinion tends to be fairly monolithic and supportive of military action if the received information justifies the action. In contrast, public opinion becomes more polarized when the public conversation contains discordant voices, particularly if the media covers this substantial opposition to the war (Berinsky 2007; Brody 1991; Zaller 1992: chap. 9; Baum and Potter 2015). Thus, the *elite consensus* thesis suggests that rally periods emerge when, as the cannons roar, the leaders of the opposition party either explicitly support the president's foreign and military policies or refrain from criticizing the commander-in-chief to avoid being perceived as unpatriotic by members of the electorate (Zaller 1994a), instead delaying criticism until the ramifications of the war become clear (Groeling and Baum 2008). Under these conditions, the rally-round-the-flag effect emerges when a large portion of opposition party members and independent voters shift to supporting the president based on the information and cues the public receives from opinion leaders, which is biased in favor of the president and his military policy (Berinsky 2007; Brody 1991, 1994, 2002; Zaller 1992, 1994b).[3] According to this view, a rally-round-the-flag effect is simply a reflection of a consensus among the elite, which the media then transmit to the public.[4]

While the mass media and the rhetoric of political leaders certainly play a crucial role in the rally phenomenon, there are at least three reasons the *elite consensus* argument is not a sufficient explanation for the rally-round-the-flag phenomenon. First, the argument fails to acknowledge that public opinion is co-produced from below. Certainly, opinion leaders and ordinary citizens do not play equal parts in public opinion formation. Indeed, as Ari

Adut (2018: x) noted, the public sphere "is marked by an incredible asymmetry between the few who act and the multitude who watch." Still, as forcefully argued by Feldman, Huddy, and Marcus (2015: 2), a purely top-down theory of public opinion formation misses the fact that "Americans can sift through complex information and arrive at an independent political judgment under the right conditions" (although perhaps the word "independent" is a bit too strong). Feldman and coauthors supported their argument by showing that in the case of the 2003 invasion of Iraq, a significant opposition to the war evolved prior to the invasion, especially among Democrats, but also among independent voters who learned about the issue from various national and local news sources. As a result, and in contrast to the elite consensus argument, public opinion about the invasion of Iraq was more polarized than the views expressed by the political elite.

Second, people utilize significant agency when choosing which sources of "news" to read, listen to, or watch. During rally periods, people may consume certain media content (e.g., "patriotic" TV channels) not because it is the only content available to them, but because the content fits their previously established attitudes about foreign policy and military issues, a phenomenon known as the "gratification effect" (Katz, Blumler, and Gurevitch 1973). More precisely, the general public might have already adopted a specific frame of interpretation that leads people to focus on the implications of a war or security crisis for the value of the nation (i.e., its sense of self-worth and the respect it receives from other nations), to receive and absorb information selectively, and to overlook dissenting voices. In addition, when the public adopts this frame of interpretation, its member expect the political elite to close ranks and present a unified front to the outside "enemy of the nation" (Groeling and Baum 2008).

In other words, the *elite consensus* argument might mistake cause for effect: during a rally period, the lack of oppositional voices may be the *product* of the rally, which forces members of the opposition to hold their tongues to avoid appearing "unpatriotic" and seeming to betray the "national interest" (Hetherington and Nelson 2003: 38). Further, there might be a feedback effect between the public and "opinion leaders" during rally periods: an emerging consensus among the political elite about the president and the military policy convinces many ordinary citizens to rally around the flag; in turn, the media and politicians from both sides of the aisle make an extra effort to show patriotism and support for the government, and mute criticism, in order to satisfy their audience who are already rallying around the flag, thus further boosting the rally effect.

A third limitation of the elite consensus argument is that theories that focus on the role of the political elite and the media tend to overemphasize their power to persuade the public because these theories assume that most members of the public are cold-minded information processors (Taber 2003) and generally ignore the emotional aspect of attitude formation. Indeed, the elite consensus argument can be combined with the rational public argument discussed in the previous section. Taken together, the two arguments suggest that rally periods occur when the information provided to the public by the media and the political elite is biased in favor of military action, such that the public does not receive sufficient information to accurately assess the cost–benefit ratio (Page and Shapiro 1992:173).

More generally, the rationalist assumption that underlies much of the extant research on public opinion in the United States has become increasingly problematic in light of studies revealing that affective reactions are central to people's judgments (e.g., Adolphs and Tranel 1999; Bechara et al. 1994; Bechara, Damasio, and Damasio 2000; LeDoux 1996; Lehrer 2009), including the formation of political attitudes (e.g., Marcus, Neuman, and MacKuen 2000; Neuman et al. 2007: multiple chapters). Ample empirical evidence about political attitude formation has challenged the rationalist assumption that underlies both the rational public argument and the elite consensus thesis. Specifically, studies have found that the way individuals process the information they receive depends on their preexisting emotional state or "mood" (e.g., Aday 2010; Druckman and McDermott 2008), as well as their affective reactions to the information and cues they receive (e.g., Gross, Brewer, and Aday 2009; Marcus 2000; Miller 2007; Way and Masters 1996).

Realist Approaches

In the field of international relations, the realism paradigm views the world as a competition between selfish states for power and resources. Thus, this theoretical framework posits that the core interest of modern states is the quest for greater power (see Donnelly 2000 for a review).

The Security-Concerned Public Approach

Although realism has not produced an explicit explanation for the rally-round-the-flag phenomenon, the security-concerned public argument, which shares the core assumptions of realism, focuses on public opinion in the United States and can serve as an explanation for the rally phenomenon. Several scholars have suggested that the US public is more likely to support military initiatives that are perceived as being aimed at maintaining or regaining national interests, especially national security (Kohut and Toth 1994, 1996; Nincic 1997; Rielly 1979; Western 2005).[5] Thus, while the rational public thesis assumes that the public is motivated to support or oppose a military policy based on the likelihood the policy will succeed, the realist argument assumes that support or opposition is based on how important the public considers the policy to be for national security. Susan Brewer (2011: 3) summarized this idea concisely: "When Americans are called upon to fight, they want to know why Americans must kill and be killed. They expect their leaders to prove that war is right, necessary, and worth the sacrifice."[6]

The realist argument has a straightforward implication for explanations of the rally-round-the-flag phenomenon—it suggests that the core factor driving rallies is concern about national security (Huddy et al. 2005). Importantly, this is a "sociotropic" concern for the security of the entire nation, rather than concern for personal security.[7] However, this explanation for the emergence of rally outcomes is based on a problematic assumption, namely that individuals actually *know* what national security interests are and that they are capable of assessing the extent to which the security of the nation is at risk.[8] The realist explanation thus assumes the main thing that needs to be explained: how the public identifies and defines national interests during rally periods, and how a consensus about the need to protect certain "national interests" emerges among members of the public. For example, why was "fighting communism" a foreign policy objective that nearly every American supported during the Cuban Missile Crisis in 1962, but many Americans viewed with suspicion during the invasion of Grenada in 1983?

This question hints at the subjective and fluid nature of people's beliefs about national interests. National interests are not objective facts that individuals simply "know," but rather subjective *beliefs* (Kaufman 2001; Rousseau 2006; Rousseau and Garcia-Retamero 2009) that people acquire via ideological and political socialization. For example, one US citizen may believe that having the strongest military in the world is a core national interest, while her fellow American considers reducing federal expenditures (including military expenditures) to be the nation's most important goal. Further, people's beliefs about certain national interests can change in response to circumstances. Even in times of war or security crisis, a person does not simply "know" that national security is under threat, but develops this attitude as an "emotional belief" (Mercer 2005, 2010)—that is, a belief that is constituted and strengthened by a person's affective reaction to the war and to the rhetoric that links the war to collective national identity (Mercer 2010: 2).[9] By ignoring the emotional basis of the rally-round-the-flag effect, a realist explanation might follow the pattern of rationalist explanations, mistaking cause for effect: Wide agreement about the definition of national interests and the need to protect those interests is not the cause of rally periods. Rather, this type of consensus emerges through the rally processes.

The Manipulation of Threat Approach

In the aftermath of the September 11 attacks, several political psychologists, political scientists, and sociologists developed a novel explanation for the subsequent rally; they argued that the rally reaction had emerged in response to strong *feelings* of threat to national security (Huddy, Feldman, and Cassese 2007; Kam and Ramos 2008; Lambert et al. 2010; Perrin and Smolek 2009; Schildkraut 2002).[10] Other scholars extended this argument, claiming that opinion leaders had fostered a sense of threat to national and personal security among the public in order to provoke a rally reaction. Indeed, studies have shown that US presidents garner more public support for aggressive foreign policy when they frequently mention threats to national security (Cramer and Thrall 2009; Gadarian 2010; Kaufmann 2004; Willer 2004).[11,12]

While arguments that point to "threat inflation" by the political elite (Thrall and Cramer 2009) as the root cause of rally-round-the-flag reactions gained some traction after the September 11 attacks, which were an unprecedented security crisis, these arguments cannot explain the emergence of rally periods following events that did not evoke a widespread sense of threat to either personal safety or national security.

This is a significant limitation because for several decades most US citizens have not been directly involved in military activity, and the military supremacy and geographical location of the United States have made most potential threats to ordinary citizens very unlikely to materialize. As sociologist Michael Mann noted, because the United States fights its wars abroad and there is no mandatory conscription, the mobilization of Americans (who are far from the battlefield) behind these wars resembles the behavior of sports fans cheering on their favorite team from the comfort of their living rooms (Mann 1987).[13] I argue that the main concern of these "fans" is not the nation's security, but rather its honor and how much respect it receives from other nations.

Additional Theoretical Principles

Given the limitations of the dominant approaches to public opinion, any attempt to fully explicate the rally-round-the-flag phenomenon must consider alternative principles that can serve as the foundations of an explanation for the emergence of rallies. The following sections highlight two such principles, which a few studies have begun to establish and which the next chapter develops in further detail. First, as an alternative to realism's assumption that the public's concern centers on threats to collective security, studies of the rally phenomenon should consider people's concerns about the collective value of the nation, as well as the circumstances that foster these concerns. Second, rather than assuming that political attitudes are driven by rational information processing, any thorough explanation must pay close attention to the emotional underpinning of political attitudes and the resulting rallies.

Symbolic Concerns as the Driver of the Rally Effect

The concerns that underlie the rally-round-the-flag phenomenon are mostly related to the symbolic value of the home nation, namely its honor (the nation's sense of self-worth) and its prestige (the extent to which other nations appreciate "our" nation). In rally periods, this type of concern triggers even those whose personal safety is not threatened to experience strong emotions that motivate them to rally behind the national leadership. The success of the George W. Bush administration in mobilizing most of the public—including many Democratic voters—to rally behind the invasion of Iraq in 2003 is one example of this process (I discuss this series of events in detail in Chapter 5). The Bush administration achieved success by portraying the invasion of Iraq as a conflict between the good, democratic America and the evil, totalitarian Iraq, which was depicted as the snake's head in the so-called axis of evil (Brewer 2011: chap. 6; Krebs and Lobasz 2009; McCartney 2004). I show that while Bush's rhetoric certainly fostered security concerns among the public, the rally behind Bush and the war in Iraq was driven primarily by concerns about the nation's symbolic value vis-à-vis its despised enemies. This interpretive framework suggested that the United States had to defeat Iraq in order to reclaim national honor after the humiliation of the September 11 attacks, and to earn the respect of other nations by leading the global "war on terror."

The Importance of Emotions

While I am critical of the "manipulation of threat" argument, one element of the approach is particularly useful—its emphasis on the role of the sitting president, who (with the help of a loyal media) steers public opinion during rally periods. Further, the focus on personal feelings is a major step toward better understanding the rally phenomenon because this focus suggests, explicitly or implicitly, that rallying around the flag has an emotional basis.

The next steps, therefore, are to better identify the emotions that motivate people to rally around the flag and the factors that generate these emotions. Highlighting feelings of threat may seem to imply that the rally is motivated by fear, but this idea has been discredited by scholars who claim that anger, rather than fear, motivates individuals to rally around the flag. Prior studies have shown that individuals who experience high levels of fear tend to be risk-averse and thus prefer policies that minimize immediate risks (Huddy et al. 2005; Lerner and Keltner 2001; Lerner et al. 2003; Skitka et al. 2006), suggesting that fear cannot be the emotion that motivates a majority of the public to rally behind a government that is pursuing war. Instead, this line of argumentation points to *anger*—which is characterized by a sense of potency and an urge to take action in order to cope with a difficult situation and thwart the agent causing the distress—as the emotion that drives individuals to take action against enemies and to underestimate the risk associated with this action.

By differentiating the effects of anger from those of fear, this body of research has taken another major step toward better understanding the rally-round-the-flag phenomenon. Specifically, this work implies that support for the president during rally periods is motivated by a sense of collective *potency* that allows angry individuals to respond to the threat posed by the enemy by supporting the leader's action against the enemy instead of cowering in fear. However, while anger toward external enemies has certainly played a role in rally periods during America's wars and security crises, emotions that are directed inward, toward the home nation and its representative institutions, have played an even greater role in these rallies. In particular, as discussed in the next chapter, rallies behind presidents have been motivated by increased feelings of national pride, confidence in the capacity of the national leadership and the military to win wars, and hope for a better future that military actions could create.

Conclusion

This chapter has discussed several competing approaches to public opinion that offer clues to the causes of the rally-round-the-flag phenomenon. However, a close investigation of recent US rally periods in Chapters 5, 6, and 8 reveals a major limitation of these arguments: each one is contradicted by multiple instances of rallies emerging under conditions that the argument highlights as being *unfavorable* for the development of rallies.[14] For example, in contrast to the *rational public* argument, rallies emerged during the Iran hostage crisis and in the aftermath of the September 11 attacks despite the absence of any evidence of US success in these struggles, and in the 1991 Gulf War a rally emerged before the US-led coalition achieved victory. In contrast to arguments that highlight the *propagation of security concerns*, President Ford mobilized a rally in the aftermath of the *Mayaguez* incident without publicly propagating threats, and President George H. W. Bush enjoyed a surge of public support during the invasion of Panama without claiming that the country posed a military threat to the United States (he highlighted other threats). Finally, in contrast to the *elite consensus* argument, rallies emerged during the Gulf War and the Iraq War despite significant opposition to the presidents' foreign policy.

Most of the theoretical approaches to attitude formation that this chapter has reviewed share the problematic assumption that people's political attitudes are driven by the same mechanisms during rally periods and settled times: these theoretical approaches suppose that members of the public always rationally assess government policies, always prioritize national security considerations, or always seek the advice of their congressional representatives when assessing the president and his policies. In contrast, in the explanation I develop in the remaining chapters of this book, the rally-round-the-flag phenomenon represents an irregular phase of public opinion formation in which distinct mechanisms of attitude formation—in particular, emotions that are linked to national identities—come into play and motivate the public to temporarily close ranks behind the foreign policy and the government.

3

Why Do People *Really* Rally? Context, Actors, Meaning, and Emotions

Now America must wield the sword in defense of liberty, and in the very act of striking never once divest herself of that love of liberty that nurtured every son and daughter among us and is the sinew of our spirit, the pulsing of our national heart.

—From a letter sent to the *New York Times* on September 11, 2001, by Roland E. Cowden of Maryville, TN[1]

Sept. 11 proved that New York is the greatest city in the world, and now the men and women in our military will enable us to show the world that the United States is the greatest country.

—From a letter sent to the *New York Times* a few days into the invasion of Iraq by Martha and Michael Gardner of Hunt Valley, MD[2]

"Incredible Pride in My President, in My Country"

On a crisp, blue-skied Tuesday morning, Julie Dethrow, a student at Utah State University in Logan, Utah, was walking from her sorority house to her first class of the day. As she passed "Old Main"—the oldest building on campus—she noticed that the US flag was flying at half-mast. She thought that perhaps a congressperson or some other important person had passed away, but as she continued to walk, preparing to begin another day of classes, she quickly forgot about the flag. As soon as she entered the classroom, one of her classmates told her that the World Trade Center in New York City had been attacked by two airplanes that crashed into the Twin Towers. The horrifying news created a commotion in the classroom, but Julie's professor decided to hold class despite the attacks, which made her even more upset. After class, Julie rushed to the student union to watch the news on a large

Rally 'round the Flag. Yuval Feinstein, Oxford University Press. © Oxford University Press 2022.
DOI: 10.1093/oso/9780197629710.003.0003

television screen. She stayed for several hours, watching the live broadcast with other students, many of whom were weeping.

That evening at 8:30 p.m. (EST), President George W. Bush addressed the nation from the Oval Office. In his speech, he called the onslaught an attack on the American way of life and freedom and promised retaliation. Like most other Americans, Julie watched the live broadcast of the presidential address; she felt "incredible pride for my president, for my country" while watching Bush's speech. Despite being a "pretty strong Democrat," Julie was "really pleased" with the way President Bush "handled his speech and how he carried out the events and the planning throughout the rest of the week and throughout the rest of the war." After watching the national address, Julie went to her sorority house and joined her sorority sisters who were making frames for a candlelight vigil planned for the following day. After finishing the frames, she continued to watch television with her friends until late at night. Julie sensed a special atmosphere—"an aura of calm" and "a little bit more patience in the world, and a lot less anger and animosity toward each other"—among her friends that night, as they were all part of a grieving nation.

The next morning, Julie worked a shift at her job in a photo-finishing store, but no one came in. In the following days and weeks, a few people who had been in New York City on September 11 came to the store, and while waiting for their photos to be developed they shared their memories from that tragic day with the staff. In addition to images of the Twin Towers collapsing, the picture that kept coming to Julie's mind was that of firefighters raising the US flag amidst the rubble of the Twin Towers. The image made her feel proud and reminded her of the 1945 photo of a group of US Marines raising the American flag on the Japanese island of Iwo Jima.[3]

When recounting her experience a few weeks later, Julie wept as she recalled imagining the pain and horror that the people in the towers must have felt during the attacks, as well as the possible acts of heroism committed by some victims that could have offered comfort to their families but would forever remain unknown. She was scared and heartbroken for a friend she feared would have to go to war, because "while there would be no greater honor, in my mind, than to die for your country, I can't imagine losing the people I love the most." After pausing for a few seconds, Julie wrapped up her testimony by wondering how long this feeling of patriotism would last. She emphasized how impressed she was "with the people in this country, and with [the] outpouring of love that they have shown with the donating the money, and of their time and their blood, for this cause." She concluded, "I'm really, really impressed by that and I am just thankful for all those people."

Julie's recollection of her experiences, which was recorded as part of the September 11, 2001, Documentary Project about six weeks after the attacks, offers a sense of what many people in the United States felt in the aftermath of the September 11 attacks.[4] In the days after the strikes, public opinion in the United States, which is usually quite polarized (Gries 2014), became almost monolithic. President Bush's job-approval rating increased from about 50 percent before the attacks to 90 percent several days later, and almost all Americans (about 94 percent) hoped the government would take military action against those responsible for the attacks (Larson and Savych 2005: 94). In addition, the proportion of the public who said they trusted the government in Washington, DC, increased about 20 percent, eventually reaching 65 percent—the highest level since the mid-1960s (Chanley 2002). Even state and local governments enjoyed a boost in trust (Perrin and Smolek 2009).

While such a dramatic shift in public opinion cannot be fully explained by examining the experiences of one person who rallied around the flag, Julie Dethrow's testimony offers an initial glimpse of some of the core elements of rally processes in the United States: an eruption or escalation of a violent confrontation with an evil enemy monopolizes media coverage of all types; the public perceives the conflict as a matter of national honor and collective worth; many citizens engage in activities that convey their solidarity with both the victims and US security forces (such as candlelight vigils and blood drives); people across the country feel strong emotions (especially national pride) that center on the common fate of all members of the nation and their shared struggle with a vicious enemy; and ultimately, a vast majority of the public closes ranks behind the commander-in-chief, who takes or promises to take strong action against the nation's enemies. While this is a cursory characterization of rally processes based on the testimony of one college student following a single event, it is a helpful starting point from which to delve into a detailed theorization of the rally phenomenon.

Contextualizing the Rally Phenomenon: Struggles for National Honor and Prestige

At the most elemental level, the rally-round-the-flag phenomenon occurs because most members of the public are fundamentally committed to maintaining the positive symbolic value of the nation. Rallies are not the result of security concerns or rational assessments of policies (the considerations discussed in the previous chapter), but rather are motivated by concerns about national honor and the respect the nation receives from other nations. Membership in an imagined national community provides a "protective cocoon" (to borrow a term from Anthony Giddens [1991]) that helps individuals overcome the most profound existential fears of living a short, isolated, and meaningless life, which the conditions of modern life have exacerbated, as scholars in the Frankfurt School have argued forcefully (for further elaboration of this issue, see Finlayson 1998; Feinstein 2021). Consequently, most individuals carry a deep emotional commitment to protecting their home nation, which provides them with a feeling of social integration, meaning, and positive self-worth.

My theorization of the rally-round-the-flag phenomenon does not cover all aspects of the comfort that national identification offers to people in modern societies, but rather focuses on the sense of self-worth that membership in a nation provides. My theory centers on the link between people's sense of personal self-worth and their perceived collective worth as members of their nation, and highlights the conditions that make people feel that the collective national worth (and thus also their own worth) is under threat and must be protected. The rest of this section explores the foundations and components of perceived collective national worth and examines the emergence of concerns about collective worth during militarized conflicts.

The Collective Symbolic Value of the Nation and Its Members

Membership in a nation is a subjective experience that offers all members a shared valuable symbolic resource: collective symbolic worth. Max Weber (1978: 391) called this type of sentiment the "honor of the masses (*Massenehre*)." This shared symbolic value does not depend on people's objective life conditions, but rather on their subjective belief that they are members of a valuable community—even people whose life conditions are miserable share this special collective value with other members of the nation. Therefore, as Liah Greenfeld (2006) noted, because most people's sense of self-worth is closely tied to their sense of collective national worth, most members of modern societies hold a profound commitment to protecting the collective worth of their national group (see also Lebow 2008: 17). The collective symbolic value of a nation is an abstract and fluid asset, which people continually reassess in response to changing circumstances and which entails two intertwined components: the honor of the nation and its prestige. As explained in the following, in the context of militarized conflicts, concerns about national honor often develop in tandem with concerns about the nation's international prestige.

National honor is the symbolic value of the national group, which is assessed by looking inward when members of the nation gauge the degree to which their nation's actions, or the actions of institutions that represent the nation, such as the government and the military, align with or violate what people believe to be the nation's core moral standards based on historical narratives and myths. A positive evaluation of the impact of an event or policy on national honor evokes pride, while a negative evaluation evokes shame (I discuss these affective reactions in detail later, in the section about emotion and meaning). For example, in most national cultures, taking decisive action to defend the nation against attacks is considered a desirable (i.e., "honorable") action and thus makes citizens feel proud. In contrast, succumbing to an enemy's threats or adversarial actions is deemed disgraceful and thus generates shame.

In addition to embracing these broadly appealing principles, specific national cultures may nurture certain unique moral principles. For example, in the Netherlands, many citizens embrace the notion of the country's international role as a humanitarian leader, a belief encapsulated in the Dutch term *gidsland* (the guide state) (Herman 2006). Similarly, Swiss nationalism has nurtured a sense of non-divine chosenness and moral leadership (A. D. Smith 1992: 446)—or, as Roshwlad (2006: 184) put it, "choosing to be chosen"—based on the depiction of Switzerland as the paradigmatic case of direct democracy and respect for diversity through political contract (i.e., Swiss "civic exceptionalism" [Zimmer 2003]), as well as on the myth of Switzerland's choice of armed neutrality, which grants the nation a special role and respect in the international arena. In turn, these specific core moral principles and the related popular belief in cultural exceptionalism and collective mission serve as a yardstick for assessing whether a national policy is deemed honorable or disgraceful (or has no implications for national honor).

National prestige is the value obtained from others' evaluation of "us." However, for the emergence of a rally-round-the-flag effect, the crucial issue is not how much other actors (nations or non-national actors) actually respect the home-nation, but rather whether people *believe* that other actors respect or disrespect their nation. In short, national prestige is a perceived collective value based on looking outward at the nation's position in the world.

Many people hold fairly stable beliefs about the prestige of their nation that are founded on a more profound set of beliefs about cultural exceptionalism and a glorious historical legacy, which are themselves embedded in national narratives and myths (Feinstein and Bonikowski 2021). Agents of nationalism (especially schools, the media, and the political elite) often nurture beliefs about cultural exceptionalism and special collective moral virtue (Van Evera 1994: 27). Despite this context, feeling respected or disrespected by other nations is, to a significant degree, situational. For example, how the home-nation responds to a conflict with another nation or a non-national actor (e.g., a terrorist organization) can impact people's assessments of the degree to which their nation is becoming more or less respected by other nations. When an external actor's actions seem to degrade the home-nation's value, people may experience affective reactions ranging from an ephemeral feeling of embarrassment to deeper and longer-lasting feelings of humiliation and resentment toward the actor responsible for the humiliation. Humiliation and resentment motivate people to seek retaliation (in violent ethnic conflicts, these feelings make people more likely to participate in violent activities [Petersen 2002]). In contrast, people who believe that "our actions" teach other nations to respect us tend to feel elation and pride.

The relational aspect of a nation's prestige, which depends on how its members believe others evaluate them, makes prestige a precarious asset. As Liah Greenfeld noted, "no matter how much prestige one may have gained at a certain moment, one can be outdone in the next" (Greenfeld 2006: 206). In the United States, the rally-round-the-flag phenomenon has been directly related to concerns about national prestige. Specifically, rallies have emerged when conflicts seemed to challenge the United States' reputation as a proud and powerful nation and people believed that the government's reaction would effectively restore the nation's prestige. In turn, foreign and military policies that restored national prestige during conflict were widely seen as the most honorable, "American" way of dealing with challenges to US might and the respect the nation was entitled to receive as an international leader.

In settled times, the attitudes of most US citizens toward the president are driven not by pressing concerns about the nation's honor and prestige, but primarily by partisan and ideological identities, as well as the demographic characteristics—in particular, ethnicity/race, socioeconomic class, gender, education, and generation—that are associated with partisan and ideological preferences (for a review, see Bonikowski, Feinstein, and Bock 2021). However, unusual circumstances may raise public concerns about collective symbolic worth, which may in turn lead the majority of US citizens to close ranks behind a president whose foreign military policy seems likely to protect the nation's honor and prestige.

Challenges to National Honor and Prestige during War

More than any other type of event, wars and security crises tend to boost public concerns about national honor and prestige. Engaging in militarized conflict not only tests the power of the nation and its capacity to defeat enemies on the battleground, but often poses a significant challenge to the nation's symbolic value, specifically its honor and international prestige.[5] Collective honor becomes a major public concern during conflicts if people believe that core elements of their collective national identity—such as the solidarity among compatriots and their bravery and determination—are being tested by the enemy. In the context of this perception, standing firmly and united against an enemy is an honorable act of collective identity affirmation.

Wars and security crises are also likely to raise concerns about the respect the home-nation receives from other nations, including nations that are not directly involved but that observe the conflict and assess the actions of the parties involved. Concerns of this type are especially common among global superpowers, whose foreign policies and military actions are closely monitored by allies and rivals from all corners of the globe. Therefore, US policymakers and ordinary citizens may believe that even relatively limited military actions (for example, the 1961 Bay of Pigs invasion, which is discussed in Chapter 5) will have serious implications for the special international status of the United States and the respect it receives as "leader of the free world." A study of public reactions to threats made by the United States in dozens of security crises since 1945 offered compelling evidence for the symbolic meaning of US international conflicts (Snyder and Borghard 2011); investigators concluded that public opinion in the United States is concerned with national honor and the country's international reputation for political resolve, more than any other aspect of international conflicts (see also Tomz 2007).

Concerns about Honor and Prestige as Preconditions of Rally-round-the-Flag

Because the public ascribes such importance to maintaining national honor and prestige, the risk of being humiliated (in addition to concerns about US casualties and the financial cost of wars) makes many US citizens reluctant to engage in unnecessary wars and likely to be especially critical of presidents who send American troops to fight wars far from home—a tendency that has arguably increased in the aftermath of the Vietnam War (the so-called Vietnam Syndrome). However, in some cases, military actions were taken *in the aftermath of the United States suffering a major humiliation* in the international arena (as discussed in Chapters 5 and 6, military defeats and foreign attacks against major US civilian targets are common causes of humiliation). In the context of a preexisting feeling of humiliation, a public desire to restore honor and prestige through retaliation opens the way for the emergence of a rally behind a president who is beating the war drums (Snyder and Borghard 2011). To explain this tendency, I rely on principles of prospect theory from the field of behavioral economics (Kahaneman and Tversky 1979). This theory was developed to explain individual financial behavior, but can be applied to political attitude formation during a rally period based on the conceptualization (following Max Weber [1978: 395–98]) of national honor and prestige as valuable collective assets that can increase or decrease via interactions with other groups.

Prospect theory suggests that most people are usually risk averse: when making decisions, they tend to give more weight to avoiding the loss of value they already possess than to gaining value. In the context of attitudes toward engaging in wars, this principle suggests that many people deem war too risky and prefer to seek a diplomatic solution to the conflict or, if a peaceful solution is out of reach and the conflict is bearable, to allow the conflict to endure with no escalation. This hypothesized reaction has found empirical support in research that shows that US presidents who threaten to use force in international conflicts tend to suffer a "belligerence cost" in their public approval ratings [Kertzer and Brutger 2016]).

Prospect theory, however, also contends that individuals' levels of risk-aversion and risk-seeking vary by context. One of the prominent findings of prior tests of prospect theory is that risk-taking increases when people have already experienced a loss of significant value: that is, people are more willing to gamble to regain lost value than to gain value they previously did not possess. Applying this principle to political attitude formation leads to the prediction that the experience of a major national humiliation will cause a shift in many people's risk preferences: people are more likely to accept the risks involved in going to war—including the risk of suffering another national humiliation—if they hope that doing so will compensate for a previous loss of collective value due to a humiliating event.

A second scenario in which the public becomes increasingly concerned about the international prestige of the United States involves a call from the United Nations for the United States to lead the free world in a struggle against a tyrannical regime. As discussed in Chapter 8, this type of call from the international community serves as a precondition for a rally, even in the absence of a feeling of national humiliation, because a recognition of the nation's moral superiority and unique leadership position is embedded in the call. Once again, prospect theory can help explain the emergence of a rally behind a president who orders military action. A call for the United States to lead the free world in war creates a "framing effect" (Tversky and Kahneman 1981) that changes the reference point for people's evaluations of the potential risks and rewards for the international prestige of the United States. The unusual request from the United Nations raises people's expectations about the nation's international prestige to an unusually high level. In this context, a greater tendency toward risk-taking by going to war stems less from a desire to gain international prestige than from a desire to prevent the loss of the prestige already bestowed on the United States by the UN request to act as leader of the free world.

To summarize, in both scenarios—collective humiliation or a call from the United Nations—the tendency of US citizens to rally behind military action increases as people seek to either cope with a loss of symbolic value (in the case of previous humiliation) or prevent a potential loss of value (in the case of a call to lead the free world). Due to this change of mindset, many people deviate from their general tendency to punish (by expressing disapproval in opinion polls or through voting) leaders who send US troops to war, either because they hold "dovish" views on international affairs (Kertzer and Brutger 2016) or because going to war violates leaders' previous promises not to go to war (Quek 2017). Next, the text turns from a discussion of the conditions that create the potential for a rally-round-the-flag effect to an exploration of the conditions and mechanisms through which rallies have actually emerged.

Rally Processes in the Aftermath of Wars and Security Crises

During the second half of the twentieth century and the first two decades of the twenty-first century (the period covered in this book), rallies have emerged in the United States in response to a war or security crisis whenever most of the public believed that (a) core elements of the nation, namely its character and place in the world, were being tested and must be protected or reclaimed, and (b) that the president was doing a good job managing the military and foreign policy to meet the challenge and restore or protect the nation's honor and prestige. Under these very specific circumstances, the emergence of strong positive emotions that center on national membership—especially national pride, high levels of confidence in national institutions, and hope for a bright future for the nation—have driven individuals who are usually critical of the government, who identify with the political opposition, or who are not interested in politics to shift to supporting the president.

When focusing on attitude formation at the individual level, I argue that a critical aspect of the rally process is the role of emotions that lead individuals to deviate from their regular range of attitudes (specifically, to move from being indifferent toward, undecided about, or opposing the president to supporting the president). In line with sociologist Thomas Scheff's (1990) argument that leaders gain charismatic authority when they offer people a way to transform distress and humiliation into pride (see McLaughlin 1996: 254–56 for review),[6] the two elements that lie at the core of my explanation of the rally-round-the-flag phenomenon are a public desire to reclaim national honor and prestige, and leaders who are satisfying that desire through military action.

In the postwar United States, most of the events that produced rally reactions were preceded by other events, such as a major military defeat or diplomatic crisis, that generated a feeling of collective humiliation among the public.[7] As explained in the previous section, humiliating events create a public demand for the leader to take action that would restore the nation's collective symbolic value. In this context, presidents who promised to re-claim collective honor and prestige via military action evoked positive emotions among the public. These positive emotions are the primary force that motivates individuals to rally behind the president. The following sections elaborate on the role played by positive nationalistic emotions in rally periods, as well as the circumstances that lead a majority of the public to experience such emotions.

Emotion and Meaning

The emotions (positive or negative) that members of the public experience in response to a war or security crisis depend on the perceived implications of the event and "our" actions for the collective symbolic value of the nation. These perceived implications are based on two criteria. The first criterion is the perceived hierarchy between the home nation and external groups. If the home-nation is perceived as having lost power and/or status relative to other nations as a result of the focal event, individuals are likely to have a nega-tive affective reaction: a perceived loss of collective power due to an enemy's actions triggers fear, while a perceived loss of collective status elicits anger.[8] For example, immediately after the September 11 attacks, most Americans experienced negative emotional reactions—many reacted with fear because they perceived the attacks as an apocalyptic nightmare that entailed a loss of power; somewhat later, many Americans reacted with anger because they perceived the attacks as a violation of America's status as a powerful and proud nation (Kemper 2002).

In contrast, if the power and/or status of the nation is perceived as increasing as a result of the event, members of the public are likely to have a positive affective reaction. Pride is likely the most typical feeling, but reactions may also include confidence, hope, excitement, and happiness. For example, (as discussed in Chapter 9), several days after the September 11 attacks, as the rally process was unfolding, positive feelings became wide-spread in the United States (leading more and more people to join the rally) because the public believed that the government was taking firm action against terrorism and expected this action to re-establish America's might and its reputation as a proud nation.[9]

The second criterion for evaluating the implications of events for the nation's symbolic value looks inward, using the nation's idealized image (as depicted in popular narratives about the nation's history) as a yardstick for assessing whether the current actions of the nation or the institutions that serve as symbolic representations of the nation (especially the president and the military) align with or violate collective identity standards. I use the term "identity standards" (adopted from Burke 1991) to refer to how members of the nation believe that "we" *should* behave based on "our" collective identity and shared historical legacy. The perception that the nation's actions align with the nation's identity standards evokes positive emotions (especially pride), while the perception that the nation's actions contradict collective identity standards elicits negative emotions (shame, embarrassment, guilt) (Rahn, Kroeger, and Kite 1996).[10] For example, as discussed in Chapter 5, during the 1962 Cuban Missile Crisis, most Americans perceived Kennedy's tough talk and his decision to impose a marine blockade as aligning with important standards of collective national identity, including following the Monroe Doctrine, being courageous, standing behind core national principles, and not succumbing to the threats of communist enemies. This reinforcement of national identity standards was especially important in the wake of the humiliating failure of the US-sponsored coup in Cuba during the Bay of Pigs invasion—when the United States let others do its dirty work and thus did not act in a way that reflected identity standards. In the wake of Kennedy's subsequent handling of the Cuban Missile Crisis, his job-approval rating jumped from 61 percent to 74 percent.

The public's assessment of whether the nation has gained or lost symbolic value and whether current actions meet or violate the nation's identity standards is not static, but can change as events unfold and individuals reappraise the situation. For example, as described earlier, the reaction to the September 11 attacks shifted from fear, to anger, to pride (Kemper 2002). The initial negative reactions emerged in response to a perceived loss of power and status, a perception that was reinforced by the media's tendency to draw an analogy between the 9/11 attacks and the attack on Pearl Harbor in 1941 (Ross 2013: 68–73; van Dooremalen 2021: 733). The later positive reaction emerged when most Americans came to view the situation as an opportunity to celebrate the American spirit, epitomized by the actions of the United Flight 93 passengers and the firefighters at Ground Zero, as well as an opportunity for the United States to re-establish its position as a world superpower by leading a war against global terrorism. Here too, analogies to emotionally laden events in the national past, specifically World War II, were common in media broadcasts (Ross 2013). For example, the photo of three firefighters raising the US flag in the midst of the rubble of the Twin Towers echoed the iconic photo of US Marines raising the flag on Iwo Jima. As a result of the shift in the predominant interpretation of the September 11 attacks, while most Americans continued to feel furious and many felt scared (Ross 2013: chap.3), they also experienced positive emotional reactions to the actions taken on the domestic and global fronts (see also Gross, Brewer, and Aday 2009). These positive emotions led the public to rally behind the commander-in-chief.

The Actors That Steer Emotions: The Media, the Enemy, and the President

The rally-round-the-flag effect is an aggregate phenomenon, meaning that a sudden boost in presidential job-approval ratings and a sharp decline in disapproval ratings are the outcome of attitudinal shifts experienced by many individuals. Therefore, explaining the rally phenomenon requires considering the "macro" conditions that lead most of the public to experience similar rally-producing emotions at the same time. Thus, the analysis now shifts from a focus on individuals to a focus on the broader *conditions* that lead most Americans (a) to feel that the nation should reclaim its honor and its respect from other nations, (b) to believe that the president's military policy will achieve this reclamation, and (c) to experience positive emotions that motivate them to rally behind the president.

As discussed earlier, the potential for a rally behind the president increases dramatically when there is a preexisting *public feeling of national humiliation* that evokes a desire to reclaim national honor and international prestige through military retaliation. Indeed, in the period covered in this book, collective humiliation has preceded most rally periods in the United States. Further, it is likely universally true that a public feeling of humiliation is fertile soil for rally-round-the-flag processes. However, the rally-round-the-flag phenomenon may also emerge in the absence of a widespread feeling of humiliation. This scenario (discussed in Chapter 8) involves *a request from the international community for the United States to lead the free world* in a struggle against a tyrant who has violated the world order. Such a request can transform the meaning of a conflict, making it a test of the special role and status of the United States as the moral and political "leader of the free world." Within this interpretive framework, defeating the enemy is deemed necessary in order to gain the respect of other nations.

The following sections highlight three additional conditions that drive the emergence of a massive rally-round-the-flag reaction in the United States: intense media coverage of events that adopts a celebratory tone, the existence of a clear and greatly despised enemy, and presidential rhetoric that highlights the implications of a military confrontation for the symbolic value of the nation (a "nation-affirming rhetoric"). Together, these three conditions foster a desire among the public to increase collective honor and prestige and mark a clear path to achieving this goal, namely taking decisive military action against the nation's enemies.

The Role of the Media

This section examines the essential role that the news media plays during rally processes. The media is not simply a channel through which "opinion leaders" (in particular, politicians) deliver their messages to the public; foreign affairs journalists do not simply "index" the coverage to the political elite's discussion of the focal issue (Bennett 1990). Instead, in the United States and other democratic countries, the news media is composed of *actors* (i.e., individual reporters and organizations) who choose, often with a significant level of autonomy, which topics to cover and how to cover each topic.[11] Notably, while I argue that the media is an essential agent of opinion shifts during rally periods, I am not suggesting that the relationship between media coverage of events and public opinion runs solely in one direction or is otherwise simple. Experts in communication research have established that during rally periods, the media not only affects public opinion but also *reacts* to public opinion (Bennett 1994: 30)—journalists are not outsiders, but rather members of society who tend to rally with the rest of the public. In addition, during rally periods, the public and politicians, and sometimes journalistic colleagues, condemn journalists who depart from the core cultural themes of the war discourse, which can impact journalists' reporting (Hallin and Gitlin 1994: 158). With these caveats in mind, I now explore the characteristics of media coverage during rally periods and how these characteristics function as mechanisms of opinion shift during these periods.

Setting the Stage for a Rally

Mass communication outlets—the print media, radio and television news channels, and more recently online journalism and social media—play an important role in rally processes. For an event to become a rally point, the media must place the event at the forefront of public conversation and present it in a way that captures the hearts and minds of the audience (Groeling and Baum 2008; Iyengar and Simon 1994; Scheufele, Nisbet, and Ostman 2005). This section provides a rough sketch of the main characteristics of news coverage that students of communication have highlighted as especially important for the emergence of a rally-round-the-flag effect.

Most fundamentally, a military action or security crisis cannot produce a rally period if the public is unaware of the event. Ordinary citizens learn about military operations and security crises from the media, either directly—by watching TV, listening to the radio, reading print newspapers, or reading electronic newspapers or social media—or indirectly—from other people who learned about the event from the media and shared the information. Political leaders, chief among them the president, are aware of the important role of the media, and thus when seeking public legitimacy for their policies they use the media to communicate with the public.[12]

However, the media simply informing the public about an event and the actual or proposed reaction by the government does not generate a rally. Instead, during rally periods, the media steers public opinion via three mechanisms: agenda setting, priming, and framing (Groeling and Baum 2008; Iyengar and Simon 1994; Scheufele, Nisbet, and Ostman 2005). Media outlets place the security event at the top of the agenda for public discourse, making it the main issue of the day (agenda setting); the security issue and "our" reactions to it become the yardstick for evaluating political leaders (priming); and the media assigns a certain meaning to the event and reaction, which captures the public's hearts and minds (framing).

Media Events

A war or security crisis is more likely to evoke a strong rally-round-the-flag reaction among the public if media coverage takes the form of what Dayan and Katz (1992) called a "media event": nearly all news channels interrupt their routine programming and begin livestreaming commercial-free reports about the event, which they season with dramatic special announcements, as well as opinions and explanations from special experts such as retired military generals and intelligence officers.[13] This shift transforms news reports into a type of "reality theater" (Scheufele, Nisbet, and Ostman 2005: 200). News, as Carey (2002: 75) explained, becomes "a cost center and public service rather than a profit center of private pleasure" (as they are in normal times). Most importantly, the coverage during "media events" creates an impression of a "live broadcast of history" (Dayan and Katz 1992).

As a result of this type of broadcasting, a security crisis that is geographically bounded (such as terrorist attacks in one or a few specific places) or a war that is fought far from home becomes a "national" event that monopolizes the public conversation (Feinstein 2018). Almost all members of the public are watching the live broadcast of the events and eagerly listening to the discussions of the events and their expected implications in newsrooms and public addresses by national leaders and military commanders. For example, at the onset of Operation Desert Storm against Iraq in January 1991, CNN's primetime rating of 11.7 was 10 times higher than normal, and ratings for the morning news shows were up 15 percent (Hallin and Gitlin 1994); the September 11 attacks in 2001 led to a three-fold increase in the size of the average primetime cable news audience (from 1.6 million viewers in August to 4.6 million in September) (Althaus 2008: 172); and the invasion of Iraq in March 2003 led to an even larger increase in the average number of people watching primetime cable news (per minute)—from about one million in February to about 3.5 million in April (Althaus 2008: 173).

In addition to escalating the intensity of their broadcasts and gaining extremely high levels of attention from the public, the media contribute to the emergence of rally-round-the-flag outcomes by incorporating an emotional tone and expressive content in their broadcasts. Speakers and columnists discuss the events and national leaders with awe (Katz and Liebes 2007), and most forgo any criticism of national institutions (for example, in the case of September 11, the agencies that failed to prevent terrorist attacks) either because their own heightened national identification makes them believe that now is a time for national unity, or because their assessment of the public mood and their fear of the public (or their fear that their employers would punish them if they expressed critical views) lead them to err on the side of patriotism and conformity (Carey 2002: 74). Importantly, in non-rally times, the media does not usually refrain from criticizing the government during conflicts; as Baum and Groeling (2010: chap. 3) showed, the media tends to overrepresent critical views of foreign and military affairs even when the cannons are roaring (2010: 58). Therefore, closing ranks behind the president and projecting a united home front is an uncommon media approach that is unique to rally periods.

During a rally period, the media extends its impact on public opinion through a type of coverage that links the war front and the home front and transforms even wars being fought far from the United States into a collective effort and a demonstration of national unity and strength. Reporters who escort combat units highlight the soldiers' courage, patriotism, and commitment to protecting the nation, while other reporters document all types of actions civilians are taking that demonstrate the nation's support for the troops and solidarity with fellow civilians who fell victim to the enemy's violence, for example, sending letters and packages with groceries and candy to the troops, making donations, participating in blood drives, or attaching symbols such as the yellow ribbon to clothes and putting stickers and flags on cars (Hallin and Gitlin 1994; Neiger and Rimmer-Tsory 2013). Further, this type of reporting generates "interpersonal influence" (Mutz 1998), and thus even the most socially isolated individuals can develop an image of the current public mood and the dominant public views through their exposure to news coverage. The resulting image evokes a feeling of community among those who join the rally (Hallin and Gitlin 1994: 156–57) and increases the emotional burden on people who refrain from joining.

The celebratory nature of the media coverage of a war or security crisis charges the event with a special symbolic meaning, portraying it as a test of what most members of the nation perceive to be the nation's core elements: the common qualities of members (e.g., courage and determination), solidarity among compatriots, and shared values that in times of crisis bridge internal divisions and cleavages. During rally processes, the media often engages in this type of meaning-making explicitly. For example, following the September 11 attacks, the New York Times introduced a daily advertising-free section titled "A Nation Challenged" that included reports about the challenges the security forces faced in their efforts to protect the nation and fight terrorism, as well as reports about the challenges that ordinary Americans faced in the United States—for example, how to maintain positive relations between Muslim and non-Muslim Americans in the aftermath of the terrorist attacks (Carey 2002: 75).

Summary: The Role of the Media

The media plays a crucial role in rally processes because its intense and celebratory coverage of a security crisis or military action, which charges the
situation with a special symbolic meaning for collective value, evokes strong
emotions in the public.[14] However, this type of media coverage by itself is
not enough to produce a rally-round-the-flag effect. Individuals who belong
to different political-ideological camps, who usually have different affective and attitudinal reactions to media contents (Tsfati and Nir 2017), may
also have different reactions to the media coverage of a war or security crisis
(Jacobson 2010). Therefore, media events sometimes create greater political
polarization (for example, the Iraq War, while being supported by a majority
of Americans and generating a considerable rally behind the presidency of
George W. Bush, also increased political polarization in the United States—
see a discussion of this issue in Chapter 9).

I contend that although the media plays a significant role in rally processes, media coverage cannot produce a rally without the presence of several
concurrent conditions. Specifically, only when three additional conditions
are met—at least one of the preconditions discussed earlier (i.e., collective
humiliation or a call to lead the free world) is present, and two additional
conditions, which are described in the following sections, are also present—
will many people set aside ideological and political disagreements and rally
behind the president and his military policy. The following section discusses
one of these two additional conditions for the emergence of a rally in the
United States: the existence or emergence of a despised enemy.

The Role of the Enemy

We Got Him!

On December 12, 2003, during a press conference held in Baghdad, Paul
Bremer, head of the Coalition Provisional Authority in Iraq, announced,
"Ladies and gentlemen, we got him!" There was no need to explain to the
chanting audience in the room or the millions of Americans watching from
home whom the troops had captured. As a result of a massive campaign
targeting public opinion in the United States during the build-up to the
war (see Chapter 5 for a detailed discussion), the 2003 Iraq War was widely

perceived by Americans as a war against Iraq's president, Saddam Hussein. It was Hussein's head that the public wanted as a proof of America's might and superiority in the "war against terrorism" era, and Bremer's announcement satisfied that demand.

After the press conference, the US media emphasized Saddam Hussein's defeat by showing photos of American soldiers pulling Hussein out of the spider hole where he had been hiding. Major General Raymond Odierno, the commander of the infantry division that captured Hussein, said, "He was caught like a rat" (Russel and Fairweather 2003). A picture of a military doctor examining Hussein's teeth became an iconic symbol of the Iraqi dictator's defeat and humiliation. By that time, the rally-round-the-flag effect that had emerged after the invasion of Iraq was fading and President Bush's job-approval rating had sunk to the low 50s; however, for a few weeks the capture of Saddam Hussein led to a mini-rally as Bush's job-approval rating increased to about 60 percent.[15] This pattern of events raises the question: What role do enemy leaders such as Saddam Hussein play in rally processes?

No Enemy, No Rally

During the focal period (1950–2020), no rallies developed in the United States without a clear enemy. In every war or security crisis that became a rally point, most Americans either already believed that the opponent (a foreign country or organization) was an enemy of the United States or developed this conviction as the events unfolded (in the latter scenario, the rally-round-the-flag effect emerged only *after* the public identified a clear enemy). In several instances, the incapacity or reluctance of the sitting president to paint a target around a clear enemy in the aftermath of a military operation or security crisis prevented the emergence of a rally (see Chapter 7 for an extended discussion and examples). Put simply, in the United States, at least in the period covered in this book, establishing (via the rhetoric of government officials and the media) a public belief that a specific country or organization is an enemy of the United States that must be defeated through military action has been a *necessary* condition for the emergence of a rally-round-the-flag effect.

What role do enemies play in the emergence of the rally-round-the-flag phenomenon in the aftermath of a war or security crisis? From a sociological point of view, the answer has two parts.[16] The first part relates to general cognitive, affective, and behavioral tendencies that humans have as members of social groups, especially during conflicts with other groups. The second part relates more specifically to membership in nations and the engagement of national groups in conflicts.

The Ingroup/Outgroup Distinction

Social identity theory (SIT) (Tajfel and Turner 1986), which is one of the most influential theories in the field of social psychology, postulates that individuals' attitudes and behavior in the context of intergroup relations are driven by their desire to maintain a distinct and positive identity vis-à-vis outgroups. Based on this principle, a profusion of studies have shown that in response to even the slightest amount of perceived competition with or threat from outgroups, and motivated by a desire to maintain a positive self-value, people display cognitive biases that favor their ingroup (i.e., increased negative stereotypes about outgroups and increased positive evaluations of the ingroup; for a review, see L. Huddy 2001) and sometimes even exhibit behavioral biases (as in experiements that ask participants to allocate a sum of money between ingroup and outgroup members; see Mummendey et al. 1992).

Social identity theory is based on the results of laboratory experiments that revealed that individuals exhibit cognitive and behavioral biases in favor of their ingroups even in the context of "minimal groups," in which membership has a very thin basis.[17] However, the basic principles of this theory can also be used to explain how individuals, as members of larger, imagined national communities, respond to situations that involve conflict or a threat to the home nation from external actors (Kalin and Sambanis 2018). Studies of public attitudes about foreign affairs and militarized conflicts have shown that militancy in foreign affairs attitudes is associated with beliefs about the home nation's superiority to other nations (Bliss, Oh, and Williams 2007; Crowson 2009; Herrmann, Isernia, and Segatti 2009; Kosterman and Feshbach 1989; Li and Brewer 2004; McCleary and Williams 2009). Both the belief that other nations are inferior to the home nation and the desire to dominate other nations (including, if necessary, by using military power against them) can be conceptualized as a special case of the general pro-ingroup/anti-outgroup bias highlighted in many social psychological studies (in particular within the SIT framework).

My own investigations in the United States and Israel have shown that one of the tendencies documented in "minimal group" experiments extends to the national context: specifically, situations that lead individuals to perceive that their national group is challenged by external enemies are likely to evoke stronger beliefs in national superiority and a greater desire to dominate these enemies by using force against them (Feinstein 2018, 2016b).[18] For example, in a 2011 experiment, US citizens who were exposed to (fake) presidential rhetoric highlighting cultural distinctions between the United States and Iran, as well as the animosity of the latter's Islamist regime toward the former, reported higher levels of national chauvinism and greater support for military action against Iran (Feinstein 2016b). These findings have straightforward implications for the study of the rally-round-the-flag phenomenon in the United States: namely, for individuals who identify with the home nation, a confrontation with an external enemy evokes cognitive biases in favor of their national ingroup and against rival outgroups, prompting them to attribute moral inferiority and sole responsibility for conflicts to the outgroup. During a stressful security crisis or war, attributing responsibility for the situation solely to the enemy evokes rage, which motivates people to seek retaliation (Schubert, Stewart, and Curran 2002: 565; Leonie Huddy, Feldman, and Cassese 2007), and in turn increases the likelihood that they will rally behind a president who orders a retaliation or vows to retaliate.

Enemies of the Nation

The social psychological approach to enmity outlined in the previous section portrays a general human tendency to apply an "us versus them" distinction and to seek to establish a moral hierarchy between the home group and groups of "others," and also highlights the exacerbation of that tendency in situations of perceived competition or conflict with an external group. This tendency is certainly an important mechanism of the rally phenomenon. However, fully appreciating the role of enemies in rally processes requires moving beyond the simple notion of a conflict between an "ingroup" and an "outgroup" and acknowledging the fact that people's views and feelings about the home-nation and its enemies are much more profound than the attitudes and feelings of participants in minimal group experiments.

Many wars and security crises involve established enemies that have a history of confrontations with the home-nation, and in these cases many people have pre-established views and feelings about these enemies.[19,20] Therefore, in contrast to the thin relationship between an ingroup and an outgroup in "minimal group" experiments, which can be characterized as ahistorical, ephemeral, and involving little to no actual engagement, the relationship with the enemy in national conflicts has a thick content: it is often historically rooted, persistent, and emotionally intense. Consequently, the opinions individuals form in war or other international conflicts are often influenced by beliefs about the different characters and profoundly different cultures of the home-nation and its enemies, and about the history of the relationship between the groups (Bar-Tal 2013).

Animosity toward a nation's enemies may be especially strong if the current conflict is seen in light of the historical struggles of the nation. In an effort to mobilize public support, national leaders often draw an analogy between past events and the present situation (Nigbur and Cinnirella 2007). During war, the rhetoric of national leaders often seeks to incite fear of and hatred for the enemy among members of the nation by provoking traumatic memories of past losses and humiliations.[21] Leaders sometimes ask the public to recall a previous confrontation with the same enemy. For example, during the Balkan wars of the 1990s, Serbian nationalist propaganda evoked traumatic memories of Croat violence against Serbs during World War II and thus provoked fear of the Croats and a desire to settle the score (Denich 1994; Oberschall 2000). In other instances, new enemies are compared to historical enemies that are part of the collective memory. For example, when President George H. W. Bush sought to mobilize public support for the Gulf War, he compared the Iraqi invasion of Kuwait to World War II and Saddam Hussein to Adolf Hitler. Drawing an analogy between Saddam Hussein and Adolph Hitler lent a sense of urgency to the plans to intervene in the crisis in the Persian Gulf because it implied that postponing the intervention would have consequences similar to those resulting from the delay of the US intervention in World War II (Winkler 2006: 114). Further, this analogy assigned the United States the responsibility to save humanity from evil forces. Years later, politicians, especially neoconservative leaders, once again compared Saddam Hussein to Hitler, this time to justify the Iraq War of 2003 (Brewer 2011: 5; Zulaika 2009: 195).[22]

Symbolic Struggles and the Embodiment of the Nation's Enemy: The Role of the Nemesis

Collective identities are always constructed through constitutive others; thus, in collective national memories, heroes and villains play complementary roles (Fine 2002). However, the differentiation between "us" and "them," which plays a banal but important part in the way people imagine their nations as having "finite, if elastic, boundaries, beyond which lie other nations" (Anderson 1991[1983]: 7), takes the form of friend versus foe only when, to quote Chantal Mouffe, the other "begins to be perceived as negating our identity, as putting in question our very existence" (1993: 3). Therefore, during rally processes, the construction of the opponent as a villain who not only fights "us" on the battle ground, but also stands against everything "we" represent, transforms the conflict from a competition over concrete interests (for example, material or geopolitical interests) to an epic symbolic struggle between good and evil. In the twentieth-century United States, this battle between good and evil has taken the more specific form of a struggle between a nation that considers itself the leader of liberal democratic civilization and the barbaric, communist, and most recently terrorist enemies of that civilization (Brewer 2011: 4).

An enemy leader whose ongoing actions are seen as humiliating the United States or defying its international leadership sometimes plays a unique role in these symbolic struggles. In the postwar era, several international figures became nemeses of the United States for extended periods: the communist regime of the Soviet Union, Fidel Castro in Cuba, the Ayatollah Khomeini in Iran, Manuel Noriega in Panama, Muammar Qadaffi in Libya, Saddam Hussein in Iraq, and Osama bin Laden (the leader of al-Qaeda). Due to the symbolic meaning that the struggles with these defiant leaders had for the nation's collective self-worth, during wars that produced rally periods, the US public considered killing the enemy's leader or capturing him and bringing him to justice in the United States one of the top priorities of military operations.

The Importance of the Hunt

On December 30, 2006, Iraqi guards executed Saddam Hussein in Camp Justice, a joint USA-Iraq military base. The media circulated both the official footage of this event released by Al Iraqiya (the state-run television news channel in Iraq), which did not show the execution itself, and an unofficial mobile phone video of the actual execution filmed by one of the Iraqi guards. While the enemy leaders remained alive throughout most of the US military conflicts in the focal period, and many even maintained political power, the war against Iraq ended with the enemy's leader becoming a sacrificial offering to the national gods.[23]

However, nearly four years after the invasion of Iraq, neither the media nor the general public in the United States was still enchanted by the war. The considerable rally-round-the-flag effect that began in 2003 had dissipated. As a result, Americans' views about the intervention in Iraq were closely tied to their partisan identities, and the Republican Party was the only group that retained high levels of support for the war and the president (Jacobson 2010).[24] Similarly, when a team of US Navy Seals killed Osama bin Laden, the mastermind behind the September 11 attacks, nearly a decade after the attacks (on May 2, 2011), the US public did not rally behind President Barack Obama, who had ordered the operation.

The absence of a rally-round-the-flag effect in the United States in the aftermath of either the capture and execution of Saddam Hussein or the assassination of Osama bin Laden shows that the enemy and its leader have the strongest influence on public opinion about militarized conflicts not after they have been defeated and humiliated at the end of a war or the conclusion of a lengthy pursuit, but rather when they are "wanted, dead or alive" during the early phases of a military confrontation. In that initial stage, the enemy (through its own statements and action, as well as the rhetoric of US leaders) fuels a self-righteous anger, feelings of national pride about an ongoing or expected retaliation, and (over)confidence and hope that a military confrontation with the enemy will reinforce the nation's honor and establish its moral superiority.

Summary: The Role of the Enemy

A necessary (but not sufficient) condition for the emergence of a rally-round-the-flag effect is the public's identification (with the help of political leaders and the media) of a foreign country or an organization as an enemy that challenges core elements of the nation and/or its value and thus must be defeated. Under these circumstances, ordinary people develop an "attitude of contempt and loathing" toward the enemy (Mearsheimer 1990: 21), and thus military retaliation against the enemy evokes positive feelings. As Barbara Ehrenreich put it, "We may *enjoy* the company of our fellows, but we *thrill* to the prospect of joining them in collective defense against the common enemy" (2011: 224; emphases in the original). However, the enemy's leader may not be captured or killed until much later (if at all), when the public's enthusiasm about the war has been replaced by either anxiety and political controversy (caused by "endless" military engagement overseas) or "politics-as-usual" attitudes (if the war has ended). In both scenarios, public opinion about the war (and other issues) is once again divided along party lines (Jacobson 2010), and thus the public reaction to the death or capture of the enemy's leader is more likely to reflect this division than to blur it.

Importantly, while the current discussion highlights the discourse that has emerged in the United States during rally periods and the actions taken by US leaders, the nation's rivals in international conflicts have also played an active and important role in rally processes. Through their actions and speech, these rivals have created possibilities for US presidents to mobilize public opinion by presenting military action as a desirable policy. As Kenneth Schultz (2001) argued, the enemy's actions (as the public perceives them) have a significant impact on the "audience cost" the government may pay in domestic public opinion for their policies; Schultz (2001) provided empirical support for this argument in his analysis of select cases of the United Kingdom's international conflicts. A bellicose enemy boosts the public's expectation that the government will stand firm against the enemy to protect the nation's honor and reputation, even if that means escalating the use of military power (see also Levy 2012: 386). In contrast, a rival deciding to drop its weapons and seek a peaceful solution reduces the cost a government bears in domestic public opinion for backing down from its previous threats to retaliate against the enemy (the 1994 US occupation of Haiti, discussed in Chapter 8, is a case in point). Therefore, one of the necessary conditions for the emergence of rallies in the United States has been presidents' success in convincing the public that a rival state or organization is an enemy whose actions challenge the nation's honor and international reputation and thus is worth fighting. The following section further explores this condition and the central role that presidential rhetoric plays in rally processes.

The Role of the President

Opinion leaders such as presidents and prime ministers have long been a central focus of the literature on the rally-round-the-flag phenomenon. Some scholars have identified opinion leaders' propagation of security threats as the engine of the rally phenomenon (Cramer and Thrall 2009; Gadarian 2010; Kaufmann 2004; Willer 2004), and along the same lines, other scholars have claimed that military operations are widely supported when they are described by official speakers and the media as "protective intervention" (Nincic 1997). However, I contend that the main driver of rallies is not the wish to defuse security threats, but rather a desire among the public to restore or enhance the nation's international prestige and its sense of worth. Thus, I argue that opinion leaders make three key contributions to rally processes via their rhetoric: constructing a credible enemy, stimulating a public desire to re-establish or strengthen the nation's prestige and self-image, and framing the nation's actions as the best way to fulfill this desire.

The Construction of a Credible Enemy

The previous section discussed the contribution of public notions about the actions and intentions of evil enemies to the emergence of rally-round-the-flag effects in the United States; however, enemies rarely "speak for themselves." Instead, the president, other government officials, or other opinion leaders cast a foreign nation or organization in the role of enemy via official rhetoric that convincingly portrays the leadership of the country or organization as an opponent of the nation that is worth fighting.[25] Thus, a key contribution that presidents and other opinion leaders make to rally processes is the construction of a credible enemy.

The example of Saddam Hussein is once again illustrative (the empirical chapters discuss other examples). During two wars—the 1991 Gulf War and the 2003 Iraq War—most Americans viewed Saddam Hussein as a despicable foreign leader and a defiant enemy who deserved to be punished through military action. Prior to 1990, however, most ordinary US citizens either did not know who Saddam Hussein was or knew he was the president of Iraq but did not consider him an enemy of the United States. In the course of only a few months in the summer and fall of 1990, during which the US government and private firms hired by the government of Kuwait (the country Iraq invaded in the summer of 1990) ran a concentrated information campaign, most Americans came to know Saddam Hussein as the epitome of evil and a bitter enemy of the United States. When the United States and its allies launched a military operation against Iraqi forces in Kuwait in January 1991, a massive majority of Americans rallied behind the war, and President Bush's public approval ratings skyrocketed. Twelve years later (in March 2003), following an intense White House campaign to convince Americans that the Iraqi government was sponsoring anti-Western and anti-American terrorism, that Iraq possessed chemical and biological weapons that could be delivered to US enemies and was on the verge of developing nuclear weapons, the US public again rallied behind the commander-in-chief (George W. Bush) and overwhelmingly supported a military attack against Iraq, which was widely seen as an opportunity to dethrone Saddam Hussein.

The Use of Nation-Affirming Rhetoric during Rally Periods

The core role of politicians who serve as opinion leaders (chief among them the sitting president; see Schubert, Stewart and Curran 2002: 778) and the media in rally processes is twofold: stimulating a yearning among members of the public for more national honor and appreciation from other nations, and framing actions taken in the name of the nation (including waging wars against enemies) as an efficient way to fulfill the desire for more honor and appreciation. Following Hutcheson and coauthors (2004: 28), I label a rhetoric that conveys this dual message as "nation-affirming rhetoric." Typically, nation-affirming rhetoric emphasizes solidarity among compatriots, the core values of the nation (the collective "soul") that are being tested by current events, the nation's strong will, and the ability of the nation to overcome any challenge.

Two examples offer an initial illustration of nation-affirming rhetoric (the empirical chapters include additional examples). When discussing the Cuban Missile Crisis in a national address shortly after the crisis broke in October 1962, President Kennedy described his firm action against Cuba (a marine blockade of the island) as "most consistent with our character and courage as a nation and our commitment around the world," and added that "one path we shall never choose . . . is the path of surrender or submission."[26] Similarly, when seeking to mobilize public opinion in favor of the Cambodian incursion in May 1970, President Nixon asked,

> Does the richest and strongest nation in history of the world have the character to meet a direct challenge of a group which rejects every effort to win a just peace, ignores our warnings, tramples on solemn agreements, violates the neutrality of an unarmed people and uses our prisoners as hostages?[27]

In both examples, the president's primary motivation when discussing the nation's struggles with enemies was mobilizing public opinion by asking the nation to show its noble character and stand up to the enemy. By highlighting the special character of the nation and its capacity to overcome challenges, this presidential rhetoric highlighted a key aspect of American nationalism: the belief in national exceptionalism. While not unique to the United States (Smith 2003) (national communities tend to see themselves as unique and as having some exceptional qualities), this belief is a core element of the national self-understanding of many US citizens.

National Exceptionalism and Militancy

A belief in national exceptionalism becomes dangerous when it develops a jingoistic hue, as some historians have noted in studies of the immensely violent phase of nationalism in Europe during the two world wars. In the introduction to *The Idea of Nationalism*, Hans Kohn noted that the belief in the cultural uniqueness of the nation often develops into a sense of pride in the nation and a belief in its superiority (1944: 5). Carlton Hayes described nationalism as

> a condition of mind among members of a nationality, perhaps already possessed of a national state, a condition of mind in which loyalty to the ideal or to the fact of one's national state is superior to all other loyalties and of which pride in one's nationality and *belief in its intrinsic excellence and in its "mission" are integral parts.* (Hayes 1926: 6; emphasis added)

By describing nationalism (i.e., national chauvinism) as a "condition of mind," Hayes implied that a belief in national superiority grows stronger under certain circumstances. Rick Kosterman and Seymour Feschbach reinforced this idea: "One cannot help but be concerned by the periodic waves of nationalism [i.e., national chauvinism] that seem to sweep nations and the accompanying receptivity to belligerent actions" (1989: 273). My previous research has shown that within a given society, national chauvinism is often more prevalent during wars and security crises than at other times, and that this shift increases the public's desire to dominate other nations, including through the use of military power (Feinstein 2018, 2016b; see also Herrmann, Isernia, and Segatti 2009). Thus, presidential rhetoric makes a key contribution to the emergence of a rally-round-the-flag by propagating a sense of national moral superiority and a desire among the public to demonstrate the superiority of the home nation by defeating defiant enemies.

During militarized conflicts, nation-affirming rhetoric may link national superiority to not only the need to stand bravely against the nation's enemies, but also the benefit to other nations from "our" great deeds. In more than one instance, a US president seeking public legitimacy for a military operation claimed that beyond its specific objectives, the operation would also benefit a broader audience because US national interests parallel the interest of other peoples in the region of the conflict or, even more broadly, the entire world. As Susan Brewer (2011: 4) noted, during the twentieth century, in order to sell some of the most ambitious military objectives to the US public, official rhetoric depicted wars as clashes between civilization and barbarism, between democracy and dictatorship, between freedom and communism, and between civilization and terrorism.[28] Indeed, several studies have found that public support for military action is higher in the United States if the action is described as part of a grand conflict (for example, a "war on terror"; see Gershkoff and Kushner 2005), or as having a revisionist agenda of bringing democracy to non-democratic regions (Baker and Oneal 2001).[29]

Portraying a military action as serving noble moral principles is necessary especially when the action is occurring in a remote region of the world, which in the minds of most Americans is not linked to national interests (as in the case, for example, of the intervention in the crisis in the Persian Gulf in 1990–1991). In this scenario, however, propagating a belief in America's cultural exceptionality and moral superiority to other nations may not be sufficient to generate a rally-round-the-flag effect because opposing ideological camps draw different operative conclusions from exceptionalism and superiority. This was the case, for example, in the NATO intervention in the crisis in Kosovo in 1999, which was quite controversial in the United States (Feinstein 2017). For some Americans, beliefs about national exceptionality and superiority are associated with support for isolationist foreign policy that is committed solely to the national interest, while for other Americans beliefs about exceptionality and superiority are linked to the conviction that the United States has a moral duty (rooted in the idea of manifest destiny) to disseminate the American political culture and way of life throughout the world by intervening in favor of oppressed people (Fousek 2000; Lieven 2004; McCartney 2004; Roshwald 2006).[30]

To overcome this ideological rift, presidents seeking to mobilize public opinion behind military interventions in remote regions of the world have claimed that these interventions were in the United States' best interest and that US interests also happened to align with the interests of other peoples, whose liberties had been infringed upon and who were dependent on America to regain their freedom. Ultimately, framing a military intervention as a moral mission may help presidents and other opinion leaders transcend the context of a troubled region, and develop a broader agenda of creating a "new world order" that revolves around America's core values. For example, the rhetoric of Woodrow Wilson after World War I and the rhetoric of George H. W. Bush in the 1990s made this leap (Brewer 2011: 4).

Summary: The Role of Presidential Rhetoric

In wars and security crises, the president is a primary agent of public opinion. Studies have shown that appealing directly to the public (via a national address) helps the president mobilize public opinion behind his leadership because the setting portrays the president as a strong national leader and the speech sets the agenda for the legislative and public conversations (Blinder 2007; Rottinghaus 2009; Firestone and Harris 2006). This section went beyond this basic insight by highlighting the *content* of presidential rhetoric during rally periods. *What* presidents say to the public about a war or security crisis and their respective policies is crucial to whether the public rallies behind their leadership.

Obviously, actions matter too—the decision as to whether to use US military power (or threaten to use this power) is key to the emergence of rally outcomes. However, action alone is insufficient because the public reacts not to an objective reality, but to the way reality is communicated to the public by the president and other opinion leaders. To successfully generate a rally-round-the-flag reaction, a presidential rhetoric must convince the public that a particular country or organization is a bitter enemy of the United States, and that the struggle with the enemy is a test of the nation's special character and superiority, and/or that the current conflict is part of grander global struggle under the noble moral leadership of United States. The term "nation-affirming rhetoric," which I borrowed from Hutcheson and coauthors (2004), captures the essence of presidents' rhetoric during rally periods.

Two findings, which I discuss in greater detail in the empirical chapters, reveal the importance of nation-affirming rhetoric for the emergence of a rally-round-the-flag effect during a war or security crisis. First, in most rallies in the period covered in this book, the sitting president used a nation-affirming rhetoric, and that rhetoric reverberated in the public conversation (one exception is the 1975 *Mayaguez* incident, which, for reasons discussed in Chapter 5, evoked a modest rally reaction despite the absence of an explicit nation-affirming rhetoric). Second, in several instances of war or security crisis, an important reason for the *absence* of a rally was the president's decision *not* to use a nation-affirming rhetoric—for example, when Eisenhower talked about the US intervention in Lebanon in 1958, his comments had an internationalist rather than nationalist tone (see Appendix 1 for a discussion of this event).

The subsequent empirical chapters expose a fascinating reality: on more than one occasion, in the aftermath of a war or security crisis, a president has employed a nation-affirming rhetoric and has marked a target around an enemy, and yet nevertheless has failed to mobilize a rally behind their leadership. Notably, the reason rallies fail to emerge in some conflicts despite the use of nation-affirming rhetoric is that this type of rhetoric is only persuasive under certain conditions (discussed at the beginning of this chapter), namely a preexisting public feeling of national humiliation or a call from the international community to the United States to lead a military campaign to restore world order. Under either of these conditions, a presidential call to the public to unite behind an honorable military action will capture the public's hearts and minds.

At a more general level, the finding that a president's nation-affirming rhetoric does not always spur a rally highlights two fundamental aspects of framing as a tool for political mobilization. First, as social movement scholars have convincingly argued, political framing is used not only to convince the audience of a particular view of reality, but also to motivate people to take action to change reality (see Benford and Snow 2000: 614–15). Therefore, to effectively mobilize public opinion, the official framing of an issue and related policy must both affect the way people understand the issue and policy (i.e., how they define the problem, its causes, and the solution) and alter how people *feel* about the issue and proposed policy.

Second, my theoretical argument in this chapter and the empirical investigation in Chapters 5–8 show that framing alone is insufficient for significant political mobilization. Even the US president, who is arguably the most powerful opinion leader in the nation, does not have an unlimited capacity to mobilize public opinion through framing. Indeed, people are not prone to shift their political opinions and beliefs based solely on the framing of an issue or situation. Instead, an individual's political attitudes and policy preferences usually represent a relatively stable loyalty to a political or ideological camp (Druckman 2001: 239–40; Gries 2014), and thus people tend to accept a particular framing of a politicized issue if it is congruent with their ideological and political views, and reject a framing if it is incongruent with their views (Tsfati and Nir 2017; Price, Nir, and Cappella 2005). Therefore, as Chapters 5–8 demonstrate, US presidents who sought to swing public opinion toward greater approval were only successful under specific and quite unusual circumstances.

The Complexity of National Identity

My explanation of the rally phenomenon in the United States centers on the symbolic value attached to a collective American national identity and highlights the circumstances under which that collective value becomes a cause for concern among the majority of the US public. However, this is not a book about American nationalism, and I certainly do not hold an essentialist assumption about the existence of a single unitary American national identity. Rather, American nationalism is much more complicated and internally conflicted than perhaps many American patriots would be willing to acknowledge (for discussions of the distinct belief systems that compose multiple national identities in the United States, see Bonikowski and DiMaggio 2016; Lieven 2004; R. M. Smith 1997). This book examines a political phenomenon that reflects a common thread running through the collective identities of most members of the American nation. This common thread creates *the potential* for strong feelings of unity and shared fate to emerge during rally periods among the public, which in more settled times is solidly divided along class, ethnic/racial, ideological, and political lines.

For most Americans, national identity includes several key convictions: (1) that the American nation is one of their primary social groups, as well as a shared feeling of identification with and devotion to the national group; (2) that America is an old and prideful nation with a unique and exceptional historical legacy and culture; (3) that the United States has a special leadership role among the nations (although there is disagreement about whether this role is desirable and how the US should preform it); (4) that in the past the American nation has had glorious moments and has done great deeds but has also gone through miserable times and has engaged in actions that were not so glorious; (5) that among the many events and periods in the nation's history, a few are emblematic of the nation's special spirit or "soul" (Meacham 2019); and (6) that the nation has always had enemies.

Many of these core beliefs (perhaps all except the belief in international leadership) are also part of most national identities outside the United States, although each carries a different weight and degree of popularity in different countries (Bonikowski 2013). Further, the content of each belief has distinct nuances in a given national group. For example, precisely which events represent glorious, traumatic, or shameful periods in the nation's history depends on a nation's specific mythology. Understanding why rally-round-the-flag effects emerge in different countries requires consideration of these nation-specific nuances. I briefly discuss these intriguing national-level differences in the conclusion of the book. First, however, I move into a comprehensive comparative historical investigation of the rally-round-the-flag phenomenon in the United States, examining the precise conditions under which rallies behind the president occurred between 1950 and 2020.

PART II
INVESTIGATION

4

A Plan for Solving the Rally Puzzle

The main question this book seeks to answer is this: Under what circumstances and via what mechanisms has the rally-round-the-flag effect
emerged in the United States? As mentioned in Chapter 1, the simple,
seemingly commonsensical answer initially offered by researchers—that
US citizens, as patriots, automatically rally behind the president during
international conflicts with US involvement—falls short of explaining
the historical pattern of events: in the past seven decades, rally periods
have been quite rare even though the United States has been involved in
many international conflicts, including more than a few armed conflicts.
Understanding *why* rally outcomes emerge requires examining precisely
when—that is, under what circumstances—rally processes have material-
ized in the past. To solve this puzzle, the next four chapters compare the
US public's reactions to major war events and security crises involving the
United States from 1950 to 2020.[1]

Three analytic principles guide this investigation and distinguish it from
other attempts to explain the rally-round-the-flag phenomenon. First, *rally-
round-the-flag periods are distinguished from periods in which presidential
approval ratings increased only slightly*. Small improvements in presidential popularity ratings are quite common and occur in response to not only
conflict situations, but also, for example, good news on the economy, small
market booms, or the passing of a popular law initiated by the president.[2]
Many previous studies have not distinguished between instances of rally-
round-the-flag and smaller shifts in presidential approval ratings. This is
especially true for studies that have sought to estimate the average effect of
certain supposed rally-producing events (e.g., the onset of wars) on presidential job-approval ratings or other measures of public opinion. However,
this common approach entails lumping together events that produced strong
rally reactions among the public, events that had little impact on public
opinion, and events that had no influence on public opinion at all. These
studies, therefore, have produced a weak type of explanations that cut across
cases: instead of distinguishing between positive cases (events that evoked

Rally 'round the Flag. Yuval Feinstein, Oxford University Press. © Oxford University Press 2022.
DOI: 10.1093/oso/9780197629710.003.0004

rally reactions) and negative cases (events that did not evoke rally reactions), they described an average (or probabilistic) effect of a certain type of event on presidential job-approval ratings.

For example, earlier studies concluded that wars that sought to restrain foreign aggressors have increased presidential popularity more, on average, than wars that aimed to intervene politically in foreign countries (Eichenberg 2005; Gelpi, Feaver, and Reifler 2009: chap. 4; Jentleson 1992; Jentleson and Britton 1998). However, while some military invasions that officially aimed to restrain foreign aggressors, such as the 1991 Gulf War, did generate rally effects, others, such as the Korean War, did not. Further, some wars of political intervention, such as the invasion of Grenada in 1983, did not produce rally effects, but another such conflict, the 1989 invasion of Panama, did produce a significant rally-round-the-flag effect in the US public.

In the jargon of quantitative research, the common approach to the study of the rally-round-the-flag phenomenon, which usually uses regression analysis of pooled polling data, is prone to making both *false-positive* errors (i.e., including events that did not produce rallies in a category of events identified as rally-producing events) and *false-negative* errors (i.e., including events that generated rallies in a category of events that do not generate rallies). Taken together, these two types of errors represent a mis-specification problem of statistical models, which has prevented researchers from developing a deeper understanding of what distinguishes events that generated a rally-round-the-flag response from events that did not generate this outcome. The next two analytic principles guiding the current study address the mis-specification problem.

The second analytic principle that guides this investigation is that *no single characteristic of events can explain their effects on public opinion* (in particular, why a rally followed or did not follow the event) because single-trait explanations inevitably lead to arguments about probabilistic or "average" effects that leave some cases unexplained. Instead, researchers must identify *clusters of conditions* that have jointly produced a rally outcome. In general, these conditions include the characteristics of events, as well as certain aspects of the official reactions to events and unique historical and geopolitical circumstances. Once again, my approach differs from past research: whereas previous studies have searched for a single characteristic that makes an event *likely* to generate a rally-round-the-flag outcome (e.g., the event is a war against a foreign aggressor or a humanitarian mission, rather than an intervention in another county's internal politics; Jentleson 1992; Jentleson and Britton 1998), the investigation laid out in the following chapters seeks to identify combinations of conditions that uniquely characterize events that generated a rally-round-the-flag response. This approach entails searching for an explanation that differentiates—definitively, not probabilistically—events that produced rallies from events that did not. Put simply, the book does not ask which conditions increase the likelihood that an event will generate a rally-round-the-flag outcome (the research question in previous studies), but rather why certain events actually generated rallies and why other events did not.

The third analytic principle of the investigation is that sometimes *no single explanation fits all seemingly similar outcomes*. In other words, while it might seem ideal to develop a singular parsimonious explanation of the rally phenomenon, it is possible that multiple pathways have led to the emergence of rallies. Most prior studies have used a nomothetic logic of inquiry (i.e., seeking an explanation that fits all cases and takes a probabilistic form or highlights an average effect), and thus have not considered the possibility of multiple pathways to rallies (which can be detected by focusing on small clusters of rallies that share distinct paths to emergence, rather than searching for a single pattern). The discussion in Chapters 5–8 reveals that while rally periods in the United States during the focal period share a common thread (namely, they were all linked to people's concerns about the nation's symbolic value), each rally-round-the-flag event emerged under specific conditions and via a distinct path of development that is either unique to the event or shared by a few but not all other rallies.

The following chapters present the findings of a comparative historical investigation (Mahoney 2003; Skocpol 1984; Stinchcombe 1978) of almost all major war events and security crises involving the United States between 1950 and 2020, including events that generated rallies and events that did not. To remain true to the three principles mentioned earlier—distinguishing between events that generated rallies and those that did not, developing a multicausal explanation, and permitting multiple pathways to rally-round-the-flag outcomes—the analysis encompassed two complementary efforts that in the jargon of comparative history are called (after John Stuart Mills) the Millian method of agreement and method of difference (Falleti and Mahoney 2015: 225). The first effort (searching for agreement between cases)

entailed a comparison of all events that resulted in rally periods, which revealed that only events that included either an attack on US civilian targets
or military action undertaken by the United States generated rallies. Other
types of events (e.g., several engagements between US jets and Soviet jets
during the Cold War) did not generate rallies. Thus, the presence of either a
US military attack or an attack on a US civilian target was a *necessary* condition for the emergence of a rally in the focal period.

The next stage of data analysis zoomed in on all events that included
at least one of the two fundamental conditions mentioned in the preceding paragraph—foreign attacks on US civilians, or military action by
the United States. Crucially, most of the events that involved one of these
incidents did *not* generate significant rally effects. Therefore, the second effort in the analysis (searching for differences between cases) entailed identifying distinct *combinations* of conditions (Thelen and Mahoney 2015: 7;
Ragin 1987) that were present only during rally processes and thus were
sufficient for the emergence of rallies. Specifically, I compared events that
generated rallies with seemingly similar events that were not followed by
rally periods. This comparison detected a few sets of conditions that represent distinct paths to the emergence of a rally-round-the-flag effect
(Chapters 5–8 discuss these paths).

Comparative historical research is an iterative process (Mahoney and
Rueschemeyer 2003: 13), in which theoretical arguments and their corre-
sponding sets of variables are repeatedly modified in an effort to produce an
explanatory model that fully (or almost fully) differentiates the outcome of
interest (in this book, rally-round-the-flag) from other outcomes (no rally).
I developed some elements of my theoretical argument (most notably, the
emphasis of on preexisting feelings of national humiliation) through such
iterative processes, in which I sought a satisfying solution to the puzzle of the
emergence of rallies in the aftermath of only a few events. Discovering two
preconditions for the emergence of rallies—a previous humiliating event or
a call from the United Nations to lead the free world—enhanced the analysis
by adding another important element in the comparative historical search for
causality: *process tracing* through the detection of sequences of linked events
(Falleti and Mahoney 2015: 229–30). For example, as discussed in Chapter 5,
neither John F. Kennedy's policy during the Cuban Missile Crisis nor the
rally of the public behind Kennedy during that period can be understood
without linking the event to the failed Bay of Pigs invasion that occurred a
year and half earlier.

Case Selection

Nearly 50 war events and security crises are examined in this study (see Appendix Table A1 for the full list of events). The initial list of events contained 57 acts of war and other security events that occurred between 1950 and 2020.[3] This list was extracted from a longer list of events using two selection criteria:[4] First, the *New York Times* reported the event on its front page, which indicates that the media placed the event high on the agenda for public conversation. This selection criterion reflects the idea that sufficient media attention is a precondition for the transformation of events into rally points (Baker and Oneal 2001; Baum and Groeling 2005; Lian and Oneal 1993), most fundamentally because the public cannot rally in response to events that people do not know about or know about but do not consider very important (which are the most likely assessments of events that are not featured in the headlines). Second, I excluded several major international events that did not involve military action by the United States or its enemy or a threat to take military action (e.g., signings of peace agreements or ceasefires); however, none of these events had an effect on the public approval of the president similar in magnitude to the effects of the events described as rallies in the following chapters.[5] Fifty-seven events met the selection criteria, but eight were eventually dropped from the list—five because there were not enough data to assess their effects on public opinion, and three because their effects on public opinion were ambiguous (however, these ambiguous cases were included in a second round of analysis[6]).

Identifying Instances of Rally-round-the-Flag

As a first step, I distinguished between rally-round-the-flag effects and reactions to events that did not include a rally-round-the-flag effect (following the first analytic principle). I made this distinction based on the original meaning of the term "rally-round-the-flag," which has been somewhat eroded in the past few decades: the term is meant to refer to *extraordinary* boosts to the popularity of presidents. To differentiate between rally periods and relatively minor increases in presidential job-approval ratings, I examined the changes in presidents' approval and disapproval ratings in the periods during and shortly after each event on this list (in addition, to ensure that no rally period was absent from the list of events, I examined the entire data series for presidential job-approval and disapproval ratings for each presidential term in the focal period). This exercise produced a classification scheme that includes four types of reactions to events.[7]

First, instances of *rally-round-the-flag* were characterized by a sudden, sharp increase in presidential job-approval ratings. In addition, rallies entailed a significant decline in presidential job-*disapproval* ratings. Taken together, these two shifts indicate that many citizens who had previously disapproved of the president transitioned to approval. The coding of rally-round-the-flag periods was a qualitative process. Because rally effects are easily noticeable in the data on presidential job-approval and disapproval ratings (as shown in Appendix, Figures A1–A13), which are usually fairly stable or change slowly (Page and Shapiro 1992), there was no need to choose a specific cutoff to distinguish rallies from smaller deviations from the general pattern of public opinion about the president. A closer look at the data reveals that rally effects are indeed substantial and thus unusual: in all but one case of rally-round-the-flag, the difference between support for the president and opposition to the president increased by at least 20 percentage points (e.g., approval increased by 11 percentage points and disapproval decreased by 10 percentage points, creating a total change of 21 percentage points). The only exception is the public reaction to the 1989 invasion of Panama, which I treat as a rally-round-the-flag event even though the difference between approval and disapproval increased by only 18 points during the invasion; however, the overall presidential job-approval rating following the invasion was extremely high (80 percent) and the disapproval rating was very low (11 percent). Table 4.1 presents the list of events that generated rally-round-the-flag effects in the examined period.

The second type of events were followed by a very small increase (1–2 percentage points) in the president's job-approval rating (which may reflect sampling variability), a decline in the approval rating, or no change. Events of this type were coded as non-rallies. The third type entailed somewhat larger increases in presidential job-approval ratings that were nonetheless too small to be treated as significant rally effects (typically, a 6–10 point increase in the difference between job approval and job disapproval, for example, the presidential job-approval rating increased by 5 points and the job-disapproval rating decreased by 3 points, totaling an 8-point change). In contrast to the effects coded as rally-round-the-flag, which only emerged following major wars or security events, these smaller improvements in presidential

Table 4.1 Rally-round-the-Flag Events

Event	Approval Rating		Disapproval Rating		Net Gain (Δapproval+ |Δdisapproval|)
	Before Event	In the Aftermath of Event	Before Event	In the Aftermath of Event	
Cuban Missile Crisis (10/22–10/28/1962)	62	74	25	14	23
Mayaguez incident (5/12–5/15/1975)	40	51	43	33	21
Iran hostage crisis (11/4/1979–1/20/1981)	31	58	55	32	50
Invasion of Panama (12/20/1989–1/31/1990)	71	80	20	11	18
Gulf War (1/17–2/28/1991)	64	89	25	8	42
September 11 attacks (9/11/2001)	57	90	34	6	61
Invasion of Iraq (3/20–5/1/2003)	58	71	38	25	26

job-approval ratings occurred not only after wars or security crises, but also in the aftermath of minor events such as the release of good news about the economy, small market booms, or the passing of a popular law initiated by the president. Further, in many cases, sampling variability was likely the true cause of minor shifts of public opinion in favor of the president. For example, polls conducted before and after President Lyndon Johnson ordered the deployment of US Marines in the Dominican Republic (on April 28, 1965) showed an increase of 6 points in Johnson's job-approval rating, which rose from 64 percent in the last week of April to 70 percent in early May. However, a closer look at the data series reveals that the rating in late April was a deviation from an almost flat trend line that had hovered around 70 percent for several months. Therefore, the suspected minor rally effect probably reflects a measurement error (in the April data) due to sampling variability. For both reasons—because many different types of events can produce smaller shifts in aggregated public opinion data and because measurement errors are more likely than robust rally effects—events that were followed by a minor increase in the president's job-approval rating were coded as non-rallies.

The fourth type of event that emerged in the focal period was *borderline cases*: a few events led to increases in presidential job-approval ratings that were quite substantial but not large enough to warrant unequivocal treatment as a rally-round-the-flag effect. For example, in 1986, an air raid on Libya was followed by 6-point increase in President Reagan's job-approval rating and a 7-point decrease in his job-disapproval rating. Chapter 7 focuses on the cases that verged on becoming rally points. The discussion of these borderline events sheds light on how certain conditions are crucial to the emergence of a full-blown rally effect—I show that these conditions were absent from the borderline cases, which share other characteristics with events that generated more substantial rally effects.

Data

To identify multiple pathways to rally-round-the-flag, each represented by a specific cluster of conditions (following the second and third analytic principles), I used an original variable-rich data set, which I compiled from two types of sources: First, I reviewed an extensive collection of secondary resources (primarily academic articles and books) about specific events, historical periods, and the presidencies of US presidents. Second, to reconstruct the official framing of events, to assess the reactions of political actors other than the government, and to evaluate the intensity and content of media coverage, I reviewed the coverage of each event in three major newspapers: the *New York Times*, the *Los Angeles Times*, and the *Washington Post*. Based on this data collection process, the information about each event includes an extensive characterization of the event (e.g., the type of event, the official policy goals, how many American casualties resulted from the event, if any), the reactions of opinion leaders (the president, the media, and politicians from both sides of the political spectrum), the pertinent historical and geopolitical circumstances surrounding the event, the economic conditions in the United States at the time (e.g., the unemployment rate and the level of public economic optimism or pessimism prior to the event), and the contemporary political conditions (e.g., presidential job-approval ratings before the event and whether the government was divided by political party).

The following chapters present a narrative about the emergence of rally-round-the-flag outcomes based on the results of the data analysis. While the analysis included dozens of events, only some are discussed at length in the following chapters, while others are mentioned briefly or are not mentioned at all. Specifically, the discussion centers on the focal events in the second stage of data analysis: these are the events that generated a rally-round-the-flag effect, as well as several events that share key features with rally-producing events yet did not generate this effect. When discussing the focal events in Chapters 5–8, I present examples of the primary materials (e.g., the texts of presidential speeches and news reports, and findings of opinion polls) that I used to reconstruct the development of each event, its historical context, and the reactions of government leaders, the media, and the public. The discussion also includes quotes from letters that members of the US public wrote to the press. These quotes demonstrate the plausibility of my retrospective reading of historical situations by showing that laypeople indeed shared the meanings I attribute to historical events in real historical time; however, they are not part of the empirical materials analyzed in the study.

As mentioned before, all the rallies discussed in this book share a common thread: the rally behind the commander-in-chief stemmed from the public's desire to maintain or restore the nation's collective honor and prestige through military action. Yet despite this commonality, there are multiple pathways to the emergence of a rally. Chapters 5, 6, and 8 discuss three distinct pathways to a rally-round-the-flag effect. In the first two pathways (Chapters 5 and 6), the public rallies behind the president when its members are led to believe that taking military action against an enemy is necessary to claim national honor and the respect of other nations. Specifically, in the first pathway (Chapter 5), a prior international fiasco nurtures a popular belief that the United States has been humiliated and must demonstrate its military might in order to reclaim national honor and prestige. In the second

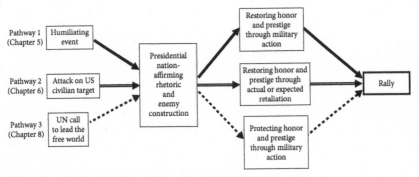

Figure 4.1. Pathways to rally-round-the-flag effects.

pathway (Chapter 6), a feeling of collective humiliation and a desire to retaliate emerges in the aftermath of a major attack against US civilian targets. The third pathway (Chapter 8) is farther afield from the first two. In these cases, a rally emerges when the United States leads coalition forces in a military operation authorized by the UN Security Council because the public believes that fulfilling the role of "leader of the free world" will reinforce the nation's collective honor and prestige. Figure 4.1 illustrates the three pathways to a rally-round-the-flag outcome.

5

Saving the Nation's Face

Rallies in Militarized Conflicts

Since 1950, the United States has participated in many militarized conflicts, but only four of these conflicts—the 1962 Cuban Missile Crisis, the 1975 *Mayaguez* incident, the 1989 invasion of Panama, and the 2003 invasion of Iraq—have produced rally-round-the-flag reactions among the US public. The common thread in these instances of rally is that they offered the United States an opportunity to reclaim national honor and prestige after being humiliated in prior events. In this chapter, I examine these four militarized conflicts, explaining how each came to be understood as not just a foreign policy issue, but part of a critical effort to maintain or restore the nation's collective honor and prestige (see Figure 4.1. in Chapter 4 for an illustration of this process). In three of these cases, the sitting president used nationalist rhetoric to highlight an opportunity for the United States to reclaim its collective honor and prestige. The fourth case, the *Mayaguez* incident, reveals a different pattern—in this instance, specific historical circumstances stimulated a public desire to reclaim national honor and prestige via military conflict even though the president did not use nationalist rhetoric. After discussing the four cases, I discuss three events that did not evoke rallies despite the nationalist tone of the presidential rhetoric (i.e., the invasions of the Dominican Republic, Cambodia, and Grenada). The comparison of the two sets of events—i.e., those that generated rallies and those that did not—highlights the role of two conditions that, together with presidential rhetoric that has a nationalist tone, co-produced rallies during US militarized conflicts: preceding episode of national humiliation that evoked a public desire to reclaim national honor and prestige and established enemy for the US public to unite against.

The Cuban Missile Crisis

On October 22, 1962, at 7:00 p.m., President Kennedy gave a national address from the Oval Office in the White House, in which he announced that

Rally 'round the Flag. Yuval Feinstein, Oxford University Press. © Oxford University Press 2022.
DOI: 10.1093/oso/9780197629710.003.0005

"unmistakable evidence [held by his administration] has established the fact that a series of offensive missile sites is now in preparation on that impris-oned island."[1,2] Kennedy then added that "the purpose of these bases can be none other than to provide a nuclear strike capability against the Western Hemisphere."[3] Kennedy did not explain what had led the Kremlin to take such a risky action, which could have transformed the Cold War into a hot war between two superpowers, each heavily armed with nuclear weapons.

Moscow decided to send nuclear missiles to Cuba for two main reasons (Garthoff 1992: 41–43; Lebow 1992: 169). First, Moscow sought to offset a similar action taken by the United States less than a year before: in June 1961, the United States began placing Jupiter nuclear missiles at bases around the Black Sea in Turkey, thus further tilting the balance of military power on the European front of the Cold War in favor of the United States and its allies. Second, for an extended period before the missile crisis, the Cuban government had well-founded concerns that the United States was planning an invasion to overthrow Cuba's Communist regime, and therefore the gov-ernment pleaded with Moscow to send help. Moscow's decision to install nuclear weapons in Cuba was meant to address both problems, but the US public was not informed of this context during the Cuban Missile Crisis.[4]

In his address to the nation, Kennedy described Moscow's action as "a de-liberately provocative and unjustified change in the status quo," as a violation of Moscow's assurance to the United States that military assistance to Cuba would include only defensive weapons, and as a threat to not only the United States but also other nations in the Western Hemisphere. The policy reaction Kennedy announced included several elements: quarantining shipments of offensive weapons to Cuba with the possibility of extending the quarantine to other types of cargo; increasing surveillance of Cuba and ordering the US military to prepare to take additional actions if needed;[5] a declaration that "any nuclear missile launched from Cuba against any nation in the Western Hemisphere [would be regarded] as an attack by the Soviet Union on the United States, requiring a full retaliatory response upon the Soviet Union"; a call for US allies in Latin America and around the world, as well as the UN Security Council, to back the US policy on Cuba; and a call for Chairman Khrushchev to "halt and eliminate this clandestine, reckless and provocative threat to world peace and to stable relations between our two nations . . . to abandon this course of world domination, and to join in an historic effort to end the perilous arms race and to transform the history of man." Kennedy noted that no one could predict how the crisis would develop, and thus he anticipated that "months of sacrifice and self-discipline lie ahead." However, on October 27, the nations reached an agreement that ended the crisis on October 28.

The Public Reaction to the Missile Crisis

The missile crisis immediately hit the headlines of all major newspapers and was the main topic of editorials in the following days. Television and radio stations interrupted their regular programming frequently to air special reports about the crisis (George 2003: 96), turning the crisis into a "media event" (Dayan and Katz 1992). Across the country, people were magnetized by the media broadcast of the crisis. *Newsweek* reported that "throughout the nation Americans hung by their radios and TV sets, and pressed up to television store windows. Transistor radios popped up on streets, in trains, even in theaters. There was the gnawing appreciation everywhere that this time might really be it" (George 2003: 94). The media stood almost unanimously behind Kennedy's decision to impose a marine blockade on Cuba,[6] which the editors of the *Washington Post*, for example, described as "inevitable."[7]

Reactions on Capitol Hill were similar to those in the media. Most leaders of the Republican Party (and of course the Democrats in the Senate and Congress) expressed their support for the president's policy (George 2003: 127–29). However, some critical voices did emerge during the crisis. Several prominent GOP members publicly accused Kennedy of using the crisis for political gain—they claimed that Soviet missile installation in Cuba was not a new problem, but Kennedy had chosen to disregard it until the expected elections made the propagation of a crisis politically profitable for the president's party, even if that meant putting the country at risk of nuclear annihilation (George 2003: 128–29).[8] Overall, the GOP's reaction can be described as narrow support in the context of broader criticism: while backing Kennedy's decision to impose a marine blockade on Cuba and demand that Soviet missiles be removed from the island, Republicans continued to criticize Kennedy and his record in dealing with the Cuban problem and with communism more generally.[9] The GOP's bifurcated position during the missile crisis was conveyed, for example, by former President Dwight Eisenhower's speech in Gettysburg, Pennsylvania, on October 23 (one day after the missile crisis became public): Eisenhower encouraged all Americans to support the president during the crisis, but also urged Republicans to intensify their election campaigns, explaining, "Though we support the President in foreign crisis, we do not have to support him when he speaks or acts as head of a political party; and indeed we do not . . . we are free to ask and to learn how we arrived at our present state, even in foreign affairs."[10]

The Symbolic Meaning of the Missile Crisis

Despite some criticism from members of the opposition party, especially those who wanted to see the United States take tougher military action against Cuba, the majority of the public rallied behind the leadership of President Kennedy during the crisis because the crisis became infused with a profound symbolic meaning: the installation of Soviet nuclear missiles so close to the US shore was seen as a humiliating act that challenged the credibility of the United States as a superpower (Weldes 1999: 179). In his address to the nation, President Kenney repeatedly stressed that the installation of Soviet offensive missiles in Cuba was a test of the United States' capacity to establish and maintain its status as a global superpower and as the leader of the nations in the Western Hemisphere. The media, too, bolstered the notion that the time had come for a tough response to a manipulative, untrustworthy Soviet enemy whose imperialist ambitions could no longer be held in check through diplomacy alone. While this depiction of the Soviet Union was not new, the exposure of the secret installment of Soviet nuclear missiles in the United States' metaphorical backyard intensified the public's frustration with the endless Cold War and the lack of decisive action against Moscow's repeated sinister maneuvers. The news about Soviet missiles in Cuba thus boosted an already present desire to teach the Soviet Union a lesson; as Alise George explained (2003: 119), Americans wanted "to give Khrushchev a bloody nose."

Beyond the larger context of the Cold War, the missile crisis evoked a rally reaction because of the meaning the crisis had in light of a problematic relationship between the United States and Cuba. During the years prior to the missile crisis, the "Cuban problem" had become an especially irritating issue for both policymakers and the general US public. Following the Cuban Revolution (1953–1959) that overthrew the military dictatorship of President Fulgencio Batista, policymakers in the United States had gradually defined socialist Cuba as a major threat to US national interests (Weldes 1999). They portrayed Fidel Castro and his "bearded" loyalists as agents of a conspiracy by global communism (directed by Moscow) to expand throughout Latin America and the entire Western Hemisphere (Weldes 1999). For several years prior to the missile crisis, US political discourse had increasingly portrayed Cuba as posing a dual symbolic threat: a threat to the free and civilized way of life of the family of nations in the Americas inspired by the United States, and an even broader threat to the prestige of the United States as a global superpower (Weldes 1999: 184). In that period, a series of covert operations by the Central Intelligence Agency (CIA) called "Operation Mongoose" sought to remove Castro's communist regime from power and replace it with a US-friendly regime (Weldes 1999: 67–69; White 1995: chap. 2).

In April 1961, the United States attempted to overthrow the Castro government by launching an invasion at the Bay of Pigs (Bahía de Cochinos) on the southwestern coast of Cuba. However, the invasion, which was planned and sponsored by the CIA and was executed by about 1,500 Cuban exiles, failed and was aborted after only three days. In the following months, Republicans kept the spotlight on the embarrassing memories of the Bay of Pigs fiasco via their criticism of President Kennedy for being indecisive in his policy on Cuba (Hilsman 1996: 72; White 1995: chap. 4). Some Republicans, such as Senator Homer E. Capehart of Indiana, even openly advocated for taking military action against Cuba (Kennedy 1969: 25). Consequently, in early 1962, Cuba was the only foreign policy issue on which Kennedy's public disapproval ratings were higher than his approval ratings, and most Americans wanted the United States to take a tougher stance on Cuba even before the Soviet missiles were revealed (Snyder and Borghard 2011: 453). The criticism from Republican politicians only intensified during the summer and fall of 1962 in the run-up to congressional elections, and some politicians and media commentators accused Kennedy of not responding vigorously enough to the buildup of Soviet forces in Cuba (Kennedy publicly dismissed that criticism by arguing that the weapons the Soviet Union had sent to Cuba had a purely defensive purpose; George 2003: 93, 115, 122).

In the aftermath of the Bay of Pigs fiasco, the media made a significant contribution to keeping the "Cuban problem" high on Americans' list of concerns and fostering the public's desire to settle the score with Castro. For example, on April 18, 1962, the *Washington Post* reported that Cuba had held a two-day national holiday to celebrate the anniversary of its Bay of Pigs triumph.[11] The following day, the *New York Times* dedicated part of its editorial column to a discussion of the implications of the fiasco for US foreign affairs.[12] The editors proclaimed:

> The outcome of that battle was a blow to American pride and prestige which was certainly unmatched in the history of our relations with Latin America. The monumental folly of the invasion, so far as the United States was concerned, grows with the passage of time, while the heroism, the idealism and the tragic waste of young Cuban lives were brought home to us anew with the recent trial of the captives and the ransom of the ill and wounded.
>
> [...]
>
> The invasion was more than a failure itself; it strengthened Castro in a regime that is now openly a ruthless, Communist totalitarian dictatorship. Thus, one year later, the United States faces a Cuban problem that is harder than ever to solve. At least, we presumably know now what not to do. The Castro revolution will in due time be ended by the Cubans.

Six months later, and just two weeks before the eruption of the Cuban Missile Crisis, the *New York Times* published a special report summarizing several interviews that reporters had conducted in three communities across the United States, which focused on ordinary US citizens' views on the "Cuban problem."[13] The interviews were conducted in the context of growing tensions with the Soviet Union and Cuba over arms shipments from Moscow to Havana and Cuba's announcement, in late September, of a plan to build a fishing port that would serve a joint Cuban-Soviet Atlantic fishing fleet, which the United States believed the Soviet Union would use to collect military intelligence (especially on the US missile-launching site at Cape Canaveral, Florida, and the US military installation at Guantanamo).[14]

Many of the interviewees expressed frustration with how the Kennedy administration had handled the Cuban problem and demanded stricter action against Cuba. For example, the column featured the following quotes: "I'm for kicking 'em out!" "They just keep crowding us and crowding us. How far are we going to be pushed?" "It's a mess. We're a little sick and tired of that crowd up there in Washington. We was [*sic*] crazy that we didn't stop it right at the start." "We sit here and pay our taxes while they throw mud in our faces." One interviewee made a connection between recent developments in US-Cuba relations and the Bay of Pigs fiasco, saying, "I can't understand why we didn't give these fellows help when they went over there to start with."

As if to rub salt in the wound, on October 11, 1962 (a week and a half before the missile crisis became public), the media reported that the United States would pay part of the ransom Cuba was demanding for the release of the Bay of Pigs prisoners and that the payment would come out of the CIA's budget.[15] Two days later, a Gallup Poll found that while most Americans did not support sending US troops to Cuba to help overthrow Castro, the vast majority wished the United States would do something to address the Cuban problem. Only 22 percent preferred a "hands-off" policy on Cuba.[16] Notably, when asked to explain why they objected to taking military action against Cuba, many respondents mentioned their concern that such action would further damage the United States' international reputation if the United States was branded as the aggressor in the conflict (thus deepening rather than fixing the damage caused by the Bay of Pigs fiasco).[17]

The Cuban Missile Crisis offered President Kennedy the opportunity to repair the nation's reputation (and his own reputation) by demonstrating that the United States still dominated the Western Hemisphere. As noted earlier, many Americans felt that the time had come to settle the score with Cuba's communist government and with the Soviet Union.[18] The popular desire to restore the international reputation of the United States likely influenced Kennedy's decision to impose a marine blockade on Cuba and to use threatening language against Cuba and the Soviet Union. While it is impossible to know exactly how much the public mood affected the administration's decisions, experts who have examined the deliberations that occurred in the White House and among the members of the Executive Committee of the National Security Council (ExComm) during the crisis have suggested that the administration's reaction was driven not by a sense of security threat, but rather by concerns about being perceived as weak. Specifically, those in power were committed to the Cold War doctrine that the United States should never appear weak in eyes of its enemies and were worried that the American public would punish Kennedy and the Democratic Party for showing weakness, especially when dealing with the "Cuban problem," which had been a core issue in Kennedy's 1960 presidential campaign (George 2003: 116; Snyder and Borghard 2011; Stern 2003; Lebow 1992: 164–168; Hilsman 1996: 71–74).[19]

According to Robert Kennedy (1969) (who was the attorney general at the time), initially most cabinet members thought that "an air strike against the missiles sites could be the only course" (1969: 31). After the option of imposing a marine blockade on Cuba was put on the table, several members of the administration objected, saying that the blockade would be like "closing the door after the horse had left the barn," might lead to confrontation with the Soviet Union instead of dealing with Cuba and Castro, and would probably lead to a Russian demand for the United States to remove all its missiles surrounding the Soviet Union in exchange for the removal of the missiles from Cuba (1969: 34–35). Therefore, they proposed launching an immediate air strike against Cuba, a proposition that members of the Joint Chiefs of Staff supported unanimously (1969: 36). According to Jim Rasenberger (2012: 364), the Joint Chiefs even proposed that the United States invade Cuba and oust Castro, but Kennedy, who was guided by the bitter outcome at the Bay of Pigs, decided on a firm but measured reaction.

In his rhetoric about the missile crisis, however, Kennedy did not try to downplay the importance of the event to the nation's regional and international standing and its potential implications for national honor and prestige. In his national address on the missile crisis (on October 22, 1962), Kennedy highlighted the symbolic meaning of the situation for the nation by referring to the American spirit and to the United States' commitments as a world superpower: He stated that taking strong action in response to Soviet provocation would be "most consistent with our character and courage as a nation and our commitment around the world," adding that "one path we shall never choose . . . is the path of surrender or submission."[20] The public largely embraced Kennedy's message, as shown by the considerable growth in his job-approval rating, from 62 percent before the crisis to 74 percent in the aftermath of the crisis, and the decline in his disapproval rating, from 25 percent to 14 percent. (Estimates for the latter time point are from a poll conducted about three weeks after the crisis ended. It is likely that the rally effect was even more substantial in the days and weeks just after the event.)

An alternative interpretation of these findings is that the public rallied behind Kennedy because people were deeply troubled by the missile's threat to security and believed that Kennedy was taking reasonable measures to deal with the threat. While many Americans undoubtedly experienced a sense of threat during the Cuban Missile Crisis (George 2003: chap. 3), there are at least three reasons to suspect that a sense of security threat was not the main reason for the rally behind Kennedy during the crisis. First, evidence from multiple surveys has shown that worries about safety and security were not pervasive. Based on these data, Tom Smith concluded:

> While the Cuban missile crisis was on most people's minds, the public was not overwhelmed by worries and did not dwell on concerns about death

and nuclear survival. Nor were there notable declines in psychological well-being. Instead, psychological reactions were rather mixed and muted. Positive affect was down, [but] general happiness was up, and negative affect changed little. Likewise, measures of stress and anxiety showed little alteration and clearly presented no evidence that people were traumatized or debilitated by worries over the crisis.[…] In sum, the public did not panic, was not overcome by nuclear anxiety, and remained psychologically intact during the crisis. (T. W. Smith 2003: 274)

Second, a strong sense of security threat would most likely have caused the American public to prefer a more cautious policy over Kennedy's quite aggressive reaction, which entailed a risk of escalating the standoff into a military confrontation with Cuba and perhaps the Soviet Union as well. Theoretical support for this argument comes from psychological studies, which show that strong fear causes individuals to overestimate risks and make risk-averse choices (Huddy et al. 2005; Lerner and Keltner 2001; Lerner et al. 2003; Skitka et al. 2006). For example, in a study of individuals' emotions in the aftermath of 9/11 and the 2003 invasion of Iraq, Leonie Huddy and her co-investigators found that individuals who experienced anxiety tended to perceive higher levels of risks and to be *less* supportive of taking military action (Huddy, Feldman, and Cassese 2007). These and similar findings suggest that had Americans really believed that the Cuban Missile Crisis could develop into a nuclear Armageddon, the majority would have preferred careful diplomacy over Kennedy's tough talk and relatively risky policy, which had the potential to develop into a military confrontation between the United States and the Soviet Union if the latter sought to break the marine blockade on Cuba and continue the construction of missile bases on the island. A Gallup poll conducted on October 23, 1962 (one day after Kennedy's national address), showed that only one of every five Americans believed that the quarantine of Cuba would lead to a third world war; about 84 percent of the public favored the quarantine, and only 4 percent opposed the policy (Detzer 1979: 192).[21]

Third, in his address to the nation, Kennedy explicitly downplayed the threat element, emphasizing that Americans were already used to living "on the bull's eye,"[22] and therefore the missile crisis only marginally increased an already present danger. Kennedy's actions during the Cuban Missile Crisis were widely perceived not as manipulating the public's fear but rather as sending a firm message to both Cuba and the Soviet

Union that 18 months after the invasion of the Bay of Pigs, the United States was once again ready to use force to stop any attempt to challenge its dominance in the Western Hemisphere. Indeed, the symbolic reaffirmation of America's status as an international leader overshadowed security-related fears as the perceived meaning of the crisis shifted from a narrowly defined dispute about missiles in Cuba to an epic struggle comparable to the nation's greatest historical battles. The following quote from a letter to the *New York Times* illustrates the popular understanding of the missile crisis:

> There comes a time during the historic evolution of a nation when that nation is caused to jeopardize its security in order to maintain its way of life. This seemingly paradoxical political axiom has been exemplified in this nation even in its early beginnings. We have since been "put to the test" in 1812, 1862, 1917, 1941, 1950 . . . , and have survived with our initial freedoms.
>
> Today we are forced to take a political position which not only shall determine our freedom and survival, but perhaps that of the entire world. The action taken against Cuba by our President is justified not only for security but morally: Even if the earth crumble, let justice be done![23]

Arguably, the most important aspect of public meaning-making during the Cuban Missile Crisis were the references by opinion leaders and ordinary citizens to the Monroe Doctrine.[24] Many professional reporters and ordinary citizens who sent letters to the press expressed that Kennedy's decision to impose a marine blockade on Cuba showed that the United States was again determined to act as a world superpower in the spirit of the Monroe Doctrine (Nacos 1990: 28).[25] For example, a *Washington Post* editorial published the morning after Kennedy's address to the nation explained:

> If there is any doubt in the minds of any Americans about the rightness of the course that has been taken or about the pull of history and of national interest that has taken the Kennedy Administration in this direction, they may well go back and read the Monroe Doctrine and the history out of which it grew. Actually, the great and powerful United States of 1962 has said no more than was implicit in the Doctrine proclaimed by the weak and isolated United States in 1823. Since that day the Doctrine has undergone many transformations without altering its basic premise—that the

United States will not tolerate the subjugation of any part of the Western Hemisphere by a hostile European power.[26]

While framing the crisis through a reference to the United States' epic struggle against European colonialism in the early nineteenth century did not completely eliminate worries about the security threat posed by the missiles and any potential subsequent military confrontations, this formulation nonetheless added an aspect of celebratory identity affirmation to the events by portraying the crisis as a proud re-enactment of an epic historical struggle that is considered one of the nation's finest hours.

As explained in the theoretical discussion in Chapter 3, it is precisely this type of reinterpretation of military actions and security crises that generates strong affective reactions that motivate individuals to rally around the flag. In a letter to the editor, a reader of the *Washington Post* vividly expressed the festive reaction many Americans had to Kennedy's actions and rhetoric about the crisis: "Now is the time to display Old Glory," he exclaimed, "Let's get those flags out and display our colors as they have never been displayed before. Let's show the world we are one."[27]

When the crisis ended with the signing (on October 27) of an agreement that included the removal of the missiles from Cuba and Khrushchev's public concession (on October 28), "the American spirit rose in strength and resolution," as *Time* magazine declared in a special edition on the crisis,[28] because the public believed that standing firm against communist aggression had led to a great victory that restored the international reputation of the United States, a success that both the media and the public attributed to Kennedy's wisdom and courage (George 2003: 104). The public, however, did not know that in return for the removal of Soviet missiles from Cuba, the United States promised not to invade Cuba and agreed to remove its Jupiter missiles from Turkey (Garthoff 1992: 52); that part of the agreement, which did not align with the narrative of a decisive US victory, was not divulged to the public until much later.

The Invasion of Panama

The invasion of Panama was a military invasion of a foreign country, and thus its core features differ from those of the Cuban Missile Crisis, which included a heated verbal confrontation between governments but no actual fighting between armed forces. In both cases, however, a previous international fiasco influenced the perceived meaning of an ongoing event. In the case of the invasion of Panama, the fiasco that set the stage for the rally-round-the-flag effect was the Iran-Contra affair (also known as "Irangate"), which transformed the meaning of the "war on drugs" (first announced by President Nixon in 1971 and later expanded by Ronald Reagan[29]) in the public discourse, leading to the mobilization of US public opinion against Panamanian strongman Manuel Noriega. The transformation proceeded in three stages.

Stage 1: Before the Iran-Contra Affair—the US Drug Problem and Reagan's Legitimacy Crisis

On June 12, 1986, the *New York Times* reported for the first time that General Manuel Noriega, Panama's ruler and a close ally of the United States, was involved in drug dealing and arms trafficking (Byrne 2014).[30] The Reagan administration did not deny that information. Instead, unnamed officials expressed their concerns about this issue in newspaper interviews.[31] Republican Senator Jesse Helms, a member of the Foreign Relations Committee, was first to publicly accused Noriega (in an interview on NBC News' *Meet the Press*) of being the head of the most extensive drug operation in the Western Hemisphere.[32] However, that accusation did not become the administration's official stance, and no efforts were made to remove Noriega from power. To the contrary, despite the exposure of his drug trafficking business, Noriega remained a US ally (a fact that, as we shall see, remained concealed from the public until the end of 1987).

Nevertheless, with the congressional election expected later that year, the United States' drug problem became the focal issue of discussions, legislative efforts on Capitol Hill, and election campaigns; and the topic was regularly featured on newspapers' front pages and the electronic media's primetime.[33] Within a heated political contention over how to deal with the drug problem, Reagan faced growing criticism not only from the opposition party, but also from his own party. As the election approached, many Republicans on the Hill openly expressed their concern that the administration's lack of an effective anti-drug policy would lead to a loss of electoral power.[34] These concerns were not unfounded: evidence from a public opinion poll conducted in August 1986 showed that the drugs issue had become the top public opinion concern,[35] and in November the Republicans indeed lost the majority in the Senate.

In the context of this crisis of legitimacy, taking care of the illegal drug problem—which until this point had been identified primarily as the pet project of First Lady Nancy Reagan (Elwood 1994)—became a central domestic and foreign policy issue for the administration.[36] As a foreign policy issue, the struggle with drug trafficking from Mexico and Central America included forging alliances with governments and joint military operations against drug producers and traffickers.[37] In addition, the president and other senior government officials frequently highlighted the drug problem in public speeches, in which they made having a "drug-free generation" the grand mission of the administration.[38] According to Reagan, the struggle to achieve this goal amounted to a "national crusade," an expression Reagan has first used in a joint national address with the First Lady, on September 1, 1986, in which he highlighted that fighting drugs was a matter of national dignity and a test for the nation's unity and perseverance:[39]

> In this crusade, let us not forget who we are, Mr. Reagan said. Drug abuse is a repudiation of everything America is. The destructiveness and human wreckage mock our heritage.
>
> [...]
>
> When we all come together, united—striving for this cause—then those who are killing America and terrorizing it with slow but sure chemical destruction will see that they are up against the mightiest force for good that we know. Then, they will have no dark alleyways to hide in.

Stage 2: The Aftermath of the Iran-Contra Affair

On November 3, 1986, an article in the Lebanese newspaper *al-Shariah* revealed that the CIA had secretly sold weapons to Iran—breaching the arms embargo that had been imposed on Iran since the Iran-Iraq war—in exchange for the release of seven American hostages who were being held by the Lebanese paramilitary group Hezbollah, which was sponsored by Iran. The story quickly reached the headlines of news reports in the United States and around the world (Sofaer 2003: 1083; Byrne 2014: 252; Wroe 1991: 3). Only three weeks later, it became public knowledge that the CIA used a portion of the money obtained from the arms sale to fund the "Contras" who were fighting against the Sandinista socialist government of Nicaragua.

The diversion of money from the arms deal with Iran to the Contras first became public at a media briefing held at the White House on November 25, 1986 (Byrne 2014). During the briefing, which intended to cover up the role of the president and the CIA in the affair (Byrne 2014), President Reagan claimed that his policy toward Iran was successful and said nothing explicitly about the diversion of money to the Contras. Rather, he briefly mentioned that "one aspect of the implementation of that policy," which he said he had not been fully informed of, was "seriously flawed." Reagan refused to take questions from the curious reporters. He referred them to the next speaker, Attorney General Ed Meese, for further clarification on the matter.[40] The main goal of Attorney General Meese—whose office, during an investigation of the deal with Iran, had accidentally uncovered the diversion of money received by the CIA from Iran to the Contras—was to protect Reagan and his presidency (Byrne 2014). To achieve this goal, Meese falsely claimed that the diversion of funding to the Contras was the action of a third party and that the president knew nothing about it. He said that Israel had served as the moderator in the transaction with Iran, that the Israeli representatives negotiated a payment from Iran that exceeded what Iran owed the United States for the weapons it received, and that the surplus money from the transaction was diverted (allegedly by Israel) to the Contras without the United States knowing about this initiative.[41]

Despite the Reagan administration's official denial that the United States had sponsored the Contras and authorized their engagement in drug trafficking, rumors about the CIA being directly involved in trafficking spread across the country. It remains unclear what portion of the public was aware of the Contra's drug trafficking during that period or of the CIA's involvement in dirty deals with drug lords in Latin America. However, Irangate certainly fueled the political contention over the drug problem, thus boosting the drug hysteria among the public and exacerbating Reagan's legitimacy crisis, as evidenced in the dramatic decline in Reagan's public approval ratings—from 64 percent in mid-October to 47 percent in early December 1986.[42] Even though the president experienced a legitimacy crisis due to the drug hysteria, and some high-ranking officials were already in favor of taking action to remove Noriega from power (Scranton 1991: 46), the United States did not officially portray Noriega as a wanted enemy until the beginning of 1988.

Stage 3. Publicly Turning against Noriega

On November 19, 1987, newspaper headlines across the United States announced that the congressional committees investigating the Iran-Contra affair had concluded that Reagan bore the ultimate responsibility for wrongdoing.[43] Crucially, the newspapers also revealed that Lieutenant Colonel Oliver North, a White House aide who played a major role in the Iran-Contra affair, had testified that in a meeting with Noriega on August 23, 1986, the General offered to conduct acts of political sabotage and possibly assassinations in Nicaragua for the Reagan administration to help remove the Sandinistas from power.[44] North also testified that at the direction of the president's national security adviser, Rear Admiral John M. Poindexter, he accepted Noriega's offer to conduct sabotage operations in Nicaragua that the United States would fund with profits from the sale of arms to Iran.

North was eventually dismissed from service, and the sabotage plans were never carried out, but the revelation that an official US representative had made a deal with Noriega changed the course of the US war on drugs. The war on drugs shifted from a problem confronted via a combination of law enforcement, public education programs, and a foreign policy of creating regional alliances and conducting joint military raids on drug traffickers, to a direct confrontation with a foreign leader who transformed from a secret ally into the US public's primary enemy. On February 5, 1988, the US Justice Department indicted Noriega on multiple drug trafficking charges[45] that linked him to the Medellín cartel in Colombia, which was responsible for most of the cocaine smuggled to the United States, as well as to the United States' old nemesis, Fidel Castro. Noriega then became the nation's new nemesis.

When the White House later negotiated a "plea bargain" that would lead Noriega to step down from power in return for dropping the US federal indictments against him, President Reagan faced a massive backlash in Congress, including by members of his party. On May 17, 1988, the Senate approved a resolution by a massive majority (86 to 10) that opposed any deal that included dropping the drug charges against Noriega.[46] On the same day, the Senate also decided unanimously (95 to 0) to deny economic and military aid to Panama's Defense Forces until Noriega was out of power (this was mainly a symbolic measure because aid to Panama was already suspended).[47] In a press conference held later that day, Reagan refused to comment on the negotiation with Noriega. However, one of the questions asked in the conference conveyed most clearly the public's frustration by Reagan's policy on Panama and the common desire of Americans to act more decisively to stop the collective humiliation by Noriega:

> [T]he combination of sanctions and negotiations has been going on for an awfully long time, and it seems as if the United States looks progressively weaker. Aren't you a little angry that Noriega has managed to humiliate and embarrass the United States?[48]

In the preceding months, the news media played a crucial role in making Noriega a foreign leader most Americans became familiar with and learned to hate. This change in Noriega's position in the US public discourse is evident in the extent of the national media's coverage of him in three distinct periods; the extent of media coverage is evidenced by how often Noriega's name was mentioned in the *New York Times* and the *Washington Post*. Between June 1986 (the month Noriega's involvement in drug trafficking was first publicly exposed) and November 1987, neither newspaper contained more than a fleeting mention of Noriega, with the exception of some reports of political unrest in Panama in the summer of 1987. In comparison, between November 1987 (the month Oliver North's testimony was made public) and January 1988, Noriega's name was mentioned about 10 times per month in the *New York Times* and 4–10 times per month in the *Washington Post*. Between February 1988 (the month Noriega was indicted for drug trafficking) and May of the same year, mentions of Noriega rose dramatically to 60–80 per month in the *New York Times* and 40–80 in the *Washington Post*. After this point, the newspapers' interest in Noriega declined somewhat but remained significant, with about 20–30 mentions per month in both newspapers, until the US invasion of Panama, which led to the largest boost in both newspapers' coverage of Noriega.[49]

In sum, drug trafficking from Latin America transformed from a health and crime problem into a matter of national honor and prestige through a multistage, top-down process. The Reagan administration, other politicians, and the media propagated a public feeling of humiliation and outrage about foreign drug lords' attacks on America's youth, and then depicted Manuel Noriega as the head of a snake that the United States must forcefully cut (Scranton 1991: chap. 6). This shift created the potential for a rally-round-the-flag effect in the wake of military action against Panama, which was realized after Reagan left the White House and was succeeded by his vice president, George H. W. Bush.

Going to War to Oust Noriega

After taking office, Bush intensified both the rhetoric and the implementation of the war on drugs. On September 5, 1989, in an address to the nation on the National Drug Control Strategy, Bush described drugs as "the gravest domestic threat facing our nation today," concluded that drug use was "sapping our strength as a nation," and presented a new strategy for fighting drugs. For the first time, Bush mentioned the possibility of using "the resources of America's armed forces" to fight the drug cartels in Latin American countries. Further, the address highlighted the reframing of the drug problem as an issue related to national identity and character—after an extended description of the ways drugs were harming Americans, especially children, Bush called for "a united America, a determined America, an angry America." He concluded by exclaiming, "Victory over drugs is our cause, a just cause, and with your help, we are going to win!"[50]

On December 20, 1989, President Bush appealed to nationalist sentiment when he addressed the nation to announce that the US military was invading Panama. He said that Noriega had declared a state of war with the United States, and then described an incident in which Noriega's people killed an American serviceman, wounded another serviceman, and captured and tortured a third serviceman and threatened to sexually abuse his wife. Bush then justified the military operation as necessary to save the lives of thousands of other Americans in Panama.[51] The public's reaction to the invasion of Panama was to rally behind President Bush, whose job-approval rating increased from 71 percent to 80 percent (while his disapproval rating dropped from 20 percent to 11 percent).

The invasion of Panama (which lasted six weeks and resulted in a US victory) had three official goals: "to restore democracy to Panama, to protect American lives, and to capture General Noriega and bring him to the United States for prosecution on drug-trafficking charges."[52] In the context of the administration's portrayal of the war on drugs as a critical challenge to the United States that would require both domestic measures and actions against drug lords in foreign countries, the third goal—capturing Noriega, "the drug lord"—was the one that won the hearts and minds of most Americans. For example, grieving parents of American servicemen reported finding comfort and pride in knowing that their sons had been killed or injured while fighting a just war against drug trafficking. Julie Otto, who lost her 19-year-old son in the invasion, said that he "would have felt going out to oust Noriega was the right thing to do . . . [because he] was really against drugs. We do not feel his life was sacrificed in vain. It was for a major cause." Otto's husband added that he "was proud that his son had died fighting against drugs." Similarly, Richard Turner, whose 19-year-old son returned from Panama with a head injury, said that he supported the invasion because "the drugs Noriega was dealing were killing American kids, and now maybe that'll stop."[53]

Data from multiple surveys conducted shortly after the invasion reveal the administration's success in putting a target on Noriega's back: about 80 percent of Americans supported an invasion aimed at overthrowing Noriega, even though few believed that the invasion would significantly reduce the flow of drugs into the United States.[54] Further, even after the United States achieved a military victory and Noriega became a fugitive in his own country, nearly 60 percent of Americans thought that the military intervention in Panama could only be defined as a success if Noriega was captured.[55] Thus, many Americans felt that achieving the strategic goals of the military operation was not sufficient—they demanded the head of Noriega, a dictator whom the United States had been supporting for years and who had become an enemy of the nation only after the Iran-Contra scandal's exposure of his relationship with the CIA. Stanley E. Cohen of Bethesda, Maryland, expressed this view in the following letter to the *Washington Post*:

> As we contemplate the cost of restoring something resembling decent government to Panama, it is appropriate to remember that Gen. Manuel Noriega achieved power and thrived with the support of the United States, which nurtured him for its own purposes. So it is appropriate that our president accept responsibility for disposing our own Frankenstein. It is refreshing that President Bush has the integrity to clean up this mess.[56]

To summarize, during Reagan's presidency, the drug problem in the United States became a struggle for national dignity. However, it was the transformation of Noriega in the US public discourse from a largely unknown ally into a despised national enemy (following the exposure of the Iran-Contra scandal and the dirty deals the United States had made with Noriega and the Contras) that set the stage for a rally behind an invasion of Panama. When President Bush ordered the invasion and the overthrow of Noriega, the public largely saw the action as an opportunity to restore the nation's collective honor and earn the respect of other nations after years of unsuccessful and humiliating struggle with Latin American drug trafficking. Fourteen years later, under profoundly different historical circumstances (discussed in the following), the head of another state (Iraqi President Saddam Hussein) became the target of military action that facilitated the transformation of collective humiliation into national pride.

The Iraq War

The invasion of Iraq in March 2003 led to a rally behind President George W. Bush, whose job-approval ratings increased from 58 percent to 71 percent. There was a high level of public support for the military action (initially about 76 percent), likely because it allowed the United States to overcome the sense of humiliation brought about by the September 11 attacks, as well as the frustration caused by months of futile hunting for Osama bin Laden, the leader of al-Qaeda. In the aftermath of the September 11 attacks, President Bush openly expressed his desire to capture bin Laden, declaring "I want him—I want justice. And there's an old poster out West as I recall, that said 'Wanted: Dead or Alive'" (Brewer 2011: 236).

President Bush first mentioned Iraq as part of the "axis of evil" in his annual State of the Union address on January 29, 2002, and in the months afterward he continued to place Iraq at the center of his foreign policy and rhetoric (Brewer 2011: 235–48). The invasion of Iraq thus became a test case for reclaiming the honor and might of the United States in the post–9/11 era (McCartney 2004).

To sell the plan for a "preemptive strike" against Iraq, first to the media and then to policymakers and the general public, the George W. Bush administration launched a massive information campaign, assisted by private public relations companies (Entman 2003; Gershkoff and Kushner 2005; Hersh 2003; Schechter 2004). The campaign centered on three claims: that Saddam Hussein was a supporter and sponsor of anti-American terrorism, and more specifically a collaborator of al-Qaeda, that Iraq possessed chemical and biological weapons and was able to deliver them to enemies of the US and its allies, and that Iraq was alarmingly close to developing a nuclear arsenal that would threaten the United States (Brewer 2011: chap. 6; Kaufmann 2004:6; Pfiffner 2004). These claims were not based on solid intelligence reports (Entman 2003; Kaufmann 2004: 17–28; Pfiffner 2004; Rampton and Stauber 2003), and actually contradicted the CIA and other intelligence agencies' assessment that Iraq was not cooperating with al-Qaeda, its contribution to anti-American terrorism was minor, it had a relatively limited capacity to deliver chemical or biological weapons, and thus the risk to the US was minimal, and it was not close to developing nuclear weapons (Hersh 2003; Kaufmann 2004; Pfiffner 2004; Zulaika 2009: 194–95).

The media shared the CIA's assessments with the public.[57] However, as the preparations for an attack against Iraq were gaining speed, the gap between the public assessments of CIA director George J. Tenet and those of the Bush administration narrowed. On October 7, 2002, Tenet wrote a letter to the chairman of the Senate Intelligence Committee; excerpts of the letter were made public, revealing Tenet's claim that Iraq was still aspiring to possess nuclear weapons and the country had developed closer relationships with al-Qaeda and its offshoots (Lewis 2018: 427).[58] At the time, however, there was still a significant gap between Tenet's assessment and the claims of senior administration officials (especially Vice President Cheney and Secretary of State Colin Powell) that Iraq's weapons of mass destruction (WMD) posed an imminent threat to the United States, and that Baghdad had formed a partnership with al-Qaeda. The gap continued to narrow during the final countdown to the invasion of Iraq. On February 11, 2003, in testimony given before the US Senate Select Committee on Intelligence, Tenet said, "Secretary of State Powell clearly outlined last week [at the United Nations] the continuing threats posed by Iraq's weapons of mass destruction, its efforts to deceive U.N. inspectors, and the safe haven that Baghdad has allowed for terrorists in Iraq."[59] Tenet then stated that Iraq was harboring and training terrorists linked to al-Qaeda (although he did not claim that Iraq was plotting with al-Qaeda against the United States).

In his memoir, *At the Center of the Storm*, Tenet (2007: chap. 18) admitted that the CIA never found solid evidence that corroborated the Bush administration's claims about Iraq's WMD and partnership with al-Qaeda, but he did not take personal responsibility for misinforming decision-makers and the public about Iraq. Nevertheless, Tenet offered a vivid account of how, in light of the September 11 attacks, Iraq's intentions were misconstrued and misrepresented to the public:

> After 9/11, everything changed. Many foreign policy issues were now viewed through the prism of smoke rising from the World Trade Center and the Pentagon. For many in the Bush administration, Iraq was unfinished business. They seized on the emotional impact of 9/11 and created a psychological connection between the failure to act decisively against al-Qa'ida

and the danger posed by Iraq's WMD programs. The message was: We can never afford to be surprised again. In the case of Iraq, if sanctions eroded and nothing was done (and the international community had little patience for maintaining sanctions indefinitely), we might wake up one day to find that Saddam possessed a nuclear weapon, and then our ability to deal with him would take on an entirely different cast. Unfortunately, this train of thought also led to some overheated and misleading rhetoric, such as the argument [by National Security Advisor Condoleezza Rice] that we don't want our "smoking gun to be a mushroom cloud." (Tenet 2007: 305)

Tenet's critique of government officials' misinterpretation or misrepresentation of Saddam Hussein's intentions is well founded, but it is worth reiterating that the former CIA director publicly endorsed the administration's claims shortly before the war. In any case, it was President Bush, more than any other public official, who sought to convince the public that Saddam Hussein posed an imminent threat to the United States by conspiring with the terrorists who launched the September 11 attacks. Bush used a series of national addresses to the public to communicate this message. In the final address before the war (on March 17, 2003), Bush gave Hussein a 48-hour ultimatum to leave Iraq or face military consequences, and concluded that the regime in Iraq "has a deep hatred of America and our friends. And it has aided, trained and harbored terrorists, including operatives of al Qaeda." Although Bush was commanding a coalition of countries, he justified the invasion of Iraq as a defensive act against an enemy of the United States.[60]

Despite significant public opposition to the war and criticism of the official justifications for the war from both politicians (see, for example, Brewer 2011: 248) and journalists (Feldman, Huddy, and Marcus 2015: chap. 3–4),[61] the Bush administration's public opinion campaign was quite successful in convincing a majority of the US public that Saddam Hussein was sponsoring anti-American terrorism and that Iraq was attempting to produce weapons of mass destruction that could be used against the United States and its allies (however, see Feldman and coauthors' [2015] discussion of the limits of this success, and especially the emergence of significant opposition to the war, particularly among Democrats).[62] As a result, 12 years after the Persian Gulf War, on the eve of the invasion of Iraq, Saddam Hussein was once again the man most Americans loved to hate. For example, residents of Bakersfield, California, expressed this hatred by shooting paintballs at a big picture of Saddam Hussein that they had hung on a billboard.[63]

Data from opinion polls provide a broader view of the Bush administration's success in selling the invasion of Iraq to the US public. Despite the absence of corroborating evidence for the administration's claims about Hussein and Iraq—but perhaps because the head of US intelligence did not publicly dismiss these claims—on the eve of the war, 88 percent of respondents thought Saddam Hussein was involved in supporting terrorist groups that had plans to attack the United States, and 85 percent thought that preventing Iraq from using weapons of mass destruction or providing them to terrorists was a good or very good reason for going to war.[64] Further, 77 percent believed that in the absence of military action by the United States, Iraq would use weapons of mass destruction against a neighboring country,[65] and 73 percent said that disarming Iraq of weapons of mass destruction was a realistic expectation for the war.[66,67]

During the invasion, government spokespeople and the media portrayed the military operation as a smooth process and a straightforward success. Thus, the already high levels of confidence in the government and military increased further. One week after the invasion began, an estimated 87 percent of Americans thought it was likely that the armed forces would find conclusive evidence that Iraq had WMD or the facilities to develop them,[68] 85 percent believed that the invasion would destroy Iraq's capabilities of producing and using WMD, and 88 percent said that this goal was worth the costs of going to war. In addition, 87 percent thought that making the United States safer from terrorism was worth the costs of going to war.[69] Ultimately, the success of the public opinion campaign was revealed in the 76 percent approval rating of Bush's decision to go to war.[70]

It might seem that the shift that occurred in the aftermath of George W. Bush's rhetoric and the administration's public opinion campaign is evidence for the *realist* perspective, according to which the public rallied behind Bush because he defined the war in national security terms. However, Robb Willer (2004) and others have argued that the campaign was successful not simply because it propagated security threats, but because it reframed the crisis of September 11 as part of a broader war against the United States and its values, weaving the binary distinction between the United States and its "evil" enemies into the official rhetoric (Krebs 2007; Smith 2005), which was then largely adopted by journalists (Hutcheson et al. 2004). In this way, the goal of defeating terrorist organizations transcended security concerns and became a matter of collective identity and prestige: "Evil" enemies were challenging the honor and basic values of the United States, and thus the nation was being called to defend its reputation by standing up for these values and showing the rest of the world their universal validity (Krebs 2007; McCartney 2004; Roshwald 2006: 203).

The quest to reclaim national honor and restore what many Americans believed to be their core national values and the moral basis of the United States' international leadership and authority began immediately after the September 11 attacks, when leaders and members of the media (as Chapter 6 discusses in detail) frequently compared the situation to Japan's attack on Pearl Harbor, which had prompted the United States to join World War II. This development is illustrated in the following statement from Lance Morrow (a prominent columnist for *Time* magazine) just a day after the attacks (the column was titled "The Case for Rage and Retribution"):

> A day cannot live in infamy without the nourishment of rage. Let's have rage. What's needed is a unified, unifying, Pearl Harbor sort of purple American fury ... America needs to relearn a lost discipline, self-confident relentlessness—and to relearn why human nature has equipped us all with a weapon (abhorred in decent peacetime societies) called hatred. . . . This is the moment of clarity. Let the civilized toughen up, and let the uncivilized take their chances in the game they started. (Morrow 2001)

In the aftermath of the invasion of Iraq, the editors of the *New York Times* offered the most cogent assessment of the way many US residents experienced an emotional connection between the war against Iraq and the traumatic September 11 attacks a year and a half earlier:[71]

> It would take a very set mind to judge what comes next on any ground but the success of the effort. If things go as well as we hope, even those who sharply disagree with the logic behind this war are likely to end up feeling reassured, almost against their will, by the successful projection of American power. Whether they felt the idea of war in Iraq was a bad one from the beginning, or—like us—they felt it should be undertaken only with broad international support, the yearning to go back to a time when we felt in control of our own destiny still runs strong. Of all the reasons for this mission, the unspoken one, deepest and most hopeless, is to erase Sept. 11 from our hearts.

The editors of the *Wall Street Journal* also highlighted the connection between the war and the September 11 attacks.[72] On the first day of the invasion, the paper's editorial column, titled "The Hopes of Mankind," proclaimed:

> The reservoir of public support is especially deep because it comes in the wake of September 11. Americans understand that the soldiers now fighting in Iraq are, literally, protecting us here at home from those we now know can strike our homeland all too easily. They are taking the war to the terrorists, and to their ally and patron, before they can strike here again.

Then, to highlight that the United States was not engaging in war merely to protects its own interests, but rather as a chivalrous act of saving the world, the editors quoted the message that the commander of the 1st Marine Division had delivered to his troops:

> For decades, Saddam Hussein has tortured, imprisoned, raped and murdered the Iraqi people; invaded neighboring countries without provocation; and threatened the world with weapons of mass destruction. The time has come to end his reign of terror. On your young shoulders rest the hopes of mankind.

Survey data show that the public did not lag far behind the press in assessing that the military confrontation with Iraq was an honorable mission with important implications for the United States' leadership and unique international status in the post–9/11 era. The available survey data from the period reveal a shift among the public toward higher levels of national pride and confidence, as well as the emergence of a sense of national exceptionalism and superiority. For example, a National Tragedy Study conducted by the National Opinion Research Center (NORC) documented dramatic increases in measures of national pride and confidence in government institutions immediately after September 11, 2001 (Rasinski et al. 2002; T. W. Smith, Rasinski, and Toce 2001), and Gross and colleagues found similar results using data from a different survey (Gross, Brewer, and Aday 2009). Further, using General Social Survey (GSS) data from several periods, Bonikowski and DiMaggio (2016) showed that ultranationalist beliefs—including strong feelings of national belonging and pride, high levels of hubris, and a lack of shame about any aspect of America—were much more prevalent in the

United States in 2004 than in either the pre–9/11 era (1996) or a later period (2012) (for similar findings, see T. W. Smith and Kim 2006). Finally, as shown in Chapter 9, which examines individual-level data on public attitudes during the Iraq War, Americans rallied behind President Bush not because of concerns about national security per se, but because the war was perceived as an opportunity to reclaim national honor and prestige by defeating the Iraqi regime, which the Bush administration effectively constructed as the nation's main enemy in the post–9/11 era.

In sum, the humiliation engendered by the September 11 attacks set the stage for the success of President Bush (with the help of other public figures and the media) in portraying the invasion of Iraq as an opportunity to restore national honor and prestige, which in turn led to high levels of support among the US public for the invasion and a rally behind Bush's leadership. The following excerpt from a letter sent by Martha and Michael Gardner of Hunt Valley, Maryland, to the *New York Times* a few days after the invasion contains an expression of the symbolic connection between the two events: "Sept. 11 proved that New York is the greatest city in the world, and now the men and women in our military will enable us to show the world that the United States is the greatest country."[73] A similar feeling of reassurance and pride was expressed by Gregory Jezarian of New York City: "I live in a city where many refuse to appreciate and pay homage to what our brave military men and women in Iraq are sacrificing. Yet, this is the same city that after Sept. 11 heard the comforting roar of fighter jets patrolling above us as if to say, 'It's OK.; we're on the job now.' Well, they're on the job again. And for that, I am thankful."[74]

Of course, the public rally behind Bush during the invasion of Iraq may have occurred because people made rational assessments that the invasion was a reasonable action in the context of America's war against terrorism. However, data from public opinion polls show that on the eve of the invasion, most Americans thought the war was likely to *increase* the immediate threat of terrorism in the United States, and only about 50 percent thought the war would reduce the threat of terrorism in the long run. Yet approval ratings for Bush and his Iraq policy were high—about 65–70 percent. Only a few days into the invasion (after the rally-round-the-flag effect had reached its peak), the optimism about the war's chances of reducing terrorism increased dramatically, peaking at about 70 percent.[75] Chapter 9 presents a detailed critique of the rationalist explanation for the rally-round-the-flag effect during the invasion of Iraq and shows that emotional reactions to the nationalist framing of events prompted both the rally behind the president and overconfidence about the expected outcome of the war.

The *Mayaguez* Incident

In the three cases discussed in the preceding sections, there was a preexisting widespread desire among the public to reclaim the nation's honor and reputation, and a rally emerged when a sitting president used nationalist rhetoric to frame the developing military conflict. The *Mayaguez* incident followed a different pattern. In this case, the preexisting desire to reclaim the nation's honor and reputation was extremely potent (because of the humiliation resulting from the defeat in Vietnam), and thus a rally occurred even though the president used rather laconic language to frame the conflict, rather than engaging in explicit nationalist rhetoric. Thus, the case shows that while nationalist presidential rhetoric can amplify public desire to reclaim national honor and prestige and thus facilitate a rally effect, certain historical circumstances can generate a strong desire among the public to reclaim national honor and prestige even in the absence of nationalist rhetoric. In addition, the *Mayaguez* incident shows that under certain circumstances, even relatively minor events can provoke a seemingly disproportionate reaction when they become suffused with profound meaning because they are perceived as a way to enhance the nation's honor and international reputation.

The incident began on May 12, 1975, when naval forces from the Khmer Rouge[76] seized the SS *Mayaguez*, an American merchant ship, in an international sea lane that Cambodia claimed as its territorial waters. In response, President Ford secretly ordered a military rescue operation; however, when American forces took over the vessel and attacked the adjacent island of Koh Tang, the *Mayaguez* crew was not in either location. The Khmer Rouge released the crew on May 15, probably to prevent an American attack on their ships and inland infrastructure. In a shrewd public relations maneuver, Ford appeared on national television to announce the operation. He told the US public, "The vessel has been recovered intact and the entire crew has been rescued,"[77] but said nothing about the 18 US servicemen who were killed and the 41 who were wounded during the rescue attempt. Nor did he mention that the initial rescue had been unsuccessful and the crew was freed only when the Khmer Rouge decided to release them.[78]

Ford's announcement was met by a surge of public support for the rescue operation and a dramatic increase in his job-approval rating. The available data show an 11-point increase in Ford's job-approval rating (from 40 percent to 51 percent) and a 10-point decline in his job-disapproval rating (from 43 percent to 33 percent). However, these estimates are based on data collected on May 5 and May 27. There are no data points available closer to the event. Thus, the initial boost to Ford's popularity may have been even larger. Indeed, the enthusiasm expressed in many "letters to the editor" (some cited in the following) and recorded in other studies indicates an even greater increase.

The rational public perspective would suggest that the *Mayaguez* incident was popular because it was a "cheap success." However, the historical record shows that being a "cheap success" is not a sufficient condition for the emergence of a rally effect. Other short and successful military operations that cost few or no American lives—the 1958 operation in Lebanon, the 1994 occupation of Haiti, and the September 1996 missile strike on Iraqi forces in Kurdistan—did not produce major rally-round-the-flag effects. To be sure, Ford's portrayal of the rescue operation as successful was also important,[79] yet it was not the success per se that evoked a rally point, but rather the historical context in which success was achieved: Cambodia's attack on a US civilian ship occurred in the immediate aftermath of two stinging setbacks for the US military in the Vietnam War. The military had been forced to pull out of Cambodia only a month earlier and had withdrawn from South Vietnam— a move that marked the nation's defeat in the war in Southeast Asia—only a few weeks before. The *Mayaguez* incident only added to a growing sense of humiliation. In this context, Ford's decisive reaction allowed the public to experience a sense of self-respect and pride.[80]

The scant survey data that are available support this interpretation: in a public opinion poll conducted about two weeks after the incident (May 23– 27), 74 percent of respondents agreed that "[i]f President Ford had not acted the US would have been looked on by all our allies and the rest of the world as a country that has lost its will to resist aggression."[81] While the survey data indicate that the public experienced a feeling of self-respect, this reaction is expressed most unambiguously in the many letters sent to the press following Ford's statement about the *Mayaguez* incident. For example, Jeffery Windle of Santa Monica, California, wrote, "Our actions were a symbol of our continuing strength and solidarity in spite of Vietnam, strength that should not be underrated."[82] In a letter to the *Washington Post*, Vance B. Gay of Washington, DC, wrote, " 'Hail to the chief.' Congratulations to President Ford for his swift and forthcoming action in the recovery of our ship and its crew from Cambodia. He reassured the world that the U.S.A. still carry [*sic*] the 'big stick' and the 'giant' is not asleep."[83] Perhaps Bob Nolthenius of Hacienda Heights, California, described the feeling of reassurance most concisely when he wrote: "Thanks Mr. President—we needed that!"[84]

Legislators had a similar reaction to Ford's announcement, as described by Louis Fisher:

> Although months would pass by before members of Congress had an adequate picture of what had taken place, on the very day of the recovery they rushed forward with glowing words of praise. A spirit of jingoism filled the air, and the episode became a "proud new chapter in our history." Legislators expressed pride in their country and in their President, exclaiming with youthful enthusiasm that it was "great to be an American." (Fisher 1995: 137)

The *Mayaguez* incident is the only militarized conflict reviewed in this chapter that produced a rally-round-the-flag effect but did *not* include nationalist presidential rhetoric. Given the surrounding circumstances—the loss of the Vietnam War and a humiliating attack on an American civilian target in the same region—President Ford could scarcely ask Americans to revel in nationalist pride and confidence. Nevertheless, national pride and confidence increased in response to Ford's announcement of the success of the operation precisely because of the dire historical circumstances that had compromised the national honor and international prestige of the United States. Therefore, as in the other three events discussed in this chapter—the Cuban Missile Crisis and the invasions of Panama and Iraq—in the *Mayaguez* incident, the sitting president enjoyed a rally-round-the-flag period because the general public saw an opportunity to restore national honor and reclaim the respect of other nations.

The realist perspective would offer an alternative explanation for the US public's reaction to the *Mayaguez* incident, namely that a rally-round-the-flag period emerged because the public supported the government's efforts to protect major national interests. However, while this argument may gain some traction in reference to the Cuban Missile Crisis and the invasions of Panama and Iraq, it cannot explain the public's reaction to the *Mayaguez* incident, because this relatively minor incident could not have changed the military results of the Vietnam War or altered the international standing of the United States. The *Mayaguez* incident, therefore, offers empirical support for the main argument advanced in this chapter, and in the book more broadly, that rally-round-the-flag periods emerge when events are widely perceived as opportunities to restore national honor and reclaim international prestige. In addition, the *Mayaguez* incident further establishes the principle that in the United States, the rally-round-the-flag effect results from an interaction between presidential action and historical circumstances: The geographical and temporal proximity of the *Mayaguez* incident to the loss of the war in Southeast Asia and the manipulated information that the public received from the president jointly evoked a specific interpretation of the incident that infused it with collective symbolic value, thereby resulting in a rally behind the leadership of President Ford.

The Roles of Nationalist Presidential Rhetoric and the Opportunity to Restore National Honor in the Creation of Rally Effects

The four events discussed in the preceding sections—the Cuban Missile Crisis, the invasion of Panama, the invasion of Iraq, and the *Mayaguez* incident—evoked rally-round-the-flag reactions among the US public. In three of these events—the Cuban Missile Crisis and the invasions of Panama and Iraq—the sitting president explicitly invoked popular nationalist sentiments when publicly discussing the military confrontation. In these cases, US presidents were central agents of public opinion, and their nation-affirming rhetoric served as an important path for reclaiming national honor and prestige. In the fourth conflict, the *Mayaguez* incident, a rally-round-the-flag effect emerged even in the absence of presidential nationalist rhetoric. Taken together, these four cases indicate that the core necessary condition for the emergence of a rally is not presidential nationalist rhetoric, but rather a widespread perception that the conflict offers an opportunity to restore national honor and international prestige in the aftermath of national degradation.

An analysis of the militarized conflicts that did not produce rally effects offers further empirical support for the core importance of the chance to restore national prestige and honor. These cases reveal that in the absence of an opportunity to reclaim national honor and prestige, nationalist presidential rhetoric falls on deaf ears.

Absence as Evidence: Cases in Which No Rally Effect Emerged

In the three cases discussed in the following subsections—the invasions of the Dominican Republic (1965), Cambodia (1970), and Grenada (1983)— nationalist presidential rhetoric largely failed to mobilize public support because the public did not come to believe that these military operations were honorable missions or were likely to earn international respect for the United States. In each case, even though the sitting US president engaged in nationalist rhetoric, the event did not evoke a rally-round-the-flag reaction because there was not a preceding episode of national humiliation and/or an established enemy for the US public to unite against.[85]

The Invasion of the Dominican Republic

The decision to deploy US troops in the Dominican Republic followed the eruption of violent clashes between "constitutionalists" (supporters of the former democratically elected president of the Dominican Republic, Juan Bosch) and "loyalists" (military forces loyal to the ruling junta). In his first public remarks on the invasion (on April 28, 1965), President Lyndon Johnson said that the operation was aimed at protecting the lives of Americans currently living in the Dominican Republic.[86] However, a few days later, on May 3, he addressed the nation again, this time announcing that the operation had two main goals: an immediate goal of saving the lives of thousands of American civilians and citizens of other countries who were trapped inside the conflict zone and a longer-term strategic goal of limiting the influence of communism and preventing the Dominican Republic from becoming "another Cuba." In the opening section of the address, Johnson proclaimed, "There are times in the affairs of nations when great principles are tested in an ordeal of conflict and danger," and continued by emphasizing that the primary goal of the military operation was to protect the lives of Americans. Like other US presidents who have announced military operations, Johnson mentioned that the use of US military power would also benefit other nations. However, as he concluded the address, Johnson made it clear that his main message was about the national interests and international prestige of the United States:

> Before I leave you, my fellow Americans, I want to say this personal word.
> I know that no American serviceman wants to kill anyone. And I know

that no American president wants to give an order which brings shootings and casualties and death. But I want you to know, and I want the world to know, that as long as I am president of this country, we are going to defend ourselves. We will defend our soldiers against attackers. We will honor our treaties. We will keep our commitments. We will defend our nation against all those who seek to destroy not only the United States but every free country of this hemisphere. We do not want to bury anyone, as I have said so many times before, but we do not intend to be buried.[87]

Although Johnson took a tough nationalist stance in his speech, it was not followed by a major rally-round-the-flag effect because neither the enemy nor the historical context were suitable for this development. With regard to the perceived enemy, Johnson and the top CIA officials could not explicitly take the side of the "loyalist" forces of the military junta that ruled the country (Brands 1987) in the fight against the "constitutionalists," even though they were convinced that pro-Castro communists had infiltrated the "constitutionalist" rebel forces (Brands 1987; Ferguson 1973). Thus, rather than explicitly taking a side in the conflict, Johnson placed the blame on "a band of Communist conspirators" that took over what had started as a popular democratic revolution.[88] The press then embraced and circulated this framing of the conflict (Nacos 1990: 58). This vaguely defined enemy did not pose the type of symbolic challenge that was present in the events that provoked major rally-round-the-flag reactions. Unlike Castro in Cuba, Noriega in Panama, and Saddam Hussein in the second Iraq campaign, the communist regime in the Dominican Republic did not have a historical record of engaging in confrontations with and embarrassing the United States. Consequently, Johnson's appeal to anticommunist sentiments generated only a minor rally effect—a six-point increase in his job-approval rating, which reached 70 percent, a level below the average rating for Johnson's first 18 months in office.[89]

The Cambodian Incursion

The Cambodian incursion of 1970 (May 1 through June 30) was the last major escalation of the Vietnam War.[90] President Richard Nixon faced a dual challenge when making a televised statement about his decision to invade Cambodia. First, it would be difficult to convince the US public, which was largely against the war, of the value of the invasion. Second, Nixon had a credibility problem because the decision to invade Cambodia came only 10 days after he announced that 150,000 American soldiers would be withdrawn from Vietnam within a year as part of an overall "Vietnamization" program (Nixon's plan to shift greater responsibility for the war to South Vietnam while the United States was preparing to withdraw). In an effort to convince the public that invading Cambodia was the best course of action, Nixon pointed to several areas on a large map of Cambodia, explaining that the areas had become military sanctuaries for North Vietnamese guerrilla forces that launched hit-and-run attacks against US and South Vietnamese forces. He claimed that the increasing amount of hostile activity originating from these sanctuaries left the United States no choice but to launch a joint military operation with South Vietnam in order to clear these areas in Cambodia. Seeking to portray his decision as in line with his overall goal of ending the war, Nixon described the invasion of Cambodia as "indispensable for the continuing success of that withdrawal [from Vietnam]," and essential for minimizing the number of casualties among "our brave men."[91]

Nixon surely knew that a discussion of the strategic and tactical aspects of the operation would not be enough to convince the American public to support the decision to escalate, rather than reduce, US military activity in Southeast Asia, and thus he chose to appeal to the public's national sentiment. His address included some of the most nationalistic and confrontational statements made by a president of the United States in the period covered in this book. The following two quotes from Nixon's address illustrate the hyper-nationalist tone of his speech.

> This attitude [of North Vietnam] has become intolerable. We will not react to this threat to American lives merely by plaintive diplomatic protests. If we did, the credibility of the United States would be destroyed in every area of the world where only the power of the United States deters aggression. Tonight I again warn the North Vietnamese that if they continue to escalate the fighting when the United States is withdrawing its forces, I shall meet my responsibility as the commander in chief of our armed forces to take the action I consider necessary to defend the security of our American men. The action I have announced tonight puts the leaders of North Vietnam on notice that we will be patient in working for peace, we will be conciliatory at the conference table, but we will not be humiliated. We will not be defeated.

The question all American people must ask and answer tonight is this: Does the richest and strongest nation in history of the world have the character to meet a direct challenge by a group which rejects every effort to win a just peace, ignores our warnings, tramples on solemn agreements, violates the neutrality of an unarmed people and uses our prisoners as hostages? If we fail to meet this challenge, all other nations will be on notice that despite its overwhelming power the United States, when a real crisis comes, will be found wanting.

The invasion of Cambodia seemingly had all the necessary characteristics to become a major rally point: it was a large-scale military invasion and a war escalation; there was a well-established and clearly defined enemy to fight; and the president announced the military engagement using nationalist rhetoric that portrayed the event as a test of the nation's capacity to defend its national honor and international prestige. At that time, however, the US public was not willing to accept the idea that invading Cambodia was an opportunity to restore some of the prestige the United States had lost in the prolonged war in Vietnam. Rather, the public perceived the invasion as another phase of the same messy conflict. Consequently, the public received Nixon's address with noticeable suspicion and skepticism. In a Harris Survey conducted in May 1970, 53 percent of respondents did not accept the official argument that the operation in Cambodia was limited in objectives and scope, but instead thought that the operation would extend the Vietnam War to the entire Indo-China region. In addition, 47 percent of respondents thought that Nixon had not told Americans the full truth about the situation, while only 42 percent thought that he had been frank and straightforward. Most Americans did not agree with the White House's official stance that the invasion of Cambodia would be a game-changer in the Vietnam War but rather suspected it would actually perpetuate the war: 76 percent of respondents thought that completing the mission in Cambodia would take more than a short time, only 43 percent agreed that the operation would help protect the lives of American troops in Vietnam, no more than 31 percent thought that the operation would shorten the war, and as few as 25 percent agreed that the military operation in Cambodia would make North Vietnam more willing to enter into serious negotiations in Paris.[92] Consequently, less than half of the US public (48–49 percent) supported the Cambodian incursion during the operation, and Nixon's job-approval rating, which was at a modest level before the incursion began, remained relatively steady (54–59 percent).[93]

The Invasion of Grenada

The invasion of Grenada in October 1983 is a particularly interesting "negative" case of rally-round-the-flag processes, because while the official rhetoric about the invasion highlighted concerns about the international reputation of the United States, the public discourse encompassed differing opinions about the need to use military power to protect or restore that reputation. This case, therefore, demonstrates that for a rally to emerge, the political leadership's efforts to frame military engagement in a way that calls for the public to unite behind the military operation and the leadership must be met with a willingness on the part of the public to embrace the official framing.

In March 1979, a military coup established Maurice Bishop, the head of the New JEWEL Movement (a coalition of reformist and Marxist-Leninist groups; Shearman 1985),[94] as the new ruler of Grenada. Bishop subsequently tightened Grenada's relationships with Cuba and the Soviet Union. The US government became increasingly concerned about this pro-communist partnership over the next few years as Grenada began to construct the Point Salines International Airport, which US intelligence indicated was meant to serve Soviet and Cuban aircraft. However, as in the Cuban Missile Crisis (though on a much smaller scale), the possible security threat of the Soviet Union gaining a foothold in Grenada was secondary to the symbolic meaning of this potential development: it seemed that the Soviet Union was once again playing war games in America's backyard. Therefore, the invasion of Grenada was meant to send a message to the Soviet Union and its allies that, despite the defeat in Vietnam, the United States was not a paper tiger and would not hesitate to use military power to protect its interests (Busch 2001: 207).

On October 13, 1983, a pro-communist faction led by Bishop's Deputy Prime Minister, Bernard Coard, ousted Bishop in a coup. Bishop was executed on October 19, and in response, the new Revolutionary Military Council declared a 96-hour shoot-to-kill curfew. Violent clashes erupted on October 22, 1983, in the aftermath of these events. After being informed of these developments, President Reagan became concerned that the 800 Americans studying at St. George's School of Medicine in Grenada would be taken hostage. Even in this aspect of the conflict, however, the security threat was secondary to the symbolic threat: with the humiliating experience of the 1979–1980 hostage crisis in Iran still fresh in his memory, Reagan was determined not to allow a similar situation to develop on his watch (Brands 1987; Busch 2001: 206–7; K. P. Mueller 2006: 182–84).

In a public explanation of his decision to invade Grenada, Reagan focused on two major concerns. First, he emphasized the need to block communist expansion to Grenada, describing the island as "a Soviet-Cuban colony being readied as a major military bastion to export terror and undermine democracy."[95] Reagan drew a connection between the invasion of Grenada and the bombing of Beirut barracks housing US and French service members that had occurred only four days earlier, killing 241 service personnel: He stated, "Not only has Moscow assisted and encouraged the violence in both countries, but it provides direct support through a network of surrogates and terrorists."[96] Reagan's second and more immediate concern was rescuing the US citizens in Grenada. He appealed directly to the traumatic collective memory of the Iran hostage crisis, declaring that "the nightmare of our hostages in Iran must never be repeated."[97] However, since no Americans had yet been taken hostage, the need to stop communist expansion became the dominant theme in Reagan's rhetoric about the invasion of Grenada.

Reagan had some success in provoking anticommunist sentiment: a solid majority of American supported the invasion, and Reagan's job-approval rating increased by a few points.[98] Still, the event did not become a major rally point. Even after US military forces achieved a quick success with relatively few American casualties, Reagan's job-approval rating never reached beyond modest levels.[99] The main reason for the lack of a rally is that, unlike Castro in Cuba, Noriega in Panama, and Hussein in Iraq, the regime in Grenada had not been portrayed as an enemy of the United States prior to the use of military force. Therefore, in the absence of any explicit provocation against the United States by either Grenada or its alleged communist sponsors, many Americans did not share the administration's view that Grenada was linked to the international prestige of the United States. Under these conditions, Reagan's explanation left many wondering whether the invasion was actually motivated, not by a desire to protect national interests, but rather by illegitimate considerations such as Reagan's "anticommunism obsession" and the economic interests of private corporations.[100] Further, Reagan's anticommunist message may have raised suspicion among many Americans who remembered a similar rhetoric being used to justify the Vietnam War.

An almost instantaneous condemnation of the invasion by countries across the globe, including some of the United States' closest allies (importantly, Grenada has been a Commonwealth Realm since 1974) led to significant unease among individuals who believed that America's leadership role should be based on a commitment to meet the highest international moral and legal standards. In numerous letters to the press, private citizens blamed the Reagan administration for creating a "macho" image for the United States and for alienating even friendly states by breaking international law. For example, Rollin Shelton of Los Angeles lamented, "It seems apparent that American prestige abroad shall continue at its present appalling low ebb until such time as we finally realize what others have long known. There is not one law for us and another for everyone else."[101] Joseph Koslowski of Jersey City, New Jersey, wrote,

> Our continued support for the corrupt and deadly government of El Salvador, the C.I.A.'s attempts to sabotage the Nicaraguan revolution ... our too costly adventure in Lebanon, and, in the great tradition of the Bay of Pigs, our invasion of Grenada have put the United States in the harshest light among all progressive-minded people.[102]

Harmon M. Gehr of Pasadena, California, expressed similar thoughts:

> In terms not only of world scorn but also, more sadly, of lives snuffed out, precious resources wasted, lies told and a general demeaning of human worth, there is a high moral price for the United States to pay. If we are not already bankrupt, we have sacrificed another installment of our obligation to lead the nations morally.[103]

Therefore, whereas the Reagan administration saw the invasion as a way to help restore international superpower status to the United States, many ordinary citizens were worried that the invasion would actually damage the nation's international standing and reputation.

Considering the invasion of Grenada as an isolated event might offer some support for the *realist* claim that Americans consider national interests when deciding whether to rally behind presidents and their foreign policy. However, the comparative perspective applied in this and the following chapters suggests that the public's perception of which interests are worthy of engagement in a military conflict is not a preexisting factor, but rather part of the rally process itself. The mobilization of the American public behind presidents and their decisions on military actions during the Cuban Missile Crisis, the *Mayaguez* incident, and the invasions of Panama and Iraq shows that collective interests are based on a sense of symbolic challenge to national honor and international prestige vis-à-vis pre-established enemies. In contrast, because the invasion of Grenada was launched against a foreign regime few Americans knew anything about, and because, despite Reagan's rhetoric, it was not connected in the public discourse to any preceding international humiliation, such as the Vietnam War or the Iran hostage crisis, the invasion of Grenada did not produce a rally-round-the-flag effect.

Another possible interpretation is that Grenada's incapacity to put up a decent fight, which resulted in a swift American victory, was the real reason for the lack of a major rally-round-the-flag effect. In other words, maybe the American public did not consider the invasion of Grenada a "real war." However, other military engagements in which US forces swiftly defeated much weaker opponents (e.g., the invasion of Panama) or the public was led to believe that US forces had achieved a quick and cheap victory (e.g., the *Mayaguez* incident) did evoke rallies. Thus, taken as a whole, these findings suggest that factors beyond the objective characteristics of a military engagement—namely the meanings assigned to the military engagement in the public discourse, specifically the portrayal of an engagement as pertinent to the nation's symbolic value—are crucial for the emergence of a rally-round-the-flag reaction among the public.

Conclusion

The scholars who first identified proposed the rally-round-the-flag phenomenon in US public opinion described the occurrence as Americans' automatic reaction to significant international events that entailed direct US involvement (Mueller 1970, 1973). However, this chapter showed that even though military engagements with other countries offer the most likely scenario for the emergence of rally effect, relatively few military confrontations have produced significant rally-round-the-flag effects in public opinion in the United States. Further, in some cases, even though the commander-in-chief issued an explicit call for the public to unite behind a military action, and even though this presidential rhetoric had a strong nationalistic tone, no significant rally-round-the-flag effect emerged. An analysis of the military confrontations that *did* evoke a rally-round-the-flag reaction revealed that in each case, the meaning of the event had been transformed in the public discourse, shifting from primarily a foreign policy issue to a more profound struggle to maintain or restore collective honor and reputation among the nations.

Does Support for the Troops Motivate Rallies?

This chapter's focus on rallies that emerged during or shortly after US military actions may lead some readers to wonder whether rallies behind the commander-in-chief are driven by a desire to support the troops and, in fact, if failing to rally is perceived as disloyalty to or even endangerment of soldiers in the field. Undoubtedly, many US citizens (and the citizens of most countries) feel morally obliged to support the troops during wars, and supporting the troops may motivate some people to support the commander-in-chief as well. However, the relationship between these two types of support is not straightforward. In some wars, many individuals who supported the troops did not rally behind the president (that was the case, for example, once the invasion of Iraq was complete and the initial rally effect had faded). Further, in some cases, calls to support the troops have increased in tandem with increased *opposition* to the war, as many people claimed the government was sacrificing servicepersons for unjustifiable goals (the Vietnam War is an illustrative case—see, for example, Beamish, Molotch and Flacks 1995). Overall, therefore, the moral commitment of many US citizens to support the troops is not a primary mechanism driving rallies around the flag. The next chapter reinforces this assessment by demonstrating that rallies can emerge—through mechanisms similar to those discussed in this chapter— even in the absence of significant military engagement with an enemy that might have evoked a desire to support the troops (that was the case in the Iran hostage crisis and in the initial rally phase of the September 11 attacks).

6

Standing Up Proudly

Rallies in the Aftermath of Attacks on the Nation

On March 4, 1817, as President James Monroe gave his first inaugural address, he declared, "National honor is national property of the highest value."[1] As the previous chapter showed, national honor is so important to the public that rally-round-the-flag reactions developed in response to military actions whenever previous events that prompted a public mood of collective humiliation in the United States fed a widespread desire to restore national honor and reclaim the respect of other nations—the perception that national honor had been violated proved to be fertile soil for presidents seeking to mobilize public support for their leadership by ordering the use of military power against the nation's enemies. However, rally periods have also emerged in contexts beyond military intervention. This chapter focuses on rally periods that emerged in the aftermath of security crises, namely foreign attacks on US civilian targets. Two such rallies occurred in the United States in the time period covered in this analysis: the first in response to the Iran hostage crisis, and the second in the immediate aftermath of the September 11 attacks. Like the rallies that emerged in response to military conflicts (described in Chapter 5), these rallies were rooted in a desire to restore national honor and reclaim international respect. In both cases, the sitting president portrayed the events as attacks against the entire nation, and characterized retaliation as a way to overcome collective humiliation by revealing the American spirit and showing the world the United States' might (see Figure 4.1 in Chapter 4 for a graphical illustration of this process). In the case of two other foreign attacks on US civilian targets—the bombing of the World Trade Center in 1993 and the bombings of US embassies in Kenya and Tanzania in 1998—no rally developed. This chapter examines all four events to identify the factors that facilitate a rally-round-the-flag reaction in the aftermath of a security crisis. In addition, the chapter offers an initial exploration of why rallies developed after attacks on civilian targets but not after attacks on military targets.

Rally 'round the Flag. Yuval Feinstein, Oxford University Press. © Oxford University Press 2022.
DOI: 10.1093/oso/9780197629710.003.0006

In more than one sense, the Iran hostage crisis, which began on November 4, 1979, and lasted 444 days, and the September 11 attacks that occurred in 2001 are two very different events. The Iran hostage crisis played out abroad and did not claim any American civilian lives (eight servicemen were killed in a failed rescue mission on April 24, 1980), while the September 11 attacks took place on American soil and claimed thousands of American civilian lives. Not surprisingly, because of these profound differences, the hostage crisis spurred a weaker rally effect than the September 11 attacks. Despite their differences, however, the two events share several characteristics that place them in the same category of rally-round-the-flag events: both events involved attacks against US civilian targets with a high symbolic value, and in both cases the sitting president struck a nationalist tone by calling on the nation to reveal its glorious character and express national unity and solidarity with the victims, and by promising to retaliate against the enemies who had attacked the United States.

The Iran Hostage Crisis

On November 4, 1979, some 3,000 Iranian demonstrators seized the US embassy in Teheran and took 63 staff members hostage; three additional hostages were taken from the foreign ministry office. Thirteen of the captives were released within a few weeks, but 52 remained in captivity for over a year, until January 20, 1981 (one captive, the vice consul, was released in July 1980).[2] In the months leading up to the event, tensions had become heightened between the United States and the Ayatollah Khomeini regime, which had come to power in the Iranian Revolution (January 7–February 11, 1979) after overthrowing the monarchical regime led by Shah Mohammad Reza Pahlavi, who was an ally of the United States.[3] In Iran, anti-American sentiment had increased after the deposed Shah arrived in the United States from exile (on October 22, 1979) to receive medical treatment for cancer. Despite President Carter's announcement that the Shah had been authorized to stay in the United States only temporarily and for the sole purpose of receiving medical treatment, the move raised suspicion among Iranians that the United States was granting permanent asylum to the Shah, who was expected to be tried and likely executed upon returning to his homeland. On November 1, Ayatollah Khomeini declared: "The United States, which has given refuge to that corrupt germ, will be confronted in a different manner by us."[4] Three days later, a crowd of furious protesters seized the US embassy in Teheran and took the hostages.

At the onset of the hostage crisis, a sense of outrage permeated the public conversation, not only because Iranian demonstrators had seized the American embassy in Tehran and had taken dozens of hostages, but also because President Carter's reaction—using restrained language and addressing the crisis via diplomatic negotiations conducted behind closed doors—was widely seen as rubbing salt in the wound. Prominent news outlets encouraged this view of the situation. For example, on November 6, the *Washington Post* editors counseled against "pussycat acquiescence in the reckless way the Iranian authorities-cum-mob are behaving" (alluding to the Carter administration's prior actions—refusing to hold the Ayatollah's regime accountable for the attack on the US embassy in Teheran and expressing gratitude for the Iranian government's promise to help keep the hostages safe), while also advising the administration to take action that would not endanger the lives of the hostages.[5] Columnist Joseph Kraft was even more blatant in his criticism of Carter's soft, "pusillanimous" approach to Iran, proclaiming, "Partisans of Jimmy Carter like to say he doesn't panic in a crisis. The test now being posed in Tehran raises the question of whether he does anything."[6] A few days later, the *New York Times* editors, while advising against any immediate risky attempts to rescue the hostages, nonetheless highlighted the broader implications of the United States' reaction to the hostage situation for the nation's international standing: "This episode promises to trigger a heated debate about America's standing in the world. The nation's purpose ought to be clear even before it knows whether its tactics were right."[7]

The many letters ordinary citizens sent to the press during the crisis offer insights into the public's mood in the aftermath of the seizure of the embassy in Teheran. The letters reveal grave public concern about the damage that the crisis and Carter's reaction to it were causing to the United States' international reputation. In a letter to the *Washington Post*, Samuel Intrater of Bethesda, Maryland, wrote:

> The development in Iran, and this country's response thereto, have brought into focus a bitter historical reality: the end of our role as a world power. For if a pipsqueak country like Iran can with impunity invade the territory of our embassy, take American citizens prisoner, and thumb its nose at us,

then clearly we have become a paper tiger, incapable of protecting our property, our interests and our citizenry.

Michael C. Smith of Washington, DC, also expressed a sense of national humiliation, lamenting, "I am sick and tired of every other country spitting in our face. How long will Americans endure this sort of treatment? . . . The time has come for us to stand up and be proud to be Americans." Some people specifically expressed their disappointment and outrage about Carter's subdued reaction to the crisis. For example, Raymon Queein of Washington, DC, complained: "The handling of the crisis in Iran by the Carter administration is cowardly and disgraceful. . . . This is the United States, not some two-bit country that has to beg for peace. Dammit, we can demand peace and we can back the demand with force."[8]

In this climate of disappointment and indignation, Carter's job-approval rating remained low, about 30 percent. The public outrage did not go unnoticed by the White House. Harold Saunders, the Assistant Secretary of State for Near East Affairs, recalled that the administration felt strong pressure from the public to pursue national honor, even if doing so meant risking the safety of the hostages (Saunders 1985). According to Snyder and Borghard (2011: 447), this pressure from the public pushed Carter to shift away from the diplomatic tenor of his rhetoric toward Iran and adopt a more belligerent tone.

Carter publicly addressed the hostage situation for the first time on November 12, when he gave a short speech from the White House in which he barred the purchase of oil from Iran. Although Carter assured the public that his administration was using "any available channel to protect the safety of the hostages and to secure their release," the tone of his speech was restrained and non-confrontational. Carter commended the public for showing restraint during the crisis, and asked the American people to help the government conserve energy (oil) in order to reduce the impact of the cessation of Iranian oil imports on the US economy; he did not mention or even hint at the possibility of using military force against Iran. However, the tone of Carter's rhetoric changed dramatically over the next few days. On November 15, the president faced the cameras again, in a speech at the annual convention of the American Federation of Labor and Congress of Industrial Organizations (AFL-CIO) in Washington, DC. The speech, which some reporters described as "the toughest speech of his Presidency,"[9] was directed to the entire nation and was covered in the national media. As the following excerpt demonstrates, Carter asked Americans to unite as members of a proud nation that remains true to its core principles and is determined to protect its honor:[10]

> I want to speak with you and all Americans about some fundamental principles upon which our nation was founded and which we must never forget. To some, these ideals may seem at times to be old-fashioned or outmoded. But we've been clearly reminded in recent days that these principles mean just as much to us now as they have ever meant, during any times of critical decision in the history of our nation. These fundamentals have old names to which we must continually give new meaning: names like strength, courage, patriotism, independence, the love of freedom, human rights, justice, concern for the common good.

Carter blamed the Iranian government for the hostage situation, saying, "For a rare time in human history a host government has condoned and even encouraged this kind of illegal action against a sovereign territory and official diplomatic relations of another nation." He described the hostages as "our nation's loyal citizens and faithful representatives," and stressed that "every American feels anger and outrage at what is happening to them, just as every American feels concern for their safety and pride in their great courage." Carter concluded the speech by reinforcing his call for national solidarity and his promise of a honorable and decisive reaction, asserting:

> No act has so galvanized the American people toward unity in the last decade as has the holding of our people as hostages in Tehran. We stand today as one people. We are dedicated to the principles and the honor of our nation. We have taken no action which would justify concern among the people, or among the Government of Iran. We have done nothing for which any American need apologize. The actions of Iranian leaders and the radicals who invaded our embassy were completely unjustified. They and all others must know that the United States of America will not yield to international terrorism or to blackmail.

In addition to engaging in tough talk, Carter used the speech to introduce several measures he had implemented in response to the crisis, including directing immigration authorities to review the visas of about 50,000 Iranian students in the United States and deport those who were present unlawfully, halting the shipment of oil from Iran to the United States, freezing official Iranian property and financial assets in the United States, and ordering the US ambassador to the United Nations to oppose any discussion of Iran's concerns in meetings of the UN Security Council.

In the following weeks, Carter continued to use rhetoric that sent a firm message to the government of Iran and called for national unity and perseverance at home.[11] The public largely embraced this tough talk, which Carter seemed to stand behind via his actions. As a result, Carter's job-approval rating increased sharply, peaking at 58 percent in late January 1980.[12] Although this rating is rather modest in absolute terms, it was the highest of his term, with the exception of his ratings in the "honeymoon" period during his first few months in office.[13]

To summarize, after the outbreak of the hostage crisis in Teheran, the US public did not initially rally behind Carter's leadership because he chose to use diplomatic negotiations conducted behind closed doors, rather than a public reaction that could have mobilized the public mood to rally behind an action against Iran. However, a week and half into the crisis, the public began to rally behind the president when the tone of Carter's rhetoric became more nationalistic and confrontational—pointing to the Iranian regime as an enemy of the United States; talking about American pride, courage, and honor; and expressing the United States' commitment to the lives of its citizens[14]—and thus began to align with the popular desire to reclaim national honor and respect of other nations. Eventually, Carter's reluctance to use military force prevented his popularity from reaching higher levels. Indeed, Carter's job-approval rating began to decline in February 1980 because most Americans concluded that while the president was talking tough to the Iranian regime, he was not willing to follow through on his threats. By early April, 71 percent of respondents to a public opinion poll thought that the hostage crisis made the United States look helpless (Snyder and Borghard 2011: 449), and Carter's job-approval rating had sunk to below 40 percent.[15]

September 11 Attacks

On the morning of Tuesday, September 11, 2001, 19 men highjacked four US passenger airplanes in US airspace. At 8:46 a.m. (Eastern Standard Time), the first plane (American Airlines Flight 11 from Boston to Los Angeles) crashed into the north tower of the World Trade Center in Manhattan. Just

17 minutes later, the second plane (United Airlines Flight 175 from Boston to Los Angeles) crashed into the south tower of the World Trade Center. Another 34 minutes passed before the third plane (American Airlines Flight 77 from Dulles, Virginia, to Los Angeles) struck the Pentagon in Washington, DC.[16] The conspirators had planned to fly the fourth hijacked plane (United Airlines Flight 93 from Newark, New Jersey, to San Francisco) into the Capitol building or the White House,[17] but the aircraft crashed in a field near Shanksville, Pennsylvania, when the flight crew and passengers made an attempt to regain the controls. At 9:59 a.m., less than an hour after being hit, the south tower of the World Trade Center collapsed, and 29 minutes later the north tower collapsed as well. The attacks killed 2,977 people (not including the 19 hijackers) and injured more than 6,000.[18] Almost immediately, the US government identified the Islamic fundamentalist organization al-Qaeda, under the leadership of Osama bin Laden, as the group responsible for the attacks.[19]

In the course of just a few hours after the attacks, many people who were initially emotionally stunned by the devastating events (Collins 2004) developed a strong feeling of collective humiliation (Kemper 2002; Feinstein 2020). The media's tendency to draw an analogy between 9/11 and Pearl Harbor (Ross 2013: 68–73; van Dooremalen 2021: 733) in its coverage of the events only reinforced the perception that the attacks violated America's status as a powerful and proud nation (see Chapter 9 for an extended discussion of the American public's reaction to this event). The strong feeling of collective humiliation prompted a desire to take steps to restore national honor. A letter from Roland E. Cowden of Maryville, Tennessee, to the *New York Times*, sent on the day of the attacks, expresses this desire to take action:

> An act against any one American anywhere in the world is an assault upon the entire American people. Now America must wield the sword in defense of liberty, and in the very act of striking never once divest herself of that love of liberty that nurtured every son and daughter among us and is the sinew of our spirit, the pulsing of our national heart. Call upon us. Do not delay. Call upon the strength of America, and she shall do great deeds.[20]

President Bush did indeed call upon the American nation. On the evening of the attacks, he delivered a special address; speaking to the entire nation, he referred to the events as an attack on the American way of life and freedom and he promised retaliation. In the following days, during visits to the sites of the attacks and memorial services for the victims, Bush repeatedly expressed his commitment to retaliating against those responsible for the attacks.

In the days and weeks after the attacks, the administration depicted Osama bin Laden and al-Qaeda as the enemy and repeatedly asserted that they must be defeated. Although Bush did not mention which terrorist organization was responsible for the hijackings in his initial address on the evening of the attacks, on September 12 the media reported that intelligence agencies had determined that Osama bin Laden was responsible for training and directing the hijackers. Bush's promise of retaliation gradually began to focus on al-Qaeda. In an address to Congress on September 20, he explicitly accused al-Qaeda of attacking the United States on September 11; identified Afghanistan as the sanctuary from which al-Qaeda had launched the attack; and officially declared a "war on terror." This declaration was widely acclaimed among ordinary citizens and politicians from both parties. As a result, Bush's public job-approval rating increased over this period, first sharply and then gradually, eventually reaching 90 percent (see Chapter 9 for an extended discussion of this process).

The Role of Official Rhetoric

In Chapter 5, I argued that during military conflicts, strong rally-round-the-flag reactions emerged when presidents used a nation-affirming rhetoric that highlighted the symbolic meaning of the event for the nation's honor and prestige and promised to reclaim honor and prestige through military retaliation against the nation's enemies; here, I make a parallel argument about the role of official rhetoric in rally development in the aftermath of major attacks against US civilian targets. As shown earlier, a nation-affirming rhetoric was crucial for the emergence of a rally-round-the-flag effect during the Iran hostage crisis (i.e., a rally developed only after President Carter's rhetoric became nation-affirming). Was presidential rhetoric also crucial for the emergence of the rally-round-the-flag result in the aftermath of the September 11 attacks? It is reasonable to speculate that the rally-round-the-flag effect was a direct response to the horrific events and had little to do with the official rhetoric about the attacks. Perhaps the same rally-round-the-flag effects would have emerged in the aftermath of the attacks even if President Bush had *not* used nationalist language and had refrained from declaring a war against terrorism. However, two developments suggest that the rally may not have developed in the absence of Bush using nationalist rhetoric.

First, the emergence of a rally in the aftermath of the Iran hostage crisis, which did not involve any casualties of US civilians, implies that the development of rallies may not be rooted in the extent of the actual damage done by an attack (nonetheless, extensive damages might make rally effects more pronounced), but rather in the symbolic challenge to the nation posed by a successful attack against US civilian targets and symbols of the United States' sovereignty and might. Bush himself highlighted the symbolic meaning of the September 11 attacks when he declared that "terrorist attacks can shake the foundations of our biggest buildings, but they cannot touch the foundation of America."[21] Second, as discussed earlier (and in greater detail in Chapter 9), the rally behind Bush did not develop immediately after the attacks, but emerged gradually as the public's interpretation of the situation shifted from an apocalyptic nightmare to an opportunity to display the American spirit, epitomized by the actions of the passengers on United Airlines Flight 93 and the firefighters working at ground zero (Feinstein 2020; Carey 2002). These two points provide only partial and circumstantial evidence for the link between the nation-affirming content of presidential rhetoric and the development of a rally reaction. Firmly establishing the existence of a causal relationship between the two would require knowing with certainty what would have occurred in this "counterfactual" (in the jargon of historical research)—how the public would have reacted to the September 11 attacks had President Bush chosen not to play the nationalist card.

Negative Cases

Of course, it is impossible to travel back in time and change the course of history to answer "what if" questions about the development of rallies. The next-best alternative to this maneuver is to examine how the public reacted when a sitting president's response to a major attack against a US civilian target (events of a lesser magnitude than the September 11 attacks that nonetheless could have become rally points) did not have a nationalist tone. In the period covered by this book, two major attacks against US civilians constitute such "negative cases": the bombing of the World Trade Center in New York City on February 26, 1993, which killed six adults and one unborn child and injured more than 1,000 people, and the bombing of the US embassies in

Kenya and Tanzania on August 7, 1998, which killed almost 300 people (including a dozen Americans) and wounded about 5,000.

These two events share key characteristics with the September 11 attacks and the Iran hostage crisis: all four events involved US civilian targets that had great symbolic value. In the attacks in Iran and later in Kenya and Tanzania, the targets were US embassies, which are symbols of state sovereignty. In the World Trade Center and September 11 attacks, the targets symbolized the central position of the United States in the international economy (the World Trade Center) and its military might (the Pentagon). Although all four cases share these key characteristics, the Iran hostage crisis and the September 11 attacks produced rally effects, but neither the 1993 World Trade Center bombing nor the attacks against the embassies in Kenya and Tanzania led to a rally period. I argue that no rallies developed in the latter cases because President Clinton's responses to these attacks did not have a nationalist tone and thus downplayed the need to reclaim national honor and prestige and promised no retaliation.

1993 World Trade Center Bombing

On February 26, 1993, a group of Islamist terrorists who identified themselves as members of the "Liberation Army" exploded a truck bomb beneath the north tower of the World Trade Center in New York City. The attack, which killed six civilians and an unborn baby, was a protest against the United States' interference in the Middle East, in particular the assistance it was providing to Israel. President Clinton chose not to portray the bombing of the Word Trade Center as an attack on the entire nation, instead framing the explosion of a 1,200-pound bomb in a Ryder truck parked in the garage beneath the World Trade Center building[22] as a matter of law enforcement. Perhaps Clinton chose this rather narrow interpretation because the bombing was the first terrorist attack perpetrated by radical Muslims in the United States, and because an event of this magnitude could still reasonably be contained within a "law enforcement" framework.[23] Clinton's effort to contain the event rather than amplify its impact on public opinion is evident in the fact that he addressed the nation in a radio address rather than a televised address. Clinton stressed that he would use "the full measure of federal law-enforcement resources" to hunt for those responsible for the blast.[24]

Thus, because Clinton portrayed the World Trade Center bombing as a law enforcement matter, and because there was no clear enemy that could become a target for public animosity, no rally-round-the-flag period developed in the aftermath of the attack (in fact, Clinton's job-approval ratings dropped slightly, from 64 percent before the World Trade Center bombing[25] to 59 percent after the bombing[26]).

The Bombings of the US Embassies in Kenya and Tanzania

Five and a half years after the World Trade Center attack, terrorists once again struck highly symbolic targets—this time the US embassies in Nairobi, Kenya, and Dar es Salaam, Tanzania. The attacks, which were perpetrated by the Egyptian Islamic Jihad (EIJ), killed 224 people, including a dozen US citizens, and wounded more than 4,500. EIJ launched the attacks in response to the Central Intelligence Agency offering assistance to the Albanian government for capturing or killing Islamic militants who were linked to the EIJ and living in Albania, and the United States asking the Egyptian government to take harsh action against EIJ members after they were extradited to that country (Mayer 2009: 114). On August 5, 1998, Ayman al-Zawahiri, an EIJ leader[27] whose brother was captured in Albania and transported to Egypt for interrogation (the Egyptian government sentenced both brothers to death in absentia), published a letter in a London Arab-language newspaper in which he promised to retaliate against the United States "in a language they will understand" (Mayer 2009: 114). Two days later, the US embassies in Kenya and Tanzania were bombed.

Despite the extent of the attack, no rally emerged in the aftermath of the bombings because President Clinton did not initially use nationalist rhetoric, and even when he began to adopt such rhetoric, he did not focus his response on a clearly defined enemy. When Clinton addressed the nation after the bombings, this time via television, he did not use nationalist language and did not initially identify a clear enemy. Instead, in a relatively short statement, he defined the attacks as abhorrent acts of terrorist violence and promised to bring the people responsible for the attacks to justice.[28] Two weeks later, when Clinton announced that the United States had launched a retaliatory missile strike against suspected al-Qaeda training camps and chemical factories in Sudan and Afghanistan, his language took on a much more nationalistic and confrontational tone. He drew a stark distinction between the American nation and the terrorists, stating:

> The radical groups affiliated with, and funded by Osama bin Laden . . . share a hatred for democracy, a fanatical glorification of violence, and a horrible distortion of their religion to justify the murder of innocents. They have made the United States their adversary precisely because of what we stand for and what we stand against.

Clinton concluded by emphasizing core US values, saying, "We will defend our people, our interests and our values. We will help people of all faiths, in all parts of the world, who want to live free of fear and violence."[29] Following his address, about 75 percent of the public supported the missile strike.[30] Despite this widespread support for the strike, Clinton's approval ratings did not change much in the days and weeks after the bombings (available data indicate a slight decline, from 66 percent to 62 percent) because the strike was a relatively limited operation that did not involve direct contact with enemy forces (unlike the military actions discussed in Chapter 5 that did produce rally reactions);[31] and while in his national address Clinton mentioned bin Laden as a sponsor of anti-American terrorism, killing bin Laden was not one of the missile strike's declared goals. Further, in the period that passed between the attacks on the US embassies and the retaliatory US missile strike, the focus of media coverage and public conversation shifted to the investigation of the Clinton–Monica Lewinsky affair, and a limited operation against a few suspected terrorist camps was insufficient for generating a rally reaction the US public.[32]

What "Negative Cases" Reveal

To summarize the argument presented in this chapter, rally-round-the-flag reactions emerged in response to major attacks against US civilian targets only when the sitting president used nationalist rhetoric that publicly conveyed (and indeed propagated) a sense of collective humiliation, and simultaneously promised to take action that would restore national honor and prestige. Attacks against US civilian targets, even when they cause a great deal of damage and claim the lives of many Americans, do not necessarily lead the public to rally behind the president. Some scholars have claimed that

the public is likely to be especially excited about the president and his military policy when a major victory is achieved on the battlefield (see especially
Eichenberg 2005). However, foreign attacks that claim the lives of many US
civilians or take living hostages represent the opposite scenario—a major *defeat* of the nation at the hands of its enemies—which may lead some people
to lose trust in the government that failed to protect US citizens rather than
rally behind the government.

This discussion of four attacks against US civilian targets shows that the
president can choose how to publicly respond to devastating attacks against
US civilian targets, and that this choice may determine whether a rally-
round-the-flag effect emerges. Rallies have followed presidential decisions
to employ a nation-affirming rhetoric—that is, a rhetoric that propagates
the public feeling of collective humiliation while also outlining a way to increase national honor and gain more respect from other nations through
military action (this was the case in the aftermath of the September 11
attacks and in part of the Iran hostage crisis). In contrast, when a president
has not highlighted the implications of attacks against US civilian targets for
the nation's honor and international prestige (which occurred in Carter's
initial reactions to the hostage crisis, and Clinton's reactions to the World
Trade Center bombing and the attacks on the US embassies in Kenya and
Tanzania), there was no emergence of a "let's get behind the president"
public mood, and some people even felt that the president's reaction added
insult to injury.

Why Haven't Attacks on Military Targets
Generated Rallies?

This chapter has focused on attacks against US civilian targets, both attacks
that prompted a rally-round-the-flag effect (the Iran hostage crisis and
the September 11 attacks) and those that did not (the World Trade Center
bombing and the bombings of the US embassies in Kenya and Tanzania).
During the focal period, there were also several attacks against US military
targets that claimed the lives of many service members or involved US soldiers
being taken hostage. These attacks include the *seizure of the USS Pueblo* by the
Democratic People's Republic of Korea (DPRK) (a US intelligence ship was
seized on January, 23, 1968, and was released only after the United States formally admitted and apologized for spying on the DPRK); the *Tet Offensive* (an

extensive surprise attack by North Vietnam and the Viet Cong against South Vietnamese, US, and allied targets, which began on January 30, 1968, claimed the lives of over 1,000 US service members, and escalated the Vietnam War[33]); the *Beirut barracks attacks* (on October 23, 1983, two suicide bombers drove trucks containing explosives at a building that housed US and French military personnel, killing 241 American service members as well as 58 French military personnel and six French civilians); the *Khobar Towers bombing* (on June 25, 1996, a truck bomb explosion killed 19 US airmen and wounded nearly 500 in Khobar, Saudi Arabia); and the *Hainan Island incident* (on April 1, 2001, 24 US aircrew members were detained by China for 10 days after their intelligence airplane, which was operating 70 miles off the Chinese shore, collided with an interceptor aircraft). None of these attacks on military targets was followed by a rally-round-the-flag period.

Because the United States has a sharp institutional separation between military and civilians and no mandatory military service, attacks on service members may not provoke the same moral outrage among the public as attacks on civilians. However, the available data cannot be used to assess this argument, because with one exception, sitting presidents did not use explicitly nationalist language to frame any of these attacks on US military targets, and thus the essential trigger for a rally-round-the-flag effect was absent.

The one case in which the sitting president responded to an attack on a US military target with nationalist language was the Beirut barracks attack on October 23, 1983. President Reagan may have chosen to play the nationalism card in this instance because he knew US forces would be launching an invasion of Grenada the following morning and wanted to set the public mood for this military action. In his first statement about the Beirut attack, Reagan described the US mission in Lebanon as vital to American interests. He asserted that the mission was "central to our credibility on a global scale" and declared, "the United States will not be intimidated by terrorists."[34] Three days later, Reagan's nationalist tone intensified: while addressing the nation about the invasion of Grenada, he drew an explicit connection between the invasion of the Caribbean country and the bombing of US military installations in Lebanon, over 6,000 miles away, by stressing that both countries were sites of terrorist violence sponsored by Moscow, and promised that the American nation could not and would not "dishonor the soldiers who died in the attacks."[35]

Despite the severity of the Beirut barracks bombing and the nationalistic tone of Reagan's rhetoric, no rally-round-the-flag period followed the attack, probably because Reagan did not (and perhaps could not) blame a specific organization for the attack, making it a target for collective rage; instead, he made vague references to the perpetrators as "terrorists" and "criminals." Had there been a distinct enemy to blame, perhaps a decision to retaliate against this enemy would have motivated the public to rally around the flag.

As noted previously, the available data cannot be used to rule out the possibility that in the focal period rally outcomes did not emerge in response to attacks against US military targets because the public tends to be less outraged by attacks against the military than by attacks against civilian targets. However, the overall argument put forward in this chapter and the evidence presented to support this argument suggest that if, in response to major attacks against American military targets (especially attacks that claimed the lives of many service members), the sitting presidents had publicly applied a nationalist framing to the events and had ordered a retaliatory attack against a clearly defined enemy, public opinion would have rallied behind the commander-in-chief and the military operation.[36]

Conclusion

At first glance, the rally-round-the-flag reactions to the Iran hostage crisis and the September 11 attacks may appear to be predictable, even self-evident, responses to devastating adversarial actions taken against US civilians. In response to this type of attacks, most people are outraged and feel solidarity with the victims. Closing ranks behind the national leader may seem like an expected outcome of the public mood. However, the analysis of major attacks against US civilian targets that did not produce significant rally reactions ("negative cases") shows that the rally-round-the-flag effect is not an automatic reaction to this type of events. Instead, the emergence of a rally effect depends on the national leadership (in particular the president) making a decision to employ a nation-affirming rhetoric. Such rhetoric highlights the negative consequences that an attack on US civilian targets has for the most precious symbolic assets of the home nation—its sense of honor and the respect it receives from other nations. Further, a nation-affirming rhetoric entails a promise of military retaliation and thus marks a path toward fortifying the nation's honor and prestige.

7

On the Verge of a Rally

Borderline Cases

*Our reluctance for conflict should not be misjudged as a failure of
will. When action is required to preserve our national security, we
will act. . . . No arsenal or no weapon in the arsenals of the world is
so formidable as the will and moral courage of free men and women.
It is a weapon our adversaries in today's world do not have. It is a
weapon that we as Americans do have. Let that be understood by
those who practice terrorism and prey upon their neighbors.*

—From President Ronald Reagan's inaugural
address on June 20, 1981[1]

Chapter 6 discussed two major rally-round-the-flag periods that emerged in
the aftermath of attacks on US civilian targets: the first and more modest rally
period occurred during the Iran hostage crisis in 1979–1980, and the second
rally, which was more intense and longer, developed in the aftermath of the
September 11, 2001, attacks and the US declaration of a "war on terror." Three
incidents that occurred in the 1980s while Ronald Reagan was in office—the
hijacking of TWA Flight 847 in June 1985, the air raid on Libya in April 1986
following a series of terrorist attacks against civilian targets in Europe, and
the bombing of Pan Am Flight 103 in December 1988—serve as a contrast
to the events covered in Chapter 6. Like the hostage crisis and September 11,
these events were seen by many in the United States as being part of a struggle
with anti-American "international terrorism." However, while the reactions
to these three events were on the verge of becoming significant rally points,
they eventually generated only minor increases (6–7 percentage points) in
the president's job-approval rating. Reagan's approval ratings peaked at 65
percent in the aftermath of the hostage situation in Lebanon, 68 percent after

Rally 'round the Flag. Yuval Feinstein, Oxford University Press. © Oxford University Press 2022.
DOI: 10.1093/oso/9780197629710.003.0007

the air raid on Libya, and 63 percent following the bombing over Lockerbie, Scotland.

The discussion of these three borderline cases addresses two questions: (1) Why did presidential approval ratings increase following the events? and (2) Why were the increases more moderate than the rally-round-the flag effects discussed in the previous chapters? The answer to the second question can refine the understanding of the conditions under which and processes through which rally-round-the-flag effects emerge in the United States.

The Historical Context

The Reagan administration came to power on the heels of the 444-day Iran hostage crisis and promised to forcefully resist terrorism. However, in the administration's first year, Reagan's tough talk was followed by little visible substantive action. In 1983, after a series of attacks—the bombing of the American Embassy in Beirut (April 18), which killed 17 Americans; the bombing of the US Marine barracks in Beirut (October 23), which killed 241 service members; and the bombing of the American Embassy in Kuwait (December 12), which was part of a larger coordinated attack on foreign installations in the country—both legislators and the general public came to see terrorism as a major credibility test for the Reagan administration (Livingstone 1988: 67). Reagan's job-approval ratings remained fairly low (41–49 percent) during most of this period; however, after the invasion of Grenada, on October 25, 1983, his approval rating increased slightly to about 52 percent and then remained fairly stable for about a year.[2]

In 1984 and 1985, as the Reagan administration began taking more substantive action against terrorist organizations and their state sponsors, the United States suffered another string of terrorist attacks, including the kidnapping of the CIA Chief of Station in Beirut (March 16, 1984); a second attack on the American Embassy in Beirut (September 20, 1984), which killed 23 people (including 2 Americans); the murder of a disabled Jewish American passenger during the hijacking of MS *Achille Lauro* (a cruise ship) in the Mediterranean Sea (October 7, 1985); a coordinated set of attacks on the Rome and Vienna airports (December 18, 1985) that killed 5 Americans and 15 citizens of other countries; and the murder of 4 marine soldiers in a café in San Salvador (June 19, 1985). The hijacking of

TWA Flight 847 on June 14, 1985, marked the peak of this wave of terrorist attacks (Livingstone 1988: 70).[3]

The Hijacking of TWA Flight 847

On June 14, 1985, two gunmen associated with the Lebanese Shiite militia Hezbollah hijacked TWA Flight 847, which carried 153 passengers and crew members, while en route from Athens to Rome.[4] The hijackers forced the pilot to fly first to Beirut, then to Algiers, and then back to Beirut. At the Beirut airport, the hijackers executed Robert Dean Stethem, a US Navy diver, and dumped his body on the runway. After refueling, the hijackers once again forced the pilot to fly the aircraft to Algiers and back to Beirut. The hijackers released most of the hostages in the first few days of the crisis, but held 39 Americans in captivity for two weeks: 32 of these passengers were moved into the custody of the Shiite Amal Militia, while the rest (who had names that the terrorists assumed were Jewish) were held by more militant Shiites affiliated with Hezbollah (Cannon 1991: 607). The hijackers' main demand was that Israel release more than 700 Shiite Lebanese prisoners the country had taken captive during its invasion of Lebanon.[5]

In response to the hijacking, Reagan made an attempt to portray the situation as "business as usual" rather than declaring a state of emergency (Cannon 1991: 606). However, things were far from usual: a military option for releasing the hostages by force seemed infeasible, and on June 16, Reagan received a letter signed by 32 of the hostages. They pleaded with him not to use military force, stating, "We implore you not to take any direct military action on our behalf. Please negotiate our immediate release by convincing the Israelis to release the 700 Lebanese prisoners as requested. Now" (Cannon 1991: 537). On the same day, the front page of the *Los Angeles Times* featured a photo of the hostage pilot with a terrorist pointing a gun to his head; the exhausted pilot told reporters that if the US government attempted a rescue, "we'd all be dead men."[6] Under these circumstances, it was extremely difficult for Reagan to order a rescue operation that would fulfill his promise to fight against terrorism. In the end, Israel announced that, although it would not negotiate with the hijackers, it would consider a US request to free the Shiite prisoners if such a request was made.[7] The hostage situation was finally resolved two weeks after it began, with the help of the president of Syria, Hafez al-Assad, and the (more secretive) assistance of the speaker of the

Iranian parliament, Hashemi Rafsanjani (Cannon 1991: 607). On June 30, the hostages were driven to Syria, where they boarded a US Air Force cargo plane and flew to an airbase in West Germany. Over the next several weeks, Israel released more than 700 Shiite prisoners, while officially maintaining that the release was not related to the hijacking.

Could this hostage situation have prompted a major rally-round-the-flag period? My (speculative) answer to this question is "yes": the hijacking of an American civilian aircraft, in the context of the multiple preceding terrorist attacks on American targets, seemed to confirm Reagan's repeated declarations that the United States was the target of a growing wave of international terrorism that challenged America's will and determination to fight its enemies and by doing so to assume leadership of the free world. The hostage situation also revived memories of the collective humiliation of the United States during the Iran hostage crisis. In addition, Reagan appealed directly to national sentiment in his address to the public (on June 19) about the hijacking. He opened with the following statement:

> One hour ago, the body of a young American hero, Navy diver Robert Dean Stethem, was returned to his native soil in a coffin after being beaten and shot at point-blank range. His murder and the fate of the other American hostages still being held in Beirut underscore an inescapable fact. The United States is tonight a nation being attacked by international terrorists who wantonly kill and who seize our innocent citizens as their prisoners.[8]

With American civilians being held hostage by terrorists and the president using explicitly nationalist language to frame the situation, only one condition for a rally-round-the flag effect was missing: a proper enemy to fight. The presence of an enemy would likely have transformed the reaction to this event into a full-blown rally-round-the-flag period. In his statement, Reagan discussed "international terrorism," but admitted that he did not know exactly who was responsible for the hijacking. In response to a question from a reporter, Reagan confirmed that Nabih Berri, the leader of Amal (a Shiite Lebanese militia and political movement)[9] and the minister of justice in the Lebanese government, had taken the hostages from the hijackers. However, the administration refrained from blaming the crisis on Berri because officials were unsure what role Berri was playing in the crisis, and knew it was possible he would be a key player in resolving the crisis (which he eventually was). Reagan was also unwilling to blame the Lebanese government—probably because the United States supported the government of Lebanon and trained its army with the expectation the army would restrain the anti-American and anti-Israeli militias of the Palestinian Liberation Organization (PLO) and Hezbollah (Baylouny 2009: 317). Administration officials eventually placed the blame for the hostage situation on a general category of individuals—"Shiites" in Lebanon—rather than any specific organization.[10] The absence of a clear enemy that could serve as a target, and the consequent lack of a counterattack by American forces, prevented the hijacking of TWA Flight 847 from developing into a major rally point.

The Bombing of Pan Am Flight 103

Terrorists launched another attack against an American civilian aircraft, this time with even more devastating consequences, on December 21, 1988: Pan Am Flight 103 from London to New York was bombed as it flew over Lockerbie, Scotland, causing the aircraft to disintegrate in midair. All 243 passengers (including 178 Americans) and 16 crew members (11 Americans) perished, and 11 others were killed on the ground. With no immediate evidence that the crash was actually caused by a bomb, and with their attention focused on the effort to free American hostages in Lebanon (who had been captured in a series of abductions in Lebanon prior to the hijacking of TWA Flight 847), the White House did not rush to point fingers at any suspected terrorist organization or sponsoring state (Simon 2001: 225–27). One week later, when British authorities confirmed that the aircraft had been destroyed by a bomb, Reagan elevated his antiterrorism rhetoric and promised retaliation. However, these were Reagan's last days in office, and president-elect George H. W. Bush adopted a more cautious rhetoric, promising that the United States would "seek hard and punish firmly, decisively, those who did this *if you could ever find them*" (Simon 2001: 227–28; emphasis in the original). As in the hijacking of TWA Flight 847, all the conditions for a major rally-round-the-flag period were present except a clear enemy that could be the target of an attack and toward which the public could channel its desire for retaliation that would restore national honor and prestige.

The 1986 Air Raid on Libya

In this final section, I discuss an event that—unlike the attacks on TWA Flight 847 and Pan Am Flight 103—did involve retaliation against a well-known enemy, and yet nonetheless did not evoke a significant rally reaction among the public. In the early hours of April 15, 1986, US bombers struck the Bab al-Azizia military barracks and compound near Tripoli, which served as the headquarters of Libyan strongman Muammar Qaddafi, as well as other targets near the capital city of Tripoli and the city of Benghazi, some of which were suspected of being terrorist training camps. In the context of America's ongoing struggle with anti-American and anti-Western terrorism, this act of retaliation could easily have generated positive feelings that motivated a rally behind the leadership of President Reagan. Furthermore, in contrast to the hijacking of TWA Flight 847 and the bombing of Pan Am Flight 103, the air raid on Libya involved military action targeting an enemy—indeed, an enemy most American already knew and despised. And yet no rally ensued in the aftermath of the raid. Given this absence of a rally-round-the-flag result despite the contentious historical context and the presence of a clearly defined enemy, the air raid on Libya is an instructive case.

The decision to initiate an airstrike in Libya was a reaction to a series of terrorist attacks that challenged America's capacity to protect its citizens and facilities abroad. Officially, the raid was a response to the bombing of the La Belle discotheque in Berlin on April 5, 1986, which killed 3 patrons (including 2 American service members) and injured 230 people (including 50 American service members). However, the decision to strike had actually been made earlier, following attacks on the Rome and Vienna airports that killed 19 people, including 4 Americans. These attacks were perpetrated by the Abu Nidal Organization, which, according to American intelligence, was sponsored by Libya (Livingstone 1988: 72; Piszkiewicz 2003: 61).

Although at least three other dictators—Ayatollah Khomeini in Iran, Saddam Hussein in Iraq, and Hafez al-Assad in Syria—sponsored more deadly terrorism than Libya during this period, Muammar Qaddafi became the main target of Reagan's anti-terrorism rhetoric (Simon 2001: 196; St. John 2002: 135). Several sources have concluded that the administration singled out Qaddafi because among all the terror-sponsoring states, Libya was the most convenient target for several reasons (Livingstone 1988: 66; Simon 2001: 196–97). First and foremost, Libya had the weakest military, and thus government officials expected an attack on Libya would be less costly than an attack on one of the other countries. Second, unlike other terror-sponsoring states, Libya was isolated from the Arab world, and unlike Iran, it was not well connected to the United Nations Security Council. An attack on Libya, therefore, was not likely to escalate into a greater diplomatic or security crisis. Third, Qaddafi was the most visible of the leaders of terror-sponsoring countries. He appeared frequently on Western news channels and did not hesitate to express anti-American views. In addition, Qaddafi's habit of wearing dresses and his eccentric mode of speech made him an ideal candidate to play the role of the villain. Indeed, many policymakers around the world considered Qaddafi to be a madman (Livingstone 1988: 66), and Reagan himself once said that Qaddafi was "not only barbarian, [but] he's flaky" (Simon 2001: 196). Due to his explicit support for terrorism and his demonization by the Reagan administration, Qaddafi became the man Americans loved to hate during the 1980s.

The air raid on Libya came as no surprise. From the beginning of 1986 onward, Reagan intensified his anti-Qaddafi rhetoric, calling him "a pariah who must be isolated from the world community" (St. John 2002: 134). In addition, the United States took several steps in preparation for a military confrontation: the US government closed the Libyan embassy in Washington, DC; suspended all economic ties with Libya; froze Libyan assets in the United States and American banks overseas; invalidated all authorizations to travel to Libya; and called all Americans residing in Libya to come home. In March, the administration stationed a flotilla of 45 navy ships off the coast of Libya and sent ships accompanied by aircraft to cross the "line of death" Qaddafi had drawn in the Gulf of Sidra, resulting in two skirmishes in which US naval forces sank two Libyan patrol ships and attacked an onshore radar installation (Livingstone 1988: 72; Piszkiewicz 2003: 61–62; Schumacher 1986).

With Qaddafi portrayed as the spearhead of anti-American terrorism, and with the relationship between the United States and Libya gradually deteriorating, the conditions were set for a rally-round-the-flag period to emerge during a military confrontation with Libya. Indeed, when the White House launched the raid on Libya, more than three quarters of the US public supported the strike, and the approval rating for Reagan's foreign policy jumped from 51 percent to 76 percent (Flamm 2009: 125; Hinckley 1988; Simons 1993: 6). However, despite the public's support for the attack, the presidential job-approval rating increased by only 6 points, peaking at 67 percent.[11]

Why didn't the air raid on Libya evoke a rally-round-the-flag effect? The answer, I argue, is that the limited scope of the raid and the lack of direct confrontation meant that the public's high expectations for Reagan's response to terrorism were not met. The raid was a limited military operation that, as Jeffrey Simon (2001: 198) explained, "almost seemed anticlimactic after all the months and years of promises of a military strike against terrorists." Two aspects of the event contributed to the anticlimactic feeling. First, the raid was not a direct military confrontation between the United States and Libya, but rather a short and limited military operation that met very little resistance. Second, Qaddafi was not killed or removed from power in the raid. Although President Reagan and Secretary of State George Schultz publicly denied that killing Qaddafi was one of the goals of the operation, the fact that Qaddafi's headquarters, which were close to his private residence, were targeted, and that two of his sons were injured and his adopted baby daughter was killed in the raid, suggested otherwise.[12] Indeed, following the raid, most Americans did not feel sorry for the personal loss the raid had inflicted on Qaddafi, whose head they wanted. In a public opinion poll conducted immediately after the results of the raid were made public, no less than 81 percent of respondents agreed with the statement, "I feel Colonel Kaddafi had it coming."[13] Therefore, even though the administration claimed that the raid was successful, and denied setting a goal to kill Qaddafi, the fact that Qaddafi survived lent a bitter taste to the mission's "success."

The discussion so far raises a question: Does the absence of a significant rally-round-the-flag reaction in a case where the public assessed a military mission as incomplete provide evidence of rational attitude formation? In other words, was the reluctance to rally behind Reagan's leadership simply a reasonable reaction to his unsuccessful policy in Libya? The *rational public* perspective (see Chapter 2 for a review) would suggest that the air raid against Libya would have developed into a major rally point if it had brought about Qaddafi's demise or at least forced him to step down.

Indeed, this interpretation cannot be completely ruled out. The dramatic increase in the public's approval of Reagan's overall foreign policy following the air raid in Libya may suggest that, in the eyes of the public, the raid marked a change in Reagan's anti-terrorism policy. In addition, the fact that Reagan's job-approval ratings increased, but only slightly, during this period may indicate that for many Americans the sense that the raid was successful was tempered by the failure to kill Qaddafi. However, several other cases provide evidence that contradicts this rationalist interpretation. Specifically, these cases illustrate that significant rally outcomes can emerge even in the absence of an immediate clear success, and thus success is *not* a necessary condition for the emergence of a major rally effect. For example, the invasions of Afghanistan in 2001 and Iraq in 2003, in which the US government sent American ground forces to dethrone terror-sponsoring regimes, evoked rally-round-the-flag reactions even before the dust of war had settled and success was visible. These counter-examples indicate that if a similar large-scale military operation had been launched against Libya, a rally-round-the-flag period would have emerged even in the absence of immediate success. In short, the limited scope and lack of direct confrontation with the enemy kept the raid on Libya from evoking enough enthusiasm and support for the president to generate a rally-round-the-flag effect.

Conclusion

Throughout the 1980s, the United States engaged in a frustrating struggle against anti-American and anti-Western terrorism. During this period, several devastating attacks that claimed the lives of many Americans evoked high levels of public outrage and strong feelings of humiliation and rage that could have produced rallies behind military actions against terrorist organizations and their sponsor states. Each of the major terrorist attacks in this period became a "media event," including a dramatic live broadcast that placed the event at the center of the public conversation, not least because the perpetrators orchestrated the attacks with a goal of stunning the media and the public in the United States and other Western countries (Weimann 1987).

In line with the argument made in previous chapters, these public feelings of outrage and humiliation created the *potential* for a rally-round-the-flag effect. However, for a rally to materialize, a humiliated public must believe that a presidential policy will put the nation on track to regain its collective honor and prestige. Such a belief emerges when the president takes or promises to take strong military action against a clearly defined enemy, whose defeat can then mark the moral superiority of the American nation and the US resolve. All the rallies discussed in previous chapters were preceded by the diffusion of a belief that presidential policy would restore national honor and prestige; however, President Reagan's reaction to the events discussed in the current chapter did not spur such a belief, and thus did not produce a rally-round-the-flag result.

8

Chivalrous Struggles

Rallies for Saving the Free World

*This is the time of all others when Democracy should prove its purity
and its spiritual power to prevail. It is surely the manifest destiny of the
United States to lead in the attempt to make this spirit prevail.*
—President Woodrow Wilson's Annual
Message to Congress, December 7, 1920[1]

On the evening of January 16, 1991, President George H. W. Bush, sitting
by his desk in the Oval Office, gave a 12-minute televised address to the nation in which he announced that the United States and its allies had initiated a military attack against Iraq. There was nothing surprising about the
announcement—it followed months of preparations that the media had
described and discussed widely. Nevertheless, Bush's statement had a dramatic effect on public opinion: overnight, the president's job-approval rating
jumped to 83 percent, an increase of about 20 points. When the ground as-
sault began just over a month later, Bush's approval rating peaked at nearly 90
percent. Did Americans rally behind Bush for the reasons discussed in the
previous chapters—because they felt an urge to reclaim lost national honor
and earn the respect of other nations? This does not seem to be the case for
the Gulf War. The United States had opened the last decade of the twentieth
century with a swift victory in Panama. Further, while the shadows of the
bloody and unsuccessful Vietnam War continued to haunt large segments of
the American public, the high levels of public support for military intervention in the Persian Gulf emerged *despite* (rather than due to) traumatic memories of Vietnam (Rowe 1991).

The reaction to the Gulf War belongs to a special category of rallies, which
are triggered when the United States seeks to fulfill its perceived role as
"leader of the free world," thus reinforcing its global prestige and honor (see

Rally 'round the Flag. Yuval Feinstein, Oxford University Press. © Oxford University Press 2022.
DOI: 10.1093/oso/9780197629710.003.0008

Figure 4.1 in Chapter 4 for a graphical illustration of this process). In the period covered by this book (1950–2020), the Gulf War was the only event that became a rally point because the American nation claimed the role of "leader of the free world." However, in other instances—specifically in the aftermath of the Cuban Missile Crisis (discussed in Chapter 5) and following the September 11 attacks (discussed in Chapter 6)—rally processes were initially fueled by a public feeling of humiliation and a desire to reclaim national honor, and then further spurred when the public embraced an official agenda highlighting the international leadership of the United States, which contributed to the legitimation of the use of military power. The United States' intervention in World War II in December 1941 is another example in which taking on the role of international leader helped spur a rally (although this occurred before the period covered in the book). Briefly, the available data suggest that after the United States declared war on Japan (December 8) and Germany (December 11), President Roosevelt's job-approval rating increased at least 11 percentage points (from about 73 percent in late November 1941 to about 84 percent in the first week of January, 1942; it is likely that Roosevelt's approval ratings were even higher in December 1941, but there are no data that can be used to examine this possibility).[2]

I once again take a comparative view to analyze the rally-round-the-flag effect of the Gulf War: I contrast the emergence this rally with the lack of a rally in other instances when the United States led an international coalition in a military invasion. The discussion focuses on the differences between the Gulf War and the Korean War (1950–1953) because none of the other internationally sanctioned military interventions during this period, which I discuss briefly in the last part of the chapter, developed into significant military confrontations, and thus the potential for the emergence of a rally outcome was much lower in these cases.

In both the Korean War and the first Gulf War, the United Nations (UN) Security Council authorized the use of military power to overturn the annexation of a country's territory by a neighboring country. The two wars had similar objectives: in the Korean War, the official mission was to compel North Korean forces to retreat to the 38th parallel north (the border with South Korea),[3] while in the Gulf War the mandate was to force the Iraqi military to pull out of Kuwait. Further, in the broader historical context, these two wars bookended the inter-bloc rivalry of the Cold War: the Korean War was the first military confrontation between the emerging Eastern and Western blocs, and the Persian Gulf War occurred during the demise of the Soviet Union in a region that had been a primary site for struggles between the two rival blocs during the Cold War. In both Korea and the Gulf War, the authorization of the UN Security Council was a prerequisite for the mobilization of public opinion in the United States because these authorizations conveyed a recognition of the United States as an international leader, thus symbolically confirming the nation's military and moral superiority. Both Presidents Truman and Bush accepted the call and led coalition interventions. Despite these similarities, however, only the Gulf War evoked a significant rally around the flag.

The Korean War: Downplaying International Leadership

President Truman's decision to intervene in Korea—first with air and naval forces (June 27, 1950) and then with ground forces as well (June 30)—was initially met with widespread approval; about 8 out of every 10 Americans supported the measure (Casey 2008: 35), although this very high level of support may have been due to the Gallup poll referring to American involvement in Korea as "military aid" (Brewer 2011: 151). Indeed, four years after the grand victory in World War II, with a fledgling United Nations that lacked the teeth to enforce its resolutions, many Americans believed it was time for the United States to lead the "free world." In letters to the press, some members of the public took an apologetic tone when expressing this view. For example, Mary Chamberlain of Broad Run, Virginia, wrote:

> In the absence of a statute of law against aggression and of a world police force capable of enforcing such law it became the unhappy duty of the United States Government as a signatory member, in good faith, of the U.N. Charter to act in the capacity of policeman for the U.N.[4]

Others enthusiastically embraced the "international policeman" role. For example, Harry Daniels of Washington, DC, wrote: "I wish to congratulate the President on his correct and courageous stand in connection with the Korean affair. . . . Mr. Truman may not know it, but he has made himself a hero among all democratic peoples in the world."[5] Using more militant language, Philip Randolph of New York declared:

> President Truman's entry into the Korean war with a big stick is the only language Communist Russia can understand. In the absence of such action,

Stalin, like Hitler, would chloroform the world with the gasses of propaganda about peace, while thrusting the sword of war through the heart of
the democratic world.[6]

Despite the high levels of public support for an intervention in Korea, the
intervention had only a modest effect on Truman's popularity. Following
the announcement of the decision to send troops to Korea, Truman's job-
approval rating increased by 9 points, peaking at 46 percent, and his disapproval rating declined by 7 points, remaining fairly high (40 percent) even
at its nadir. Why did Truman, whose job-approval rating had skyrocketed to
about 90 percent following the victory in World War II,[7] not enjoy a similar
boost in popularity after announcing the intervention in Korea even though
most of the public supported this decision?

The answer, I argue, is twofold. First, at the onset of the war, the Truman
administration played down the magnitude and importance of the events in
the Korean Peninsula, as well as the scale of the United States' involvement.
Some historians believe that Truman sought to avoid provoking war hysteria, specifically panic about the possibility of an atomic world war erupting,
which might have prompted a call from the public to launch a preemptive
strike against the Soviet Union (Casey 2008: chap. 1). Other historians claim
that Truman's rhetoric simply reflected the way his administration initially
viewed the crisis in Korea and the role of the United States in this conflict
(Lewis 2018).

In the few years before the Korean War, US foreign policy was guided by
the Truman Doctrine. The doctrine, which was announced before a joint
session of Congress on March 12, 1947, established the United States' commitment to supporting countries around the world in their struggle with
communism by providing them with financial and military assistance,
but not by sending US troops to fight in these wars (Lewis 2018: 80; Jervis
1980: 574). Further, in May 1947, Congress put the Truman Doctrine into
action by approving the provision of military and financial assistance to
Greece and Turkey to help them fight communist guerillas sponsored by the
Soviet Union (Lewis 2018: 82). Truman's initial public reaction to the crisis in
Korea, therefore, was in line with his official foreign policy and his reactions
to previous conflicts with communist entities. According to military histo-
rian Adrian Lewis, "Not until North Korea attacked South Korea did Truman
fully comprehend and accept the new duties placed upon the United States
[as the leader of the free world in the Cold War]; and even after the start of

hostilities the American people were uncertain about their new responsibilities and duties in world affairs" (Lewis 2018: 76).

US military involvement in Korea increased during the war, reflecting both the way the Korean conflict changed the Cold War doctrine of the United States (Jervis 1980) and the increasing influence of the "Domino Theory"—which postulated that any loss of a war in a region to communists could have devastating economic, psychological, and political consequences, leading to a communist takeover of other countries in the same region—on both policymaking and public opinion about the Cold War (Lewis 2018: 83). Further, at the onset of the crisis in Korea, the Truman administration not only believed that sending a large military force to fight in Korea was undesirable, but also thought that the United States' possession of nuclear weapons and provision of aerial support to South Korea would be sufficient to deter North Korea and force it to withdraw its troops, moving them north of the 38th parallel. To summarize, the United States' extensive participation in a prolonged and bloody Korean War, in which 36,574 US servicepersons lost their lives over the course of nearly three years,[8] happened *despite* the Truman administration's initial intention of providing more limited assistance to South Korea (Lewis 2018: 95).

President Truman first publicly addressed the crisis in Korea on June 26, 1950 (the day after North Korea invaded South Korea). In a short statement, he referred to the North Korean invasion as an "unprovoked aggression" and a "lawless action." He expressed the US government's satisfaction with the United Nation's determination to compel North Korea to withdraw its forces and reposition them north of the 38th parallel and vowed to support this effort. However, he did not mention any specific actions taken by his administration.[9] The following day, Truman delivered a longer address in which he noted that he had "ordered United States air and sea forces to give the Korean Government troops cover and support."[10] He also said that he had directed US forces to protect Formosa (Taiwan) from a possible communist attack and increase defense assistance to the Philippines and military assistance to France in Indochina. If Truman had a plan to intervene more forcefully in Korea, he did not share it with the public. When a reporter questioned Truman at a news conference on June 29, 1950, asking whether the United States was at war, he replied decisively, "We are not at war," and belittled the crisis, calling it an unlawful attack by "a bunch of bandits." Then, when asked whether it would be correct "to call [the international act in Korea] a police action under the United Nations," he responded, "Yes. That is exactly what it amounts to."[11] Neither the media nor politicians from the opposition party initially challenged this framing of the conflict. Further, even when criticism of the administration for not telling the public the whole truth about the war arose later, the Truman administration was able to effectively calm the public mood and distract the public from the actual scale of the war and its geopolitical consequences (Casey 2008).

Second, during the intervention in Korea, the US public did not perceive either North Korea or its political allies as enemies worth fighting, and the administration did not seek to change that perception. In June 1950, North Korea did not yet have a history of confrontation with the United States. Although the North Korean leader Kim Il Sung often used anti-American rhetoric, no military confrontations had developed, and thus North Korea had not been featured in the headlines or public conversation in the United States. Further, neither the Soviet Union nor China was initially identified as an enemy worth waging war against, because both countries had been allies of the United States in World War II, and both initially chose not to intervene in Korea. In October 1950, China decided to intervene in the conflict, becoming the largest belligerent force in the Korean War, with 1.35 million soldiers (Zhang 1995). The Soviet Union also intervened at this point, but its assistance was mostly logistic, with the exception of some covert participation of Soviet pilots in the aerial war (Xiaoming 2002).

In a national address on June 27, Truman described the broader geopolitical context of the Korean War and placed the blame on communism's expansionist agenda. He concluded, "The attack upon Korea makes it plain beyond all doubt that Communism has passed beyond the use of subversion to conquer independent nations and will now use armed invasion and war." In the period between the end of World War II and the beginning of the Korean War, US politicians had begun to feel a sense of rivalry with the Soviet Union and communism (Jervis 1980: 564). However, neither the belief that the Soviet Union should be deterred militarily in every part of the world nor the belief in a united Sino-Soviet bloc pre-dated the Korean War. Instead, these beliefs were a result of the Korean War.

So far, I have argued that for two reasons—the Truman administration's efforts to downplay the scale of the war and its meaning for US foreign affairs, and the absence of a recognizable enemy of the nation that must be defeated—most Americans perceived North Korea's invasion of South Korea as something more like a local territorial dispute than one event in the broader context of an emerging global geopolitical conflict, a view that could have transformed North Korea and its allies into enemies worth declaring war against.

However, the question remains: Could Truman have mobilized the public to rally behind his leadership by beating the drums of war and more explicitly claiming the role of leader of the free world? Several historical precedents from shortly before the Korean War suggest that this might have been possible. First, the earlier rally behind Roosevelt and his decision (in December 1941) to intervene in World War II emerged only after a long period of efforts by the president to convince the media, Congress, and the general public that the war had geopolitical importance and was relevant to the interests of the United States, and that Nazi Germany posed a direct threat to the United States (Casey 2001: chap.2). Second, Truman himself enjoyed a boost in popularity after he announced the so-called Truman Doctrine (on March 12, 1947): following the announcement, Truman's job-approval rating increased from about 49 percent in mid-January to 58 percent in mid-March and then to 63 percent toward the end of that month.[12]

To summarize, two conditions—the lack of a prior portrayal of North Korea as an enemy of the United States and of the Soviet Union and China as a "Communist Monolith" (Lewis 2018: 74) that must be defeated everywhere, as well as Truman's framing of the Korean conflict as a limited territorial dispute with minor military involvement by the United States (either to keep the home front cool or because the administration did not intend a stronger military involvement in Korea)—jointly prevented the Korean War from generating a significant rally-round-the-flag effect. Certainly, the heavy death toll America suffered during World War II and the traumatic memories carried by millions of World War II veterans played an important part, causing Americans to be less enthusiastic about the new war (Young 2010). However, the following discussion of the public reaction to the Gulf War illustrates that when a president forcefully claims an international leadership role and keeps a clear enemy in his sights, war enthusiasm can suppress even highly traumatic memories of previous wars.

The Persian Gulf War: Claiming International Leadership

The countdown to the beginning of the Persian Gulf War began when Iraqi forces invaded Kuwait on August 2, 1990. By this time, Americans were less likely to embrace the duty to serve as the world's policeman because the

Cold War was over and the traumatic memories of Vietnam still lingered. Nevertheless, the onset of the Gulf War was followed by one of the most dramatic rally effects in the history of the United States, with the presidential approval rating skyrocketing from less than 60 percent before the war to just over 80 percent at the beginning of the war and almost 90 percent when the war ended six weeks later. The initiation of the Gulf War produced the type of war enthusiasm and admiration of national leadership that are typical of wars that become rally points. The American public expressed its widespread support of the military intervention in the Persian Gulf via the types of patriotic displays so typical of popular wars, such as flag waving, community-based rallies, and long lines outside blood donation centers (Radway 2002: 479). This popular mobilization emerged, despite the relatively recent trauma of Vietnam, precisely because the two conditions that were missing in the Korean War were now present: first, a president who emphasized the geopolitical importance of the war and explicitly claimed the role of leader of the free world, and second, an enemy that Americans learned to hate and that offered a specific target, thus allowing the nation to demonstrate its international leadership by achieving a military defeat.

As the crisis in the Persian Gulf unfolded, President Bush expressed a growing commitment to use American power—first diplomatic and economic means, and if necessary military power as well—to compel the Iraqi government to withdraw its forces from Kuwait, as required by UN Security Council Resolution 660, which was passed on August 3, 1990.[13] Bush seemed determined to intervene in the crisis;[14] however, before launching an attack on Iraqi forces, he had to sell his decision to intervene in the Gulf crisis to a political elite and general public that, in the post-Vietnam era, were reluctant to support large military operations overseas. In sharp contrast to Truman's rhetoric on the Korean War, Bush's rhetoric—even in his initial national address on the Persian Gulf crisis (on August 8, 1990)—committed the United States to a significant military involvement; in the following days, the national media reported that as many as 100,000 US soldiers might be deployed in the Persian Gulf.[15] Further, Bush explicitly presented the crisis as a test of American character and international leadership:

> In the life of a nation, we're called upon to define who we are and what we believe. Sometimes these choices are not easy. But today as President, I ask for your support in a decision I've made to stand up for what's right and condemn what's wrong, all in the cause of peace.

At my direction, elements of the 82nd Airborne Division as well as key units of the United States Air Force are arriving today to take up defensive positions in Saudi Arabia. I took this action to assist the Saudi Arabian government in the defense of its homeland. No one commits America's Armed Forces to a dangerous mission lightly, but after perhaps unparalleled international consultation and exhausting every alternative, it became necessary to take this action.[16]

In this initial statement about the Gulf crisis, Bush analogized the situation in the Gulf to the situation in Europe in the late 1930s, comparing the expected US-led military action against Iraq to the allies' actions against Nazi Germany—an analogy he continued to employ in the months to come. He used the term "blitzkrieg" to describe the Iraqi invasion of Kuwait and asserted that "we succeeded in the struggle for freedom in Europe because we and our allies remained stalwart. Keeping the peace in the Middle East will require no less." He added, "as was the case in the 1930's, we see in Saddam Hussein an aggressive dictator threatening his neighbors." Bush then stressed that the Iraqi invasion of Kuwait constituted a problem for the entire world and that the international community had reached a consensus that Iraq must withdraw its forces from Kuwait. He pledged that the United States would join an international effort authorized by the United Nations to compel Iraq to withdraw its forces in Kuwait; he announced that he had ordered the deployment of air and ground forces to protect Saudi Arabia from Iraq, and noted that protecting Saudi Arabia's sovereignty was also a vital US interest.

Bush concluded his nearly 11-minute address with a passionate appeal to an American "unity of purpose":

Standing up for our principles will not come easy. It may take time and possibly cost a great deal. But we are asking no more of anyone than of the brave young men and women of our Armed Forces and their families. And I ask that in the churches around the country prayers be said for those who are committed to protect and defend America's interests.

Standing up for our principles is an American tradition. As it has so many times before, it may take time and tremendous effort, but most of all, it will take unity of purpose. As I've witnessed throughout my life in both war and peace, America has never wavered when her purpose is driven by principle. And in this August day, at home and abroad, I know she will do no less.

The leading news media embraced Bush's framing of the US intervention in the Persian Gulf as a moral duty and the fulfillment of its international leadership role. For example, the *Washington Post* announced:

> Forces are gathered under many flags, and President Bush is leading this gigantic enterprise with skill. . . . This extraordinary array of forces is drawn together from many countries by the one central conviction that it would be very bad for each of them, and for the world in general, if Iraq's invasion succeeded.[17]

Several Democratic leaders, including Senator Christopher Dodd, Massachusetts governor Michael Dukakis, and Reverend Jesse Jackson, also publicly supported Bush's policy (Dorman and Livingston 1994: 64). The majority of Americans thus embraced the president's call for unity and support, and a rally-round-the-flag effect emerged, with Bush's job-approval rating increasing from about 60 percent to about 75 percent, and his disapproval rating declining from about 25 percent to about 16 percent. This rally effect began to fade within a few weeks as the actual use of military force against Iraq was delayed, more public figures criticized Bush's policy and instead offered support for the use of economic sanctions and diplomacy to solve Persian the Gulf crisis, and media attention shifted away from the Gulf conflict to other topics such as the budget deficit (Entman and Page 1994: 84–86; Zaller 1994a: 194; Brody 1994: 216–21). However, when the Gulf War began on January 17, 1991, the Gulf crisis once again dominated the media coverage and the public discourse, and the rally behind the leadership of President Bush re-emerged in the form of unprecedented job-approval ratings of over 80 percent, which continued to increase, peaking at nearly 90 percent in March following the coalition victory over the Iraqi forces.

This dramatic rally-round-the-flag-effect was the outcome of months of preparing the public for the war. Bush's initial national address on the Gulf crisis (quoted earlier) was the kickoff of a massive information campaign conducted by the government, with the assistance of the mainstream media, during the run-up to the war (Kellner 1992; MacArthur 1992; Dorman and Livingston 1994: 64–75). The campaign that the administration presented to Congress and the general public included two crucial yet empirically questionable pieces of information. First, President Bush, other government officials, and news reporters announced that Iraq was building a large military force near the Saudi border as part of a plan to invade its militarily weak but oil-rich neighbor, Saudi Arabia. Second, the same actors claimed that the United States was seeking a diplomatic solution to the crisis in the Gulf, but Saddam Hussein adamantly refused to negotiate. The mainstream media did not check the validity of these claims, which appeared in newspaper headlines and became the main topic of special news reports, thus creating the impression that war was inevitable (Kellner 1992).

Arguably, the most important effect of the official propaganda was the construction of Saddam Hussein as the ultimate villain who must be defeated to save not only Kuwait, but also, perhaps, the entire world. Prior to the crisis in the Gulf, Saddam Hussein had rarely made it into the headlines of the American press. Even when the press covered major events such as the use of chemical weapons against Iraqi Kurds and Iranian forces during the Iran-Iraq war, Hussein's name was rarely mentioned (Lang and Lang 1994). This pattern of omission changed dramatically following Iraq's occupation of Kuwait. Three actors combined efforts to convince decision-makers and the US public that Saddam Hussein, and Iraq in general, was an enemy worthy of combat.

Two of these actors were discussed earlier: the Bush administration and the US media, which (as in previous wars) largely propagated the worldview and policy preferences of the administration (Iyengar and Simon 1994). Official speakers (including the president) and news reports reminded Americans of the Iraqi military's use of chemical gas against Iraqi Kurds and Iranian forces—but did not mention that the United States chose not to impose any sanctions on Iraq following these atrocities because Iraq was considered the "enemy of my enemy" in its war with Iran (MacArthur 1992: 38). They described atrocities committed by Iraqi soldiers in Kuwait and demonized Saddam Hussein by referring to him as "a madman," "barbarous," "a beast," and "a monster" (Kellner 1992: 63). At the same time, Hussein played the role of "evil" leader perfectly when he promised to engage in the "Mother and Father of all Battles" against the "Devil in the White House" (Taylor 1992: 6). Furthermore, government officials and members of the media frequently compared Hussein to Adolph Hitler (Kellner 1992; Taylor 1992; Dorman and Livingston 1994: 69–71). According to Dorman and Livingston (1994: 71), between August 2 (the day Iraq invaded Kuwait) and January 15 (the day President Bush authorized military action against Iraq unless it withdrew its forces from Kuwait) the *Washington Post* invoked the Saddam-Hitler comparison in 121 stories and the *New York Times* invoked the comparison in

107 stories. However, President Bush employed the Saddam-Hitler comparison more than any other public figure who spoke about the war. For example, on October 24, 1990, in an interview with Thomas Freidman at the *New York Times*, Bush said: "I'm reading a book, and it's a book of history, a great big thick history about World War II, and there's a parallel between what Hitler did to Poland and what Saddam Hussein has done to Kuwait."[18] This comparison implied that postponing intervention in the Gulf would have consequences similar to delaying intervention in World War II (Winkler 2006: 114).[19] The analogy further dictated that the United States and its allies had a moral duty to use their military power to defeat the Iraqi forces and not waste time on a futile search for a diplomatic solution or any sort of compromise. Bush used this logic in his interview with the *New York Times*:

> What happens in Baghdad matters in Burlington, because our concern, far beyond the price of oil, is the fate of sovereign nations and peoples. There's a moral underpinning, a strong moral underpinning of what's happened in the United Nations and we've stood up unanimously against Saddam Hussein's aggression—a world order, free from unlawful aggression, free from violence, free from plunder.

In summary, as Susan Brewer (2011: 7) explained, "To rally Americans around the flag, officials have manipulated facts, exaggeration, and misinformation." Official speakers and the media were not alone in the effort to persuade the US public that Saddam Hussein and his regime were an enemy worth fighting. Private US-based firms hired by the government of Kuwait played a major (although not widely acknowledged) role in mobilizing support for military intervention among members of the US public (Gardner 2010; Kellner 1992; MacArthur 1992). According to a report by the Center for Media and Democracy's PRWatch, the Kuwaiti government hired a few dozen public relations, law, and lobbying firms, including the then-largest public relations firm in the world, Hill and Knowlton, which launched "the largest foreign-funded campaign ever aimed at manipulating American public opinion" (PRWatch, the Center for Media Democracy 2011). According to Douglas Kellner (1992) and Jarol Manheim (1994: 138–42), Hill and Knowlton used every trick in the bag of propaganda tactics, including presenting manipulated photos and videotapes to the media as reliable reports of atrocities committed by Iraqi soldiers in Kuwait. The campaign reached a climax on October 10, when a 15-year-old girl, Nayirah, gave a tearful testimony in front of the House Human Rights Caucus. She stated that as a volunteer at a hospital in Kuwait City she had witnessed Iraqi soldiers taking infants from their incubators, stealing the incubators, and leaving the babies to die on the floor. With the exception of her first name, no details about Nayirah's identity were revealed, supposedly for the safety of Nayirah and her family. None of the reporters covering the testimony attempted to confirm Nayirah's identify or find any evidence to corroborate her testimony, which was initially backed by Amnesty International; had they done so, they would have discovered that Nayirah was the daughter of the Kuwaiti ambassador to the United States, Saud Nasir al-Sabah, and a member of the Kuwaiti royal family, and that her testimony had been fabricated by Hill and Knowlton's public relations experts (Kellner 1992: 68). The "baby killing" theme was immediately picked up and adopted by President Bush as well as other politicians and the media, who combined it with other stories of atrocities, such as accounts of Iraqi soldiers shooting civilians on the streets of Kuwait City and raping Kuwaiti women (Gardner 2010: 232; Kellner 1992: 65; Winkler 2006).

As a result of the massive information campaign, public attitudes in the United States gradually shifted to encompass greater animosity toward Saddam Hussein and more support for using military force to intervene in the Persian Gulf. For example, in mid-November 1990, only 46 percent of respondents to a Gallup/Newsweek Poll thought that US forces should engage in combat if Iraq refused to leave Kuwait and restore its former government. Within three weeks, support for intervention had increased to 56 percent, and by the second week of January 1991, support for military intervention in the Persian Gulf had reached 62 percent.[20]

Perhaps the development that made the events in the Persian Gulf seem truly relevant to Americans was the 110-day hostage crisis that began on August 25, 1990, when hundreds of US citizens and other foreigners in Iraq and Kuwait were taken hostage by the Iraqi Republican Guard. Initially, the Bush administration downplayed the hostage crisis, but in late October 1990, the administration, concerned about the lack of public support for a military intervention, began disseminating detailed accounts of the hostages' plight (Winkler 2006: 104, 110). For many US citizens, the situation revived traumatic memories of the Iran hostage crisis (which occurred in 1979–1980) and incited a desire to respond forcefully in order to avoid another humiliation (Gardner 2010: 233). However, all hostages were released by mid-December (about a month before the United States and allies initiated the attack against

Iraq), and thus pushing Iraqi forces out of Kuwait and restoring the latter's independence remained the sole mission of the coalition force.

After a months-long intensive campaign that presented Saddam Hussein as the embodiment of evil who must be dethroned, when the United States and allies finally launched a strike on Iraq, most Americans viewed the action primarily as a war against Saddam Hussein. In a nationally representative survey conducted by the *Los Angeles Times* on January 17–18, 1991 (one day after the air strike phase of the Gulf War began), no less than 63 percent of the respondents said that they would not consider it a victory if all Iraqi forces left Kuwait but Saddam Hussein remained in power in Iraq.[21]

The Gulf War thus became popular because official rhetoric, supported by the media and private public relations companies, successfully presented the war as the fulfillment of the United States' manifest destiny to lead the free world, advanced a public view of Saddam Hussein as the embodiment of evil (a view that was certainly grounded in the reality of Hussein's brutal dictatorship), and portrayed President Bush and US forces as knights fighting evil forces on behalf of the oppressed. This perception of America fulfilling an honorable historical mission appeared, for example, in the following two letters sent to the press. Jo Ann R. Paddock of Montgomery, Alabama, wrote:

> History should record it as "the war that united 28 nations against Iraq's madman Suddam [*sic*] Hussein; restored calm and confidence within the Persian Gulf; and demonstrated American military superiority and bravery under the courageous leadership of President George Herbert Walker Bush."[22]

Similarly, Mike Greece of New York wrote:

> History will judge that the U.S. fulfilled its *destiny in thwarting the dark side* [emphasis added] with orchestrated precision, humanity, technology, diplomacy, perseverance, morality and intelligence.[23]

The claim that the widespread support for President Bush and the Gulf War was based on the public's enthusiasm about potentially claiming the "leader of the free world" status is further supported by a striking anomaly in public opinion at the time of the intervention. Since the Vietnam War, public support for interventionist policies has usually remained at about 65 percent, while support for more isolationist policies has remained steady at about

30 percent; during the Gulf crisis, however, support for the interventionist position jumped to about 80 percent, while support for the isolationist position declined to less than 15 percent (Holsti 1998: 142).

To summarize, in sharp contrast to the Korean War—when Truman seemed to take on the "leader of the free world" role quite reluctantly and North Korea was not yet widely recognized as an enemy of the United States or part of a Communist Bloc that must be defeated—the intervention in the Persian Gulf was preceded by President Bush's active pursuit of an international leadership role and a massive public relations campaign attempting to persuade the US public that Saddam Hussein was a force of evil. These conditions, in turn, made the goal of "taking down Saddam" a test of the capacity of the United States to fulfill its international leadership role effectively and demonstrate its might and honor in the global arena. The result was the type of enthusiasm about taking military action against enemies that stimulates rally-round-the-flag periods.

As mentioned earlier, some readers may wonder whether the US public's enthusiasm about the intervention in the Persian Gulf stemmed from the opportunity that the Gulf War provided for Americans to confront the shadows of the Vietnam War and eliminate the "Vietnam Syndrome" by winning a major international war. However, this seems like a *post hoc ergo propter hoc* interpretation that reflects US media coverage, which connected the Gulf War to the loss in Vietnam only *after the United States' victory* in the Persian Gulf (on February 28, 1991). For example, in March 1991, a *Wall Street Journal* headline declared, "Victory in Gulf War Exorcises the Demons of the Vietnam Years" (Cumings 1994: 118). President Bush also echoed this theme in his speech to the American Legislative Exchange Council on March 1, 1991, which he concluded with the statement, "By God, we've kicked the Vietnam Syndrome once and for all."[24] However, while the desire to overcome the Vietnam Syndrome (which in the previous chapters I referred to as a desire to reclaim national honor and prestige) may have guided the attitudes of some of the more militaristic segments of US society (Kellner 1992; Shaw and Martin 1993), there is no evidence that the Gulf War was linked to the Vietnam War in the broader public conversation, indicating that most Americans did not view the use of military power against Iraq as an opportunity to reclaim the national honor and prestige that were lost in Vietnam (Rowe 1991).

The emergence of a rally-round-the-flag effect during the Gulf War highlights the central role of the political elite (chief among them the president) who manipulate public opinion to garner public support for military action. However, as the previous chapters demonstrated, efforts to manipulate public opinion do not always succeed. Rather, presidents are able to mobilize the public behind their leadership when external circumstances allow their rhetoric to win the hearts and minds of their compatriots. In the Gulf War, the international consensus that the Iraqi invasion of Kuwait was unacceptable, combined with the United Nations' authorization of the war, allowed President Bush to mobilize public opinion behind the leadership role of the United States.[25] In fact, in an effort to bolster US public opinion during the buildup to the Gulf War, the Bush administration had actively sought UN approval and then highlighted this approval in its communications to the public (Zaller 1994b: 258).

Receiving authorization from the United Nations, therefore, is an important precondition for the emergence of a rally behind a president who assumes an international leadership role in militarized conflicts. However, the last section of this chapter shows the necessity of another precondition: the existence of a stubborn and sufficiently powerful enemy who can put up a fight strong enough to be considered a serious test of US international leadership and might. The earlier discussion of the rally during the Gulf War highlighted the importance of this condition, and the following analysis of two UN-authorized military missions in which the absence of a suitable enemy prevented the emergence of a rally-round-the-flag offers further support for the necessity of a powerful enemy.

UN-Authorized Missions That Did Not Evoke a Rally

In addition to the Korean War, two additional times that the United Nations asked the United States to lead a coalition of countries to war—Operation Restore Hope in Somalia in December 1992 and Operation Uphold Democracy in Haiti in September 1994—failed to trigger a significant rally effect in the United States. The mission that UN Security Council Resolution 794 assigned for the operation in Somalia was not to restore international order by fighting a defiant regime (as in Korea and the Persian Gulf), but rather to open and protect supply routes for international aid. Further, several experts have argued that President Bush's decision to move forward with military intervention in Somalia was genuinely motivated by a humanitarian desire to stop the mass killing and famine (perhaps in contrast to his decision about the Gulf War) (Burgess 2002; Hirsch and Oakley 1995; Baum 2004).

On December 4, 1992, in his address to the nation about the invasion of Somalia, Bush declared that the invasion had a limited humanitarian mission: "to enable the starving to be fed."[26] In addition, in contrast to the Gulf War, the conflict in Somalia included no clear enemy to defeat, with the exception of vaguely defined "armed gangs" (or "thugs," as they were often labeled in news reports) that blocked the routes for humanitarian aid. Consequently, the US public perceived the invasion of Somalia not as a test of the international hegemony of the United States, or specifically of Bush's "New World Order" doctrine that had crystallized during the run-up to the Gulf War (for further examination of this doctrine, see Sick 2018: 298), but rather as a chance to use the United States' military power for humanitarian purposes, just as Bush had presented it. As a result, while the vast majority of Americans approved of this military operation, their approval did not translate into a rally behind President Bush. In the days following Bush's national address, about three-quarters of the American public approved of the way Bush was handling the situation in Somalia and his decision to send troops to Somalia, but only about half of the public approved of the way Bush was handling his job as president.[27]

On July 31, 1994, only four months after US forces withdrew from Somalia, the United States was once again appointed by the UN Security Council to lead an international military intervention, this time with the goal of restoring democracy in Haiti by forcing the ruling military junta to step down (United Nations Security Council Resolution 940). However, on September 19, just a few hours before the military operation in Haiti was to begin, the Clinton administration reached an agreement with General Raoul Cédras, the ruler of Haiti, which allowed the United States to occupy Haiti without using force. It is impossible to know how public opinion in the United States would have coalesced if Cédras had decided to put up a fight instead of stepping down peacefully. Given that the general public knew very little about Haiti, despite a long history of US intervention in Haitian politics (Hendrickson 2002: 43–45), it is likely that resistance by Cédras would not have posed a symbolic challenge capable of generating a significant rally-round-the-flag effect. Further, the intervention in Haiti came less than two years after the traumatic intervention in Somalia, which left Americans with the memory of bodies of dead American soldiers being dragged through the streets of Mogadishu. For these reasons, on the eve of the invasion of Haiti, most Americans did not consider the Caribbean nation worth spilling American blood for (Brecher and Wilkenfeld 1997: 533; Girard 2004: 4), and thus the potential for the emergence of a rally-round-the-flag effect was small.[28]

Conclusion

This chapter outlined a third pathway to the emergence of a rally-round-the-flag effect and examined one instance in which this type of rally developed—after the Gulf War—as well as three instances in which such a rally failed to emerge—the Korean War and the US military interventions in Somalia and Haiti. To recapitulate the main argument, when the international community asks the United States to lead an effort to restore the world order, this call puts the moral and military supremacy of the United States and its unique status as a global leader to the test. However, for this type of international crisis to transform into a rally-round-the-flag effect, the US president must publicly embrace the role of leading the free world, and the conflict must include an opponent who is willing to put up a fight and has been constructed as a national enemy against whom Americans can unite to demonstrate the power of the nation and its moral virtue.

9

War That Feels Good

The Role of Emotions in the Emergence of Rally Periods

Now America must wield the sword in defense of liberty, and in the very act of striking never once divest herself of that love of liberty that nurtured every son and daughter among us and is the sinew of our spirit, the pulsing of our national heart.

—An excerpt from a letter that Roland E. Cowden of Maryville, Tennessee, sent to the *New York Times* on September 11, 2001[1]

Sept. 11 proved that New York is the greatest city in the world, and now the men and women in our military will enable us to show the world that the United States is the greatest country.

—An excerpt from a letter that Martha and Michael Gardner of Hunt Valley, Maryland, sent to the *New York Times* a few days into the invasion of Iraq[2]

Most parts of this book focus on the conditions that have prompted certain events to trigger major rallies around the flag, and thus in previous chapters, the unit of analysis has been events (wars and security crises). However, the primary indicator used to identify a rally in public opinion—the presidential job-approval rating—is an aggregate measure composed of the attitudes of individual citizens. Therefore, a sudden increase in that rating (that is, a rally-round-the-flag effect) is the cumulative outcome of widespread changes in individual-level attitudes. In this chapter, I shift the unit of analysis to individuals in order to identify the affective (i.e., emotional) mechanisms by which (under the conditions specified in the previous chapters) certain events motivate individuals to support the president, eventually creating a rally-round-the-flag effect.

Rally 'round the Flag. Yuval Feinstein, Oxford University Press. © Oxford University Press 2022.
DOI: 10.1093/oso/9780197629710.003.0009

In contrast to rationalist arguments, which assume that policy preferences are the result of rational assessments of policies based on the available information, studies in political psychology have found that people often use their affective reactions to events and policies as informational shortcuts for attitude formation—that is, the attitudes individuals express reflect the way they *feel* about an event or policy (for a review, see Clore, Gasper, and Garvin 2000). During rally periods, strong affective reactions lead some of the individuals who do not usually approve of the president and/or his foreign policy (typically, members of the opposition party and independent voters) to approve of both the leader and the policy (Rahn, Kroeger, and Kite 1996).

Certainly, many people experience painful emotions such as anxiety and grief in response to a security crisis or war. However, this chapter's investigation of individuals' attitudes during two rally periods—the first in the aftermath of the September 11 attacks and the second during the invasion of Iraq—suggests that a rally behind the president is motivated not so much by painful feelings about the enemy's violent actions or threats, but rather primarily by pleasant feelings of national pride, confidence, and hope, which are evoked among the public when the president promises to restore national honor and gain the respect of other nations through military action. For example, the two excerpts that open this chapter, both from letters that ordinary US citizens sent to the press during rally periods, convey a strong feeling of pride about the use of military power against the nation's enemies. While Chapter 3 provided the theoretical grounds for the proposition that positive emotions are at the core of rally formation, the current chapter provides empirical support for this proposition.

The chapter focuses on the two main components of my theoretical argument: the crucial role of emotions in motivating individuals to rally behind the president, and the connection between the emotional reactions that occur during a rally process and the meanings individuals attribute to events and policies. I analyze data from public opinion surveys to test these central assertions of my argument as well as the prominent competing theoretical explanations for rallies (discussed in Chapter 2), which suggest that people rally around the flag when they make a rational assessment and conclude that a military policy is likely to succeed with a fairly low cost in American lives, when they have major security concerns, and/or when they experience strong negative feelings about a national enemy.

An Empirical Test of Rally Explanations

To trace the mechanism by which certain events trigger changes in individuals' attitudes during rally periods, I use survey data collected during a period when most of the public rallied behind President George W. Bush's leadership. The most significant phase of this rally period occurred in the aftermath of the September 11 attacks and at the onset of the Afghanistan War, when the president's approval rating skyrocketed to nearly 90 percent. Although this surge was followed by a decline, President Bush and his "war on terror" policy enjoyed the support of a solid majority of the US public for two years, including during the invasion of Iraq. The data analyzed in this chapter are drawn from two nationally representative data sources on public attitudes that were collected during the long rally period after the September 11 attacks and contain information about emotions: a Gallup poll conducted a few days after the invasion of Iraq[3] and the Threat and National Security Survey (TNSS), which included three waves in the years after 9/11 (in the aftermath of the September 11 attacks, in October and November 2002, and during the combat phase of the Iraq War).

Figure 9.1 shows the trend line of President Bush's job-approval ratings from his inauguration in January 2001 through the beginning of 2004. The

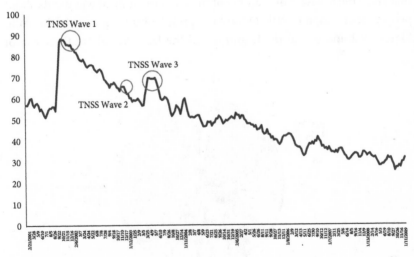

Figure 9.1. Job-approval ratings for George W. Bush across the two terms of his presidency (3-point moving average).

three periods during which the data used in this chapter were collected are circled. The data analysis proceeds in three steps. First, I use data from two time periods, the aftermath of the 9/11 attacks and the weeks surrounding the invasion of Iraq, to identify the determinants of individual-level public support for the president, thus testing my argument about the role of nation-centered emotions against competing arguments. Second, I use data from the invasion of Iraq to focus on the role of emotions; specifically, I estimate the effects of two types of emotions—positive emotions about the war and negative emotions about enemies of the United States—on support for the president. In addition, I assess whether emotional reactions to the war were associated with national identification. Third, I analyze longitudinal data to explain the decline in Bush's popularity over time in order to test my argument that during rally periods political attitudes stem from concerns about the nation and positive emotional reactions to policies that promise to alleviate these concerns.[4]

What Factors Determine Public Support for the President?

I begin the exploration by analyzing data from a Gallup opinion poll conducted during the invasion of Iraq because this poll included questions that allow me to assess the validity of the main theoretical arguments about people's motivation to rally behind the president during war. As shown in Figures 9.2 and 9.3, at the beginning of the Iraq War about three out of

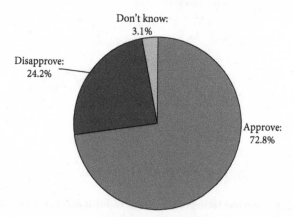

Figure 9.2. Percent of Americans who approve/disapprove of the way President Bush is doing his work. Gallup Poll, March 22–23, 2003 (US adults).

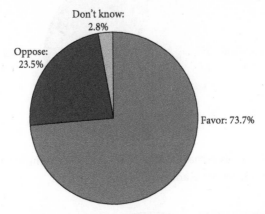

Figure 9.3. Percent of Americans who favor/oppose the war with Iraq. Gallup Poll, March 22–23, 2003 (US adults).

every four Americans supported the president and the war. What motivated people to rally behind the invasion of Iraq and President Bush? Chapters 2 and 3 outlined theoretical arguments that propose three distinct possible motivations for rallying behind the president during war or security crisis.

The first type of argument asserts that rallying is motivated by a rational assessment of both the chances that an ongoing or anticipated military action will succeed and its expected outcomes; specifically, people who believe that victory over the enemy will likely be achieved relatively quickly and will come at a reasonable cost are the most likely to rally behind the military action and the commander-in-chief. Figures 9.4–9.8 illustrate Americans' evaluations of a range factors related to the war as well as possible outcomes of the war. Figures 9.4–9.7 show that during the combat phase of the Iraq War most Americans believed that the war was going well, the United States was winning, the war would only last several weeks or a few months, and the number of US casualties would not exceed several hundred. Figure 9.8 further suggests that most Americans did not believe that the war would develop into a larger, bloody war or that the US economy would suffer severe negative consequences due to the war.

The second type of argument highlights people's concerns about security threats. The two far-right columns in Figure 9.8 show that while a solid majority of Americans thought it was likely the United States would experience terrorism in the future, only a minority were concerned about becoming a victim of terrorism themselves.

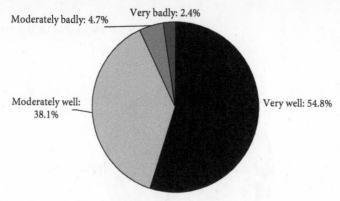

Figure 9.4. Responses to the question "How is the war going for us?" Gallup Poll, March 22–23, 2003 (US adults).

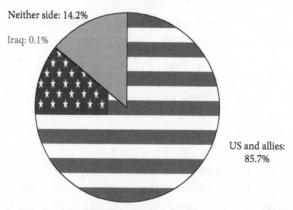

Figure 9.5. Responses to the question "Who is winning the war in the Persian Gulf?" Gallup Poll, March 22–23, 2003 (US adults).

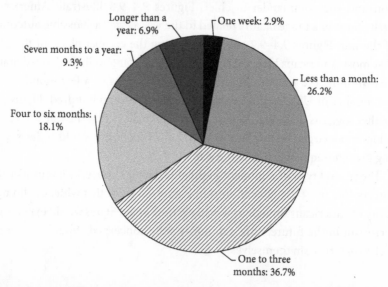

Figure 9.6. Predictions of the duration of the war. Gallup Poll, March 22–23, 2003 (US adults).

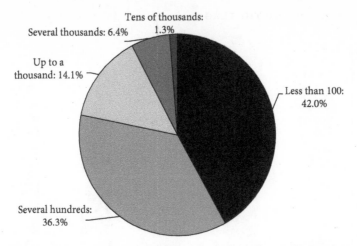

Figure 9.7. Predictions of number of US casualties. Gallup Poll, March 22–23, 2003 (US adults).

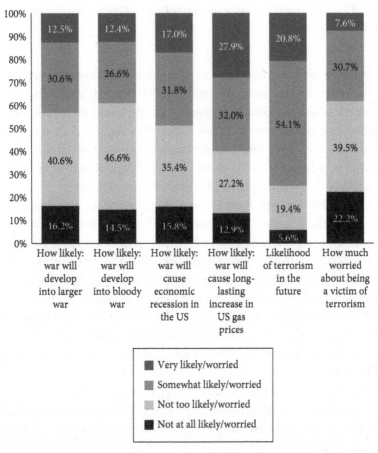

Figure 9.8. Assessments of threats and the likelihood of negative war outcomes. Gallup Poll, March 22–23, 2003 (US adults).

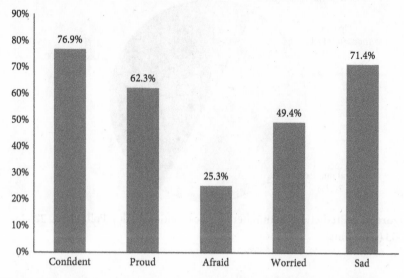

Figure 9.9. Affective reactions to the war with Iraq. Gallup Poll, March 22–23, 2003 (US adults).

The third type of argument, the one I develop in this book, centers on the positive emotions that stem from membership in a nation and that people experience when they believe an ongoing or anticipated military action will restore or enhance the nation's honor and prestige. Figure 9.9 shows that positive feelings (i.e., pride and confidence about the war) were prevalent and mixed with sadness (probably about the loss of American lives in the war), while relatively few in the public felt afraid because of the war.

To adjudicate between these three explanations of the emergence of the rally-round-the-flag effect at the onset of the Iraq War, the survey data were analyzed using logistic regressions with the president's job-approval rating as a binary outcome: the outcome variable is coded "1" for survey respondents who said that they approved of the way George W. Bush was doing his job as president, and "0" for those who said they disapproved. The independent variables were grouped by their affinity to the three theoretical approaches, and each group of variables was tested in a separate model that also included the control variables; a final model combined all statistically significant independent variables.[5]

Figure 9.10 presents the results of the regression models. The circles represent regression coefficients that estimate the likelihood (measured in log-odds) of approving of the way the President Bush was doing his job.

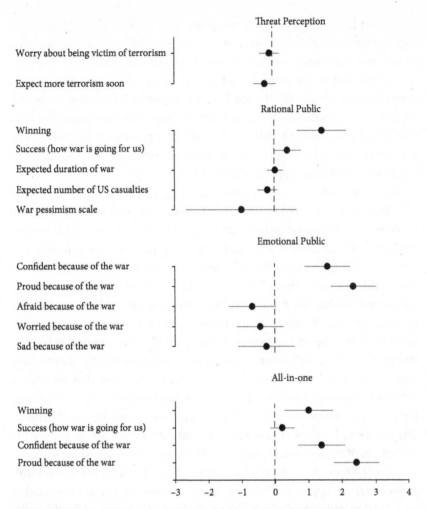

Figure 9.10. Coefficients and 95% confidence intervals from logistic regression models of president job approval. Gallup Poll, March 22–23, 2003 (US adult citizens).

A positive coefficient for a variable means that a higher score on the variable is associated with a higher likelihood of approving of the president's work, and a negative coefficient means that a higher score on the variable is associated with a higher likelihood of *disapproving* of the president's work. Each coefficient is crossed by a horizontal line marking a 95 percent confidence interval. A confidence interval entirely on one side of the dashed line that marks the zero point on the *x*-axis indicates that the regression coefficient is statistically significant at the 0.05 level or below (this means that the focal variable is likely to be associated with approval/disapproval of the president's work not only in the sample of individuals who took the survey but also in the entire US adult population). In contrast, if a confidence interval crosses the dashed line, the regression coefficient is not statistically significant (which means that a finding of an association between a focal variable and approval/disapproval of the president's job may not be generalized from the sample to the larger US population). For the full list of regression results, see Appendix Table A2.

The results of the first model show that support for President Bush was not associated with perceived security threats: the coefficients for both perceived likelihood of additional terrorist attacks and perceived personal threat are weak and not statistically significant (due to data limitations, measures of the fear and anger that might result from the threat were not included in this part of the analysis, although they are added in a later stage). The results of the second model offer some support for the rational public thesis because respondents who thought that the United States was winning the war were more likely to support the president. However, the meaning of this result is ambiguous, especially because the data were collected shortly after the war began when there was not yet sufficient evidence to show that the United States was winning. Therefore, the idea that "our" military was winning may represent an emotional belief (Mercer 2010) based on increased national identification. Further, in contrast to the rational public thesis, neither the perception of success, nor the expected duration of the war, nor the expected number of American casualties has a statistically significant association with presidential job approval. The third model contains all five items related to emotional reactions to the war. The results reveal that support for the president has a strong association with positive emotions (pride and confidence) but no statistically significant association with negative emotions. In addition, the third model fits the data much better than the previous two models (this is evident from the comparison of the Bayesian information criterion [BIC] values in Appendix Table A2). The last model contains all explanatory variables that were statistically significant in Models 1–3. The results provide empirical support for my argument about the key role of positive emotions about the war in motivating people to rally behind the commander-in-chief. Feeling proud about the war is the strongest predictor of approving of the president's work. Feeling confidence is the second strongest predictor, and belief in a US victory is the third strongest. The coefficient for success assessment (the primary indictor of the rational public argument) is weak and not statistically significant.

To determine whether the findings discussed so far are unique to the case of the Iraq War, I also analyzed nationally representative data on emotions collected in the Threat and National Security Survey (TNSS) poll conducted by Schulman, Ronca, and Bucuvalas and the Stony Brook University Center for Social Research shortly after the September 11 attacks, during the heyday of the rally behind President George W. Bush and the "war on terror," as well as the Afghanistan War. In this survey of 1,549 Americans, which was fielded between October 15, 2001, and March 2, 2002, no less than 87.4 percent of respondents said that they approved of the way the president was handling his job.

Figure 9.11 shows that during the period of data collection for this survey (October 15, 2001–March 2, 2002), most members of the US public reported experiencing positive feelings of national pride, security, and confidence, but at the same time were concerned about the terrorist threat to national security (although they were less worried about their personal safety). To what extent was the widespread approval of Bush's leadership motivated by concerns about national security, and to what extent was it driven by positive national feelings? To answer this question, I conducted a second set of logistic regressions similar to those described earlier with the president's job approval as a binary dependent variable. However, these models did not test the rational public thesis because no pertinent questions were included in the TNSS. Figure 9.12 presents a summary of the findings. For the full list of regression results, see Appendix Table A3.

The first model in Figure 9.12 examines whether in the aftermath of the September 11 attacks, rallying behind the president was associated with the experience of security threat. Although 87 percent of respondents said they were somewhat or very concerned about the possibility of another terrorist attack on US soil, these individuals were not more likely to support the president than people who reported lower levels of perceived threat; further, an individual's level of concern about personal safety was not associated with their approval of the president's job. Of all the variables in this model, only concern about terrorists' use of chemical or biological weapons against the United States has a statistically significant positive association with support of the president.

The second model tests variables related to emotional state. Only "confidence" has a statistically significant positive coefficient. None of the negative

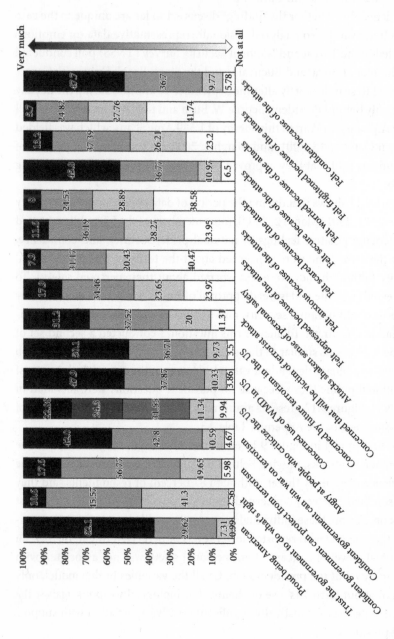

Figure 9.11. Reactions to the September 11 attacks among US adult citizens.

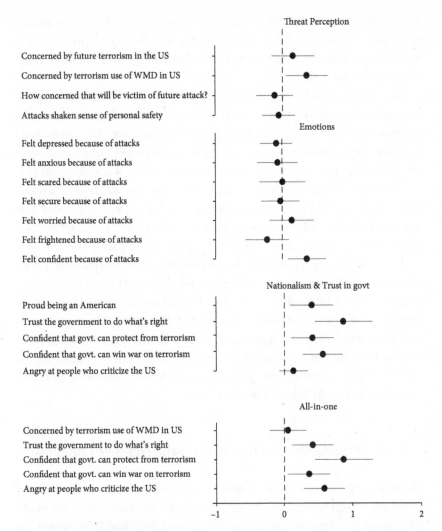

Figure 9.12. Coefficients and 95% confidence intervals from logistic regression models of president job approval (US adult citizens).

Source: "Public Reactions to the Events of September 11," Stony Brook University Center for Survey Research, October 15, 2001–March 2, 2002.

emotions is statistically significant. The third model further explores the effects of positive emotions as well as the degree of national identification. This model fits the data much better than either of the previous models (see their BIC values in Appendix Table A3), and four of the independent variables in the model have highly significant coefficients: being proud to be American, trusting the government to do what's right, and having confidence in the government's capacity to protect its citizens and win the war against terrorism. The last model combines all statistically significant covariates from the first three models; only the variables from the third model remain statistically significant.

These results indicate that the rally behind President Bush following the September 11 attacks was motivated primarily by widespread emotions of national pride and confidence. The data used in this stage of the analysis do not allow for a systematic test of my argument that positive emotions *emerge* during a rally process in response to the development of a widespread perception that current events and policies increase (or will likely increase) collective honor and prestige. However, an analysis of two additional data sets, one collected only a few hours after the September 11 attacks[6] and another collected a week later,[7] show that the US public's level of confidence in the president's capacity to handle the crisis increased significantly during this period. Correspondingly, presidential job-approval ratings increased 17 points on the first day after the attacks, climbed an additional 18 points toward the end of the first week, and peaked following the onset of the war in Afghanistan.[8] These findings, although incomplete, suggest that a gradual emotional transition from agony and anxiety in the initial hours after the attack to a more positive and optimistic outlook in the following days and weeks drove the rally behind President Bush.

Differentiating the Effects of Positive and Negative Emotions

The next step in the analysis assesses the relative effects of two types of emotions—anger toward the enemy and positive emotions about the home nation—on the development of the rally behind President Bush during the invasion of Iraq. In this step, the outcome and predictors are measured as latent variables, meaning that a given variable does not correspond to a single survey item, but rather is based on respondents' scores on a set of items. The assumption behind this approach to measuring emotions is that individuals who experience similar affective reactions may use different labels to express their feelings. Treating emotions as a latent variable assumes that each of a latent variable's components (i.e., each question about a distinct emotion label) refers to the same underlying emotion. Estimating latent variables reduces measurement errors (relative to measuring an emotion via a single survey question, as in the previous step of the analysis). For example, the latent variable that measures fear of terrorism averages a respondent's answers to three questions asking about the extent to which they felt nervous, scared, and afraid about terrorism (for a list of observed variables and their coefficients, see Appendix Table A4).[9]

The data for this step of the analysis were drawn from the third wave of the TNSS, which was conducted immediately after the invasion of Iraq (March 20–April 9, 2003; 354 respondents) and following the conquest of Baghdad (May 21–June 13, 2003; 375 respondents). Figure 9.13 presents the univariate distributions of all the variables used in the analysis of Wave 3 data. The figure shows that during the invasion of Iraq, the levels of public approval of President Bush and the war were very high (this rally effect spilled over to other domains, as evident in the relatively high level of approval of Bush's economic policy). When asked about their feelings during this period, most respondents reported having negative feelings (anger, hostility, disgust) about anti-American terrorism and Iraq's president Saddam Hussein, and having positive feelings (pride, hope, enthusiasm) about the US military action against Iraq. A sense of security threat (due to potential terrorism) was also quite prevalent among members of the public during the invasion of Iraq (a large majority of respondents reported feeling nervous and many also felt scared).

The Relative Effects of Positive and Negative Emotions

Figure 9.14 presents the results of a model that estimates the direct effects of latent variables measuring emotions on the latent variable measuring support for the president.[10] Latent variables are represented by ovals. Solid arrows represent coefficients that are statistically significant at the $p \leq 0.05$ level and dashed arrows represent coefficients that are not statistically significant at this level. All coefficients are presented in standardized form to allow comparison of their magnitudes. The model contains six latent variables: confidence in the government's capacity to fight terrorism, positive emotions about the war, fear of terrorism, anger about terrorism, anger toward Iraqi President Saddam Hussein, and support for President Bush (the outcome).

The variables that measure confidence in the government's ability to fight the war on terror and positive emotions about the war in Iraq are strong and statistically significant predictors of support for the president. In contrast, fear of terrorism has a *negative* association with support for the president, which may indicate, as Huddy and coauthors argued (Huddy, Feldman, and Cassese 2007), that anxiety makes individuals less likely to support a war, and

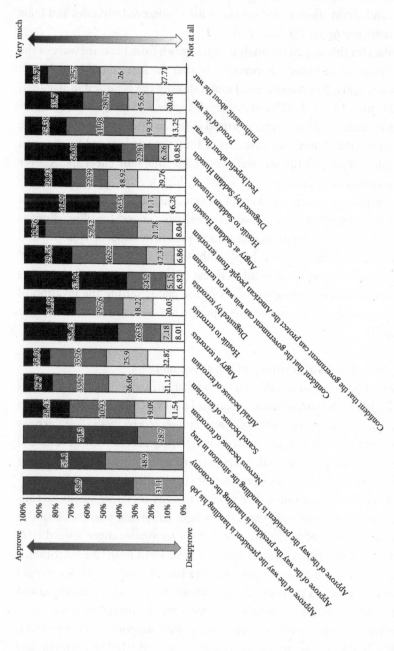

Figure 9.13. Distributions of variables included in the SEM analysis of Wave 3 TNSS data.

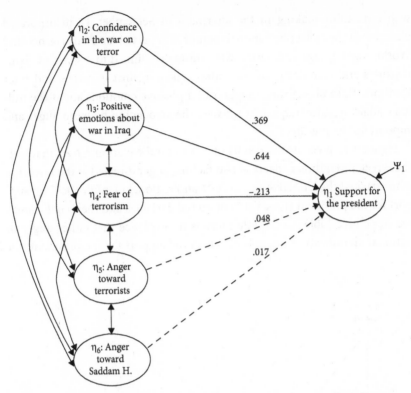

Figure 9.14. SEM of emotions as predictors of support for President George W. Bush (TNSS, Wave 3).

in turn less likely to support the president. Finally, the associations between each of the two "anger" variables and support for the president are weak and not statistically significant.

Further Consideration of the Impact of Anger

Although the analysis in Figure 9.14 does not provide evidence for a direct effect of anger on support for President Bush during the invasion of Iraq, there are two reasons to believe that anger may have had an *indirect* effect on support for the president. First, because anger is an important motivation for aggressive behavior in conflicts (Huddy, Feldman, and Cassese 2007), Americans whose anger toward the terrorists motivated them to seek retaliation likely experienced positive feelings about going to war, and in turn increased their support of President Bush when he satisfied their demand for retaliation. Second, as Ross explained (2013: chap.3), for many Americans whose meaning-making in the aftermath of September 11 incorporated elements of the collective national memory (in particular, Pearl Harbor and World War II), rage and hatred were intimately linked to a sense of righteousness and confidence in the actions taken against terrorists and their sponsors. Both observations suggest that positive emotions about the military attack against Iraq might mediate the association between anger and support for the president.

Figure 9.15 presents the results of a structural equation model that tests the direct and indirect effects of two factors, anger directed at the terrorists who attacked the United States in 2001 and national identification, on support for the president (for a list of observed variables and their coefficients, see Appendix Table A4). While there is no evidence that either anger or national identification has a direct effect on support for the president, the

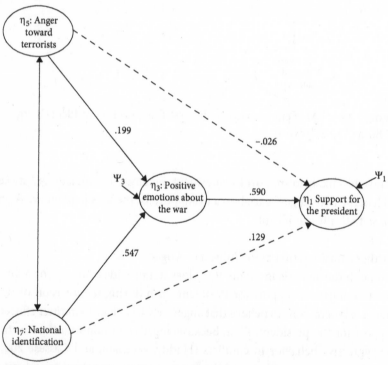

CFI = 0.97, SRMR = 0.031, RMSEA = 0.104, Yuan-Bentler's Corrected AGLS Test Statistics
P <.49

Figure 9.15. Direct and indirect effects of anger and national identification on support for President George W. Bush (TNSS, Wave 3).

results suggest that both variables affect support for the president *indirectly* via their associations with positive emotions about the war in Iraq. Notably, the national identification coefficient is almost three times larger than the anger coefficient. Thus, while anger's effect on presidential support was mediated by an individual's positive emotions about the war, such positive emotions were primarily the result of an intense identification with the nation, rather than anger directed at the nation's enemies (the combination of rage toward terrorists and positive feelings about the war in Iraq was especially common among those who embraced the official White House rhetoric accusing Iraq of sponsoring terrorists; the next section explores this rhetoric in more detail).

While positive emotions about foreign policy may also motivate individuals to support the president in peacetime, members of the opposition party and independent voters are less likely to experience these emotions outside a rally period. Therefore, the rally-round-the-flag effect occurs when positive emotions about the president and his foreign policy cross party lines because of a widespread increase in national identification and an experienced or anticipated affirmation of collective self-worth. The analysis in the following section offers further support for this argument by comparing public opinion at three points in time and showing that the rally effect declines when nationalism loses potency and is replaced by the partisanship that so thoroughly shapes public opinion in non-rally periods.

What Accounts for the Decline of a Rally-round-the-Flag Effect?

I have argued that positive emotions emerge among a large portion of the population during war or in the aftermath of a security crisis when there is a widespread desire among the public to restore or enhance the symbolic value of the nation (i.e., its honor and prestige) and the president has convinced most people that taking military action against an enemy will increase (or is already increasing) the nation's value. An ideal analysis of this phenomenon would trace the effects of a rally period on people's attitudes toward the home nation by comparing attitudes before and during a rally period. However, because most of the events that lead to rally periods are unforeseeable, this type of analysis is rarely feasible; indeed, no such data exist for the period investigated in this chapter. An alternative option is to analyze data collected during and after a rally period, which allows the empirical identification of the attitudes and affective reactions that distinguish those individuals who supported the government and its military policy only during the rally period from those individuals whose levels of support or opposition remained relatively stable (Feinstein 2018). The longitudinal portion of the TNSS data permits this type of alternative analysis.

The analysis in this section compares data from Wave 1 of the TNSS (i.e., data that were collected during the rally periods that followed the September 11 attacks) with data from Waves 2 (collected in late 2002) and 3 (collected during the combat phase of the Iraq War). In the second and third waves, public support for President Bush remained high (around 70 percent). Therefore, the investigation focuses on *differences* in support between this relatively modest phase of the rally and the more dramatic phase in the months after the September 11 attacks.[11] Specifically, I explore what caused about 20 percent of the public who supported President Bush after the September 11 attacks to *stop* supporting him in the following months. This approach offers a good indication of which factors motivated individuals to rally behind Bush when that rally was at its peak, and why some of these individuals were reluctant to join the second rally behind Bush during the Iraq War.

Figure 9.16 presents the results of models estimating the change in public support for the president between the first wave of the TNSS and Waves 2 and 3 (the circles mark the coefficients estimating the changes from Wave 1 to Wave 2 and the triangles mark the coefficients estimating the changes from Wave 1 to Wave 3). The outcome variable (change of individual's assessment of the president) is coded "1" if the respondent moved from approving

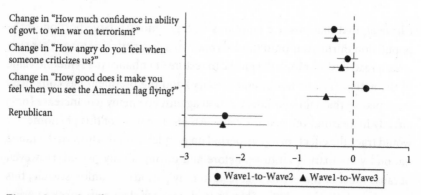

Figure 9.16. Coefficients and 95% confidence intervals from logistic regression models of attitude change.

to disapproving of the way the president was doing his work, and "0" oth-erwise.[12] The independent variables are scales representing individual-level change in answers over time. Models were estimated using logistic regression, so the coefficients represent the estimated likelihood (measured in log-odds) of moving from approval to disapproval as a function of the independent variables (a positive coefficient means that an increase in a respondent's score on an independent variable is associated with a greater likelihood of shifting from approval to disapproval of President Bush's work). For the full list of re-gression results, see Appendix Table A5.

Two variables—change in exposure to the media and change in sense of personal safety—had no statistically significant effect on declining sup-port for the president in either model (these variables were dropped from the models because of missing values),[13] indicating that the public did not stop supporting the president because people lost interest in media reports (as arguments that center on the intensity of media coverage and the con-sumption of news by the public in rally periods suggest), or because the in-itial fear of terrorist threat subsided (as arguments that highlight security threat suggest). Instead, both models suggest that, relative to individuals who maintained a high level of confidence in the president over time, those who became less confident in Bush's capacity to win the war on terror were more likely to stop supporting him at a later point.

Was this loss of confidence the result of a rational reassessment of the chances for success, perhaps prompted by the ongoing futility of the hunt for Osama bin Laden at this point in time? If so, there would have been a decline among both Democrats and Republicans (as well as independents). However, there was no significant decrease in support for either the war or the president among Republicans (Jacobson 2007). Indeed, in the current models, the coefficient for the variable "Republican" is negative and statis-tically highly significant (indicating that Republicans were much less likely than Democrats to shift from approval to disapproval of President Bush). Jacobson (2010) also found evidence that contradicts the rationalist argu-ment: a cognitive bias associated with partisanship emerged during this pe-riod such that Republicans suppressed information from the media about the real premises of the war in Iraq, while Democrats eagerly absorbed any negative information about the war. Taken together, these results indicate that the president's popularity decreased not because people across the po-litical spectrum lost confidence in his military policy due to rational assess-ment of its outcomes, but rather because political party was replacing the nation as the main reference group in people's political assessments (see also Kam and Ramos 2008).

The model comparing data from Waves 1 and 3 of the TNSS further supports this argument because the two coefficients directly related to national identification are statistically significant. Relative to respondents whose answers remained stable, those who reported feeling less angry with people who criticized the United States in Wave 3 than in Wave 1, as well as those who reported feeling less enthusiastic when seeing the US flag at the latter time, were more likely to stop supporting the president (while the decline in individuals' scores on these variables began before the invasion of Iraq, their effects on support for the president became statistically significant only after the invasion).[14]

To summarize, the findings suggest that some of the rally effect of the September 11 attacks diminished when the initial upsurge in national identification waned and the "war on terror" lost much of its potency as an interpretive framework that unified the nation. By the time the government decided to invade Iraq, the discourses of the media and the political elite already included profound disagreement about whether the decision to attack Iraq was wise and just (for a review, see Feldman, Huddy, and Marcus 2015).[15] On one side of the debate, the White House (beginning during the buildup to the invasion of Iraq) publicly accused Iraq of sponsoring anti-American terrorism and developing weapons of mass destruction. The discourse that sought to justify a preemptive strike against Iraq also included direct references to collective identity, describing Iraq and terrorist organizations in the "axis of evil" as a force that challenged the core values and honor of America, and calling on Americans to stand up for their values, demonstrate the universal validity of these values to the world, and defend the United States' international reputation as "leader of the free world" (Krebs and Lobaz 2007; McCartney 2004; Roshwald 2006: 203; for and additional discussion, see Chapter 5 of this book). On the other side of the debate, critics questioned the wisdom of shifting the focus away from the war in Afghanistan, which was clearly the harbor for al-Qaeda's terrorism, to Iraq, and highlighted the fact that an invasion of Iraq was not sanctioned by the United Nations and thus the world would likely see the United States as a bully (Jacobson 2010)—this criticism intensified after American troops stationed in Iraq found no evidence of weapons of mass destruction.

These two competing sets of claims resonated differently with the distinct core nationalist beliefs held by different subsets of society and thus produced different emotional reactions. The White House's framing of the invasion as part of America's war against terrorist enemies found more resonance (and thus produced positive emotions) among members of the political right, where a "Jacksonian" ethnoreligious nationalism, which highlights the need to protect the American nation against external and internal enemies and maintain the United States' supreme international power and status, is especially prevalent. In contrast, this framing of the invasion evoked anger rather than positive emotions for many Democrats (as well as some independent voters) who held a "Jeffersonian" creedal nationalist belief, which assigns the United States the task of defending other peoples against authoritarian oppressors, because members of this group viewed the invasion as conflicting with the United States' identity standards and reputation as a positive international leader (Feinstein 2017).[16]

Figure 9.17 presents evidence that supports this interpretation: almost all Republicans reported feeling proud and hopeful about the war and a majority reported being enthusiastic about the war, while only a small minority reported feeling angry or disgusted by the war. In contrast, Democrats reported much lower levels of pride, hope, and enthusiasm, and relatively higher levels of anger and disgust.

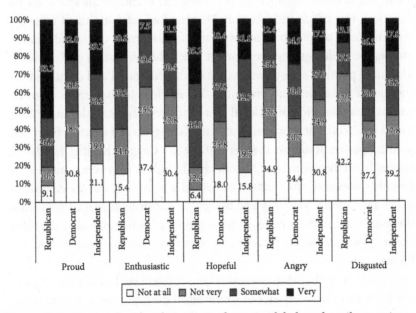

Figure 9.17. Respondents' endorsement of emotion labels to describe reaction to Iraq War, by political party (TNSS, Wave 3).

Conclusion

This chapter has zoomed in on the factors that motivate individuals to rally behind the president. An analysis of survey data collected during and between two rally periods—the aftermath of the September 11 attacks and the 2003 invasion of Iraq—showed that the rally effect emerged when the majority of the public embraced a nationalist framework that reaffirmed collective identity and generated positive emotions such as pride in the nation, confidence in the capacity of the elected leadership and the military, and hope for a better future that military action would bring about.

The public response to the September 11 attacks demonstrates how the synchronization of emotions among members of the public, based on shared interpretations of the situation and the collective reaction, produces a nationwide rally behind the president and his military policy. Popular interpretation of an event tends to be more homogenous (and thus more likely to produce a rally) if the discourse of the political elite is relatively monolithic (Berinsky 2007; Brody 1991; Zaller 1992: chap. 9). This was indeed the case in the aftermath of the September 11 attacks.

Only a few hours after the attacks, President George W. Bush delivered a national address in which he described the events as an attack on the American way of life and freedom. He promised retaliation and reassured the American people that "terrorist attacks can shake the foundations of our biggest buildings, but they cannot touch the foundation of America."[17] The entire political elite, as well as the media, embraced and circulated this framing of the events and presented the reactions to the attacks as an exemplary manifestation of national unity and perseverance (Alexander 2004; Tiryakian 2004). For example, members of Congress and senators from both political parties stood on the steps of the US Capitol, holding hands and singing "God Bless America." Members of the public, who were initially emotionally stunned (Collins 2004), embraced a bipartisan call for Americans to exhibit national solidarity and bravery in the struggle against terror, and the result was a massive increase in the president's job-approval rating (from about 50 percent shortly before the attacks to about 85 percent shortly after the attacks).[18]

In contrast to the "elite consensus" thesis (discussed in Chapter 2), I do not think that the emergence of a rally effect during a war or security crisis requires the leadership of the opposition party to support the president and his policy (or avoid explicit criticism). Nevertheless, the rally effect is likely to be stronger when the members of opposition party close ranks behind the president (as happened after the September 11 attacks) than when they voice significant opposition through the media. Increased polarization may even occur during rally periods, because subgroups within the political elite and the media send contrasting messages that resonate with the distinct core nationalist beliefs held by different subsets of society, and the members of these societal subsets, in turn, assign different meanings to the event and thus experience different affective reactions (Feinstein 2017).[19] Public reactions to the 2003 invasion of Iraq included both a rally and increased polarization (Feldman, Huddy, and Marcus 2015). The invasion evoked a rally reaction among certain segments of the American public while reinforcing the division between the political right and left, which embraced contrasting interpretations of the meaning of the invasion for American identity standards and the nation's international reputation, and thus felt differently about the war.[20]

CONCLUSION

10

Moving Forward

Directions for Future Research on the Rally-round-the-Flag Phenomenon

The core argument of this book is that a rally-round-the-flag effect emerges *when a broad swath of the public perceives events as having positive and highly desired implications for the nation's symbolic value.* This statement highlights two necessary conditions—a widespread desire to claim collective honor and prestige, and a widespread belief that the actions of national institutions will increase collective honor and prestige—that are jointly sufficient for the emergence of a rally in public opinion. These two conditions evoke positive emotions that nudge people's attitudes in favor of the national leadership. I believe that these core arguments also apply to rallies in countries other than the United States. However, as discussed in detail in the following, the circumstances under which a majority of the public comes to believe that national honor and prestige must be reclaimed and that the government is taking the right steps to do so may vary across countries and time. Nonetheless, in the United States in the period covered in this book, rallies emerged when fighting an enemy was perceived as either compensating for a previous humiliation or maintaining the nation's international prestige by responding to a call to lead the free world.

This summary reflects my current understanding of the rally-round-the-flag effect based on more than a decade of research. However, there is still much to be explored about the rally phenomenon. In this conclusion, I highlight six potentially fruitful research goals: identifying the factors that cause some rallies to be stronger than others, investigating rallies in other countries, conducting cross-national comparative research on rallies, exploring how national culture affects the necessary conditions for the emergence of rallies, analyzing rallies outside the context of international conflicts and wars, and examining the long-term consequences of rally periods.

Rally 'round the Flag. Yuval Feinstein, Oxford University Press. © Oxford University Press 2022.
DOI: 10.1093/oso/9780197629710.003.0010

Examine Variation in the Magnitudes of Rallies

Despite the progress made in this book and the original argument and supporting evidence presented herein, there is still much more to learn about rallies in the United States. One important topic this book did not examine in detail is variation in the size and duration of rally periods. For example, the rallies that emerged during the Gulf War and in the aftermath of the September 11 attacks were much larger and lasted longer than the rally that followed the *Mayaguez* incident. In the introductory chapter, I proposed an initial list of four conditions that may affect the magnitude of rallies in the United States: the objective characteristics of the rally-producing event (especially its intensity), the characteristics of media coverage, the reaction of the political elite, and preexisting public views of the sitting president. Future research should explore these and other possible conditions that strengthen or weaken rallies, both in the United States and in other countries.

Investigate Rallies in Other Countries

The rally phenomenon is not unique to the United States; several studies have documented significant rallies in other countries, including Britain (Lai and Reiter 2005; Lanoue and Headrick 1998; Norpoth 1987), Germany (Bytzek 2011), France (Georgarakis 2017), Russia (Hale 2018; Theiler 2017; Yudina 2015), and Israel (Feinstein 2018). There seems to be increasing scholarly interest in rallies that occur in countries other than the United States, and it is essential to continue this trend.

Notably, although the research on rallies outside the United States is still relatively limited, several studies suggest that my core arguments about rallies in the United States apply to other countries as well. For example, both studies of the rally that emerged in France after the January 2015 terrorist attacks against the Paris headquarters of *Charlie Hebdo* magazine (Georgarakis 2017) and studies of the rally that emerged in Russia in the aftermath of the March 2014 Crimea annexation (Sharafutdinova 2020; Thieler 2018; Yudina 2015) highlighted the concerns that people in these countries expressed during the rally periods about the symbolic value of their respective countries in their struggles with political Islam (France) or the democratic West (Russia). Further, during the Russian invasion of Crimea, studies have documented significant increases in national identification and pride not only in Russia (Theiler 2018) but also in Ukraine (Erlich and Garner 2021: 530; Kulyk 2016: 590). The latter set of findings reinforces my conclusion that rallies are not motivated by people's assessment of their county's success on the battlefield, but by the meaning they attribute to the struggle with a national enemy. In addition, my own investigation of the rally-round-the-flag effect that occurred in Israel during the 2014 Gaza War (Feinstein 2018) documented a significant increase in both national chauvinism and beliefs in exceptionalism. The study also revealed that these increases in chauvinism and exceptionalism were associated with attitudinal shifts toward more support for military action in Gaza and higher levels of satisfaction with Israeli prime minister Benjamin Netanyahu (that is, a rally-round-the-flag result). In sum, although this book focuses on the United States, its argument is not about American exceptionalism. Instead, with proper modifications, the book's core arguments likely apply to other countries.

Conduct Cross-National Investigations

A comparative cross-national investigation of the rally phenomenon would add much-needed nuance to the current understanding of the conditions and mechanisms that underlie the emergence of rallies. Unfortunately, the scarcity of surveys that regularly assess the public's approval of leaders in other countries is a significant obstacle to compiling a multi-country data set. Thus, future comparative research will likely need to target a select set of events for which there is enough evidence to establish the existence of rallies. Further, future research should also examine events for which there is compelling evidence for the lack of a rally (negative cases) because doing so allows the application of a compare-and-contrast investigative framework (similar to the one used in this book) to identify the unique sets of circumstances in which rallies have emerged.

Consider Variation in National Cultures

Future comparative research should consider the possibility that because historical legacies and core beliefs vary across nations, different types of events and policies are widely seen by each nation's members as increasing the nation's honor and prestige and thus are likely to generate a rally-round-the-flag effect. A case in point is the rally behind Australian prime minister Kevin Rudd following his apology to the Aboriginal people of Australia.

On February 13, 2008, Prime Minister Rudd delivered a speech in the Australian Parliament in which he apologized for the crimes European-Australians had committed against Aboriginal peoples during the "Stolen Generations" era. In his speech, Rudd described the apology as a step toward "the healing of the nation" and expressed his wish to "turn a new page in Australia's history by righting the wrongs of the past." The audience, both members of Parliament and crowds of people watching on large screens in public areas across the country, responded to the speech with loud applause and tears in their eyes (Barta 2008).[1] The speech, which was broadcast nation-wide by multiple television networks, prompted mass rallies in Australian cities. The widespread feeling of national pride and reassurance that emerged as a result of the speech led to a 9-point increase in Rudd's public approval rating, which rose from 59 percent before the speech to 68 percent after the speech.[2] In addition, an unknown number of Australian citizens had already rallied behind Rudd while he was running for office in 2007 based on his promise to apologize to the Aboriginal people.[3] In sum, as in the US rallies examined in this book, most Australians rallied behind Prime Minister Rudd because his actions and rhetoric enhanced their collective self-worth. However, in this case, the context for the rally was not a confrontation with a despised enemy, but rather an act of leadership that offered some redress for the damage done during a shameful period in the nation's history.

Look beyond Wars

Since public opinion experts first identified the rally-round-the-flag phe-nomenon, most of the research on the topic has focused on international conflicts and wars. This focus is likely still warranted as international conflicts, especially military confrontations, are the most common context for the emergence of rallies. However, rallies also emerge in other scenarios, and future research should pay closer attention to these circumstances. For example, recent scholarship has used the rally-round-the-flag concept to de-scribe the temporary increases in public trust in governments that occurred in several countries during the COVID-19 pandemic (Hamanaka 2021; Baekgaard et al. 2020; Blais et al. 2020; Esaiasson et al. 2020; Goldfinch,

Taplin, and Gauld 2021; Newton 2020; Reeskens and Muis 2020; Yam et al. 2020). However, most of these studies followed earlier research by treating rallies as an inevitable and self-explanatory outcome of crises, rather than as a contingent outcome that requires thorough investigation. Specifically, these recent studies paid little attention to the fact that a global pandemic generated rallies in some countries but not others (Yam et al. 2020). Indeed, this book's fundamental argument is that rallies are not automatic reactions to crises—not even to wars. Therefore, to understand why rallies emerge, researchers must go beyond the suspected trigger event and identify other supporting conditions.

Explore the Long-Term Consequences of Rallies

In Chapter 1, I described the potential immediate consequences rallies can have for policymaking—namely, the removal of some normative restrictions on policymaking—due to the unique atmosphere that characterizes these periods. Rallies, however, can have even more profound consequences for society. For quite a while, historians and sociologists of history have been interested in how rare events become "eventful" and bring about structural social changes (Sewell 1992). While the book did not directly engage with this issue, it hints at one of the mechanisms of eventfulness, and thus helps answer a largely overlooked question (van Dooremalen 2021: 726): How do events become socially transformative? If a rally-round-the-flag effect emerges in public opinion in response to unsettling events, the shift can facilitate radical policymaking and allow leaders to creatively employ certain cultural themes (Swidler 1986) to legitimize new policies. Jointly, the resulting policy and discourse can have long-lasting, even if unintended, impacts on society.

For example, George W. Bush promoted and implemented his "war on terror" policy with a strong tailwind of support from a rallying public in the aftermath of the September 11 attacks. However, the policy and discourse became increasingly controversial during the run-up to the invasion of Iraq and kept US society divided in the aftermath of the invasion (Jacobson 2007). The period left a deep mark on Americans. The roots of the current polarization of US society—which is characterized by deep resentment between the two political camps, whose members disagree on core elements of US nationalism, resistance to reaching across the aisle and seeking political compromise, and an increased threat to US democracy from ethno-nationalist politics—can be traced back to the policy and discourse that evolved during the post–9/11 rally-round-the-flag period (Bonikowski, Feinstein, and Bock 2021). Cultural and political polarization is only one of many possible long-term indirect effects of rallies that future research can explore. A partial list of these potential long-term effects includes a shift in the balance of political power between distinct versions of nationalism that foster competing political agendas, the development of new variants of nationalism, and greater integration or greater exclusion and alienation of some minority groups. Notably, a rally period may have more than one of these effects, as well as generating other profound changes.

Continued investigation of the rally phenomenon and its transformative cultural and political impacts is essential in light of the recent rise of ethnocentric, illiberal nationalism in many countries across the globe (Zakaria 2007; Diamond 2015; Feinstein and Ben-Eliezer 2019). Rally periods, especially those that emerge in response to militarized conflicts, can empower ethnocentric, authoritarian, illiberal, and militant actors, who point to the "will of the people" as their source of legitimacy. Importantly, however, rallies can also emerge in the context of peaceful and inclusionary policies, as the case of the rally behind Australian prime minister Rudd demonstrates. The Australian rally is an important reminder that national identification is not inevitably harmful, and that in addition to its widely discussed adverse outcomes, it also has positive expressions. In particular, national identification can motivate civic engagement and nurture feelings of solidarity across the boundaries of identity groups (Brubaker 2004: 121). Indeed, as this book shows, one of the most powerful engines driving political attitudes is the widespread yearning among the public to be part of an honorable and respected nation—leaders can employ this yearning to rally the public in the service of two very different types of outcomes: fostering social exclusion and intergroup militancy or improving intergroup relationships and helping to heal old wounds.

The Invasion of Lebanon

Like the Cuban Missile Crisis and the invasions of Panama and Iraq (discussed in Chapter 5), the US military intervention in Lebanon (on July 15, 1958) was justified by policymakers who contended the action was necessary to protect the geopolitical interests of the United States. The decision to send ground troops to Lebanon followed a series of events that convinced President Eisenhower that without military intervention, the entire Middle East would soon fall into the hands of pro-Nasserite, Arab nationalist forces, and this shift would allow the Soviet Union to become the sole dominant global force in the region (Alin 1994; Brands 1987; Dockrill 1996; Little 1996; Stivers 1987).

The chain of events began on February 1, 1958, when Egypt (led by President Nasser) and Syria (led by President Shukri al-Quwatli) announced that they were uniting as a single sovereign state known as the United Arab Republic (UAR). Iraq (led by King Faisal II) and Jordan (led by King Hussein) responded quickly, announcing that they were also creating a joint federation. Just over a month later, on March 23 in Saudi Arabia, King Saud, succumbing to pressure from pro-Nasserite forces within the country, yielded effective power to Crown Prince Faisal, whom the US administration considered a pro-Nasserite. Then, on July 14, Iraqi army officers instigated a successful coup, which ended the short-lived federation with Jordan and killed King Faisal and his prime minister, Nuri al-Said, who were considered Western loyalists. The Eisenhower administration concluded that the coup was conducted by pro-Nasserite forces, although the White House remained uncertain whether Nasser himself was involved. In light of these events, the Eisenhower administration became increasingly concerned that Arab nationalism would overtake the entire Middle East, and as a result Western influence would be removed completely, leaving the door wide open for the Soviet Union to gain influence in the region (Alin 1994; Dockrill 1996; Stivers 1987).

When Eisenhower publicly announced the landing of US marine and military forces in Lebanon, he downplayed national interests, instead using an internationalist language, probably to avoid jeopardizing his efforts to win the support of the United Nations Security Council. Eisenhower stated that the primary reason he was sending US troops to Lebanon was to help the Lebanese government preserve its independence and practice its right to self-defense.[1] The only connection Eisenhower made between the crisis in Lebanon and the Cold War was implicit—he said that the violence in Lebanon "*follows the pattern* of Communist aggression in Greece, Czechoslovakia, China, Korea, and Indochina*" (Stivers 1987: 208). By no means did he portray international communism as the primary enemy the United States would be fighting in Lebanon. Not surprisingly, given a presidential rhetoric that had an internationalist rather than nationalist tone and did not point to a clear enemy, the rally effect of the intervention in Lebanon was limited to an approximately 5-point increase in Eisenhower's job-approval rating, which reached a modest level of 57 percent.[2]

Presidential Job-Approval Ratings, United States, 1950–2020

In Figures A1–A13, the solid and dashed lines mark, respectively, approval and disapproval ratings, with the circles along these lines marking polling estimates. The thicker lines track the three-point moving averages of approval and disapproval ratings. Notable conflicts and events are labeled, with those that prompted rally periods marked in bold letters.[3]

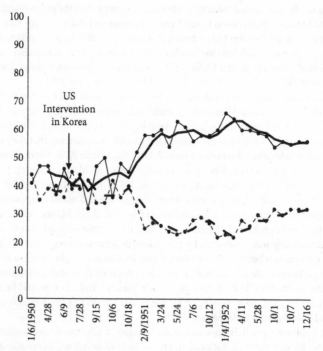

Figure A1. Harry S. Truman's job-approval and disapproval ratings (from 1950 forward).

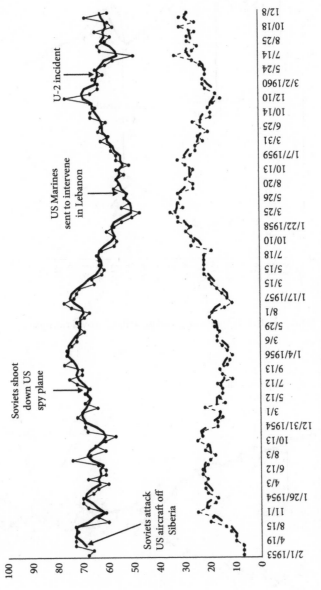

Figure A2. Dwight D. Eisenhower's job-approval and disapproval ratings.

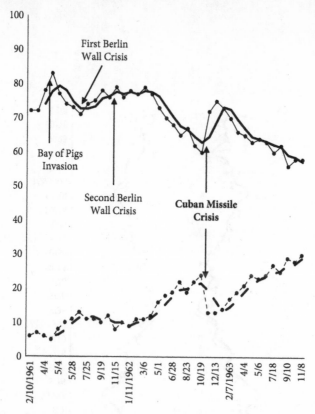

Figure A3. John F. Kennedy's job-approval and disapproval ratings.

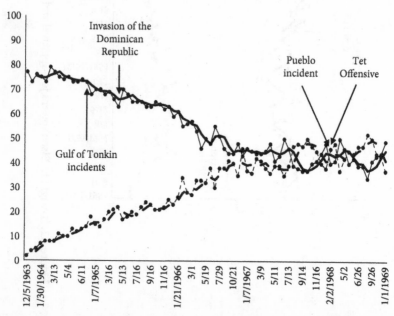

Figure A4. Lyndon B. Johnson's job-approval and disapproval ratings.

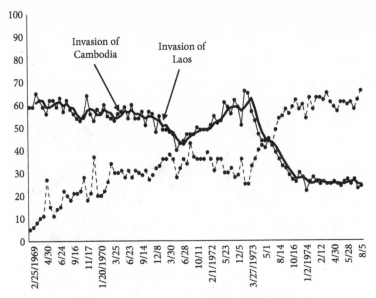

Figure A5. Richard Nixon's job-approval and disapproval ratings.

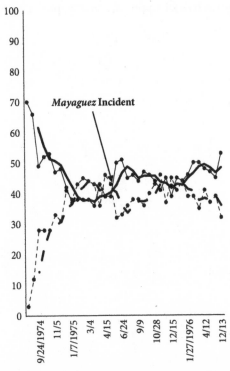

Figure A6. Gerald R. Ford's job-approval and disapproval ratings.

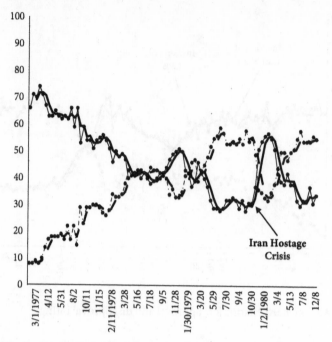

Figure A7. Jimmy Carter's job-approval and disapproval ratings.

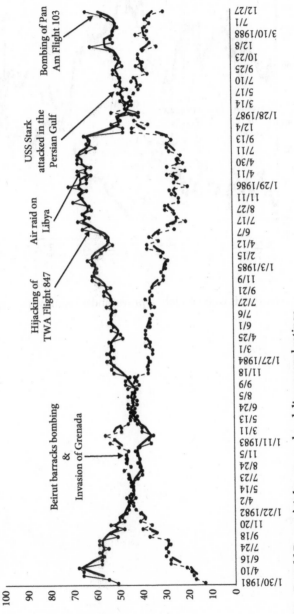

Figure A8. Ronald Reagan's job-approval and disapproval ratings.

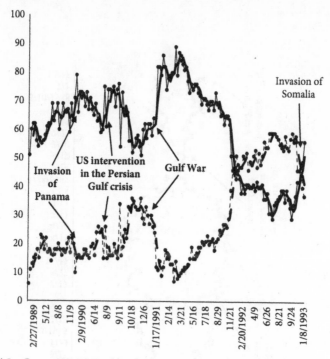

Figure A9. George H. W. Bush's job-approval and disapproval ratings.

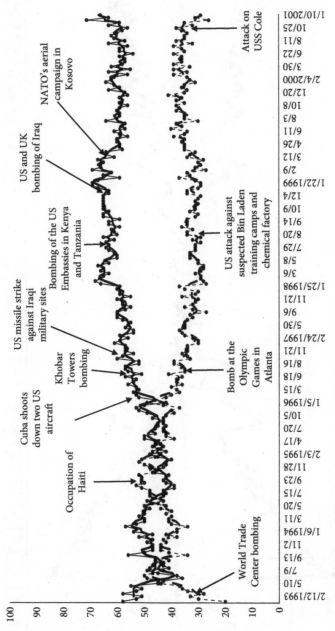

Figure A10. William J. Clinton's job-approval and disapproval ratings.

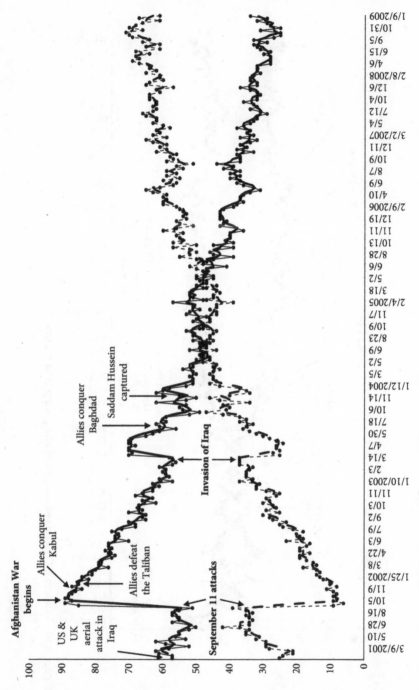

Figure A11. George W. Bush's job-approval and disapproval ratings.

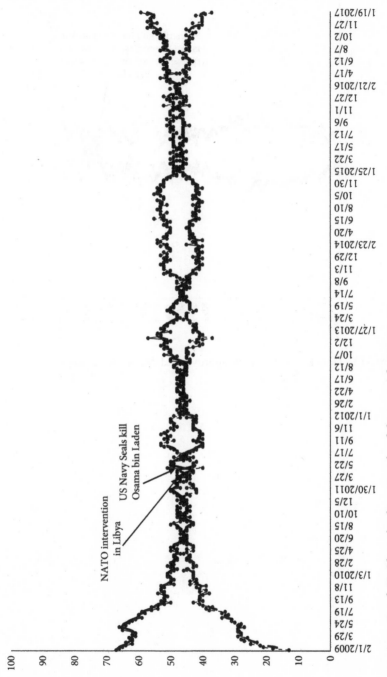

Figure A12. Barak H. Obama's job-approval and disapproval ratings.

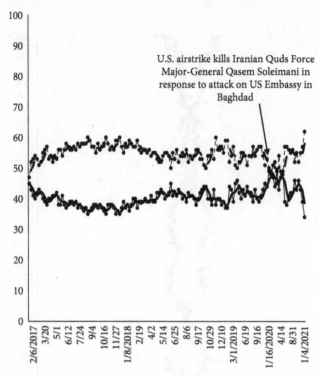

Figure A13.   Donald J. Trump's job-approval and disapproval ratings.

Table A1 List of Events and Rally-round-the-Flag Coding

Event	Date	President	Rally-round-the-Flag
North Korea attacks South Korea	6/25/1950	Harry S. Truman	No
Soviets attack US plane off Siberia	3/15/1953 (first reported 3/18/1953)	Dwight D. Eisenhower	Insufficient data
Soviets shoot down US spy plane	6/22/1955 (first reported 6/25/1955)	Eisenhower	No
Eisenhower sends Marines to Lebanon	7/15/1958	Eisenhower	Minor
U-2 incident	5/1/1960	Eisenhower	No
Bay of Pigs invasion	4/15–4/20/1961	John F. Kennedy	Ambiguous
Berlin Wall crisis	6/4–11/9/1961	Kennedy	No
Second Berlin Wall crisis	10/22–10/28/1961	Kennedy	No
Cuban Missile Crisis	10/22/1962	Kennedy	Major
Gulf of Tonkin incidents	8/2–8/4/1964	Lyndon B. Johnson	Insufficient data
Johnson sends Marines to the Dominican Republic	4/28/1965	Johnson	Minor
Vietnam draft doubled	7/28/1965	Johnson	No
Pueblo incident	1/23/1968	Johnson	No
Tet Offensive	1/31/1968 (start)	Johnson	No
Cambodia invasion	5/1–6/30/1970	Richard Nixon	No
Laos invasion	2/8/1971 (ground assault)	Nixon	No
Increase in bombing	4/10/1972	Nixon	No
Cambodia falls	4/12/1975	Gerald Ford	No
Mayaguez incident	5/12–5/15/1975	Ford	Major
Iran hostage crisis	11/4/1979–1/20/1981	Jimmy Carter	Major
Helicopter rescue plan fails	4/24/1980	Carter	Minor
Libyan jet shot down	8/19/1981	Ronald Reagan	No
Attack on US troops in Lebanon	10/23/1983	Reagan	Not major; not enough data to determine if minor
Grenada invasion	10/25–12/15/1983	Reagan	Minor
Hostage incident: TWA Flight 847	6/14–6/30/1985	Reagan	Borderline

(*continued*)

Table A1 Continued

Event	Date	President	Rally-round-the-Flag
Air raid on Libya	4/15/1986	Reagan	Borderline
USS *Stark* attacked in Persian Gulf	5/17/1987	Reagan	Insufficient data
United States downs Iranian airbus	7/3/1988	Reagan	No
Pan Am Flight 103 bombed over Lockerbie, Scotland	12/21/1988	Reagan	Borderline
US Navy downs Libyan fighters	4/1/1989	George H. W. Bush	Insufficient data
Bush sends troops to Panama and Noriega surrenders	12/20/1989–1/31/1990	Bush	Major
Gulf War	1/16/1991	Bush	Major
Operation Restore Hope in Somalia begins	12/9/1992	Bush	No
Navy launches missiles on Iraq	1/17/1993	Bush	Insufficient data
World Trade Center bombing	2/26/1993	William J. Clinton	No
Occupation of Haiti	9/19/1994	Clinton	Minor
Cuba shoots down two American civilian planes	2/24/1996	Clinton	No
Khobar Towers bombing in Saudi Arabia	6/25/1996	Clinton	No
Bomb at the Olympics in Atlanta	7/27/1996	Clinton	No
US missile strike at Iraqi military sites	9/3/1996	Clinton	No
US embassies in Kenya and Tanzania bombed	8/7/1998	Clinton	No
Attacks on suspected bin Laden training camps and chemical factory	8/20/1998	Clinton	No
Operation Desert Fox in Iraq	12/16–12/19/1998	Clinton	Ambiguous
Kosovo Air Campaign	3/24/1999	Clinton	No
USS *Cole* attacked	10/12/2000	Clinton	Minor
US and UK planes attack Iraq	2/16/2001	George W. Bush	Minor
US spy plane collides with Chinese fighter jet; crew detained and later released	4/1/2001	Bush	Minor

Table A1 Continued

Event	Date	President	Rally-round-the-Flag
9/11	9/11/2001	Bush	Major
War in Afghanistan beings	10/7/2001	Bush	Ambiguous
Capital of Afghanistan falls to Northern Alliance	11/13/2001	Bush	No
Taliban defeated in Afghanistan	12/17/2001	Bush	No
United States and allies attack Iraq	3/20/2003	Bush	Major
Baghdad falls	4/7–4/9/2003	Bush	No
Saddam Hussein captured	12/14/2003	Bush	Borderline
NATO intervention in Libya	3/19/2011	Barak Obama	No
US Navy Seals kill Osama bin Laden	5/2/2011	Obama	Borderline
US airstrike kills Iranian Quds Force Major General Qasem Soleimani in response to an attack on the US Embassy in Baghdad	1/2/2020	Donald Trump	No

Table A2 Coefficients from Logistic Regression Models of President Job Approval, US Adult Citizens, Gallup Poll, March 22–23, 2003 (standard errors in parentheses)

Explanatory Variables	Model 1 Threat Perception	Model 2 Rational Public	Model 3 Emotional Public	Model 4 All-in-One
Worry about being victim of terrorism	−0.094 (0.155)			
Expect more terrorism soon	−0.234 (0.171)			
Winning		1.452*** (0.379)		1.003** (0.368)
Success (how war is going for us)		0.412 (0.212)		0.208 (0.188)
Expected duration of war		0.0393 (0.125)		
Expected number of US casualties		−0.190 (0.151)		
War pessimism scale		−0.983 (0.853)		

(continued)

212 APPENDIX

Table A2 Continued

Explanatory Variables	Model 1 Threat Perception	Model 2 Rational Public	Model 3 Emotional Public	Model 4 All-in-One
Confident because of the war			1.593*** (0.347)	1.383*** (0.359)
Proud because of the war in Iraq			2.365*** (0.342)	2.424*** (0.343)
Afraid because of the war in Iraq			-0.677 (0.362)	
Worried because of the war in Iraq			-0.437 (0.360)	
Sad because of the war in Iraq			-0.250 (0.436)	
How closely follow news about the war	0.599** (0.180)	0.348 (0.204)	0.356 (0.230)	0.203 (0.235)
Partisan identification scale	-0.634*** (0.080)	-0.703*** (0.101)	-0.719*** (0.098)	-0.754*** (0.094)
Level of liberalism	-0.596*** (0.098)	-0.570*** (0.110)	-0.719*** (0.098)	-0.409*** (0.116)
Age 50–64	-0.556* (0.266)	-0.592 (0.325)	-0.775* (0.330)	-0.917** (0.336)
Income $30k–less than $50k	1.606*** (0.353)	1.601*** (0.462)	1.469*** (0.417)	1.385** (0.433)
Income $50k and above	0.579* (0.292)	0.379 (0.366)	0.242 (0.363)	0.036 (0.385)
College grad	-0.723** (0.247)	-0.466 (0.302)	0.148 (0.342)	0.321 (0.351)
Hispanic	0.686 (0.827)	1.284 (0.695)	1.764* (0.783)	1.519 (0.776)
Black	-2.184*** (0.409)	-1.839** (0.564)	-1.670*** (0.413)	-1.506*** (0.425)
Constant	4.069*** (0.923)	2.426 (1.301)	2.302* (1.014)	0.754 (1.098)
Observations	853	797	825	822
Chi-Square	189 (11)***	212(14)***	222(14)***	221(13)***
BIC	-312	-326	-467	-448

*p < 0.05, **p < 0.01, *** p < 0.001 (two-tailed tests)

Notes: "< $30k," "white, Asian, or other" are the omitted categories of income and race.

Table A3 Coefficients from Logistic Regression Models of President Job Approval, US Adult Citizens, "Public Reactions to the Events of September 11," Stony Brook University Center for Survey Research, 10/15/2001–3/2/2002 (standard errors in parentheses)

Explanatory Variables	Model 1 Threat Perception	Model 2 Emotions	Model 3 Nationalism and Trust in Govt.	Model 4 All-in-One
Concerned by future terrorism in the US	0.141 (0.159)			
Concerned by terrorism use of WMD in US	0.342* (0.157)			0.123 (0.141)
How concerned that will be victim of future attack?	−0.129 (0.137)			
Attacks shaken sense of personal safety	−0.070 (0.123)			
Felt depressed because of attacks		−0.061 (0.120)		
Felt anxious because of attacks		−0.043 (0.151)		
Felt scared because of attacks		0.028 (0.172)		
Felt secure because of attacks		−0.002 (0.143)		
Felt worried because of attacks		0.164 (0.161)		
Felt frightened because of attacks		−0.197 (0.177)		
Felt confident because of attacks		0.383** (0.141)		0.057 (0.135)
Proud of being an American			0.396* (0.160)	0.416** (0.154)
Trust the government to do what's right			0.857*** (0.213)	0.868*** (0.214)
Confident that govt. can protect from terrorism			0.406** (0.157)	0.363* (0.158)
Confident that govt. can win war on terrorism			0.555*** (0.150)	0.584*** (0.152)
Angry at people who criticize the US			0.127 (0.106)	

Table A3 Continued

Explanatory Variables	Model 1 Threat Perception	Model 2 Emotions	Model 3 Nationalism and Trust in Govt.	Model 4 All-in-One
How closely follow news stories about the attacks?	0.316* (0.154)	0.238 (0.159)	0.138 (0.173)	0.091 (0.174)
Days in past week read about events in newspaper?	0.129** (0.042)	0.139*** (0.044)	0.078 (0.0479)	0.0743 (0.048)
Level of liberalism	−0.191*** (0.054)	−0.215*** (0.055)	−0.067 (0.064)	−0.072 (0.0632)
Democrat or leaning Dem.	−1.595*** (0.249)	−1.580*** (0.258)	−1.608*** (0.291)	−1.647*** (0.293)
You/friends/relatives know a victim?	−0.378 (0.218)	−0.267 (0.226)	−0.193 (0.249)	−0.268 (0.247)
Constant	1.403* (0.639)	1.682** (0.731)	−3.758*** (0.882)	−3.768*** (1.005)
Observations	1294	1256	1223	1227
Chi-Square	138.2(9)***	139.5(12)***	248.9(10)***	235.1(11)***
BIC	−74	−54	−178	−157

*p < 0.05, **p < 0.01, *** p < 0.001 (two-tailed tests).

Table A4. Unstandardized and Standardized Coefficients for the Structural Equation Models Presented in Chapter 9 (Yuan-Bentler corrected standard errors in parentheses; N = 729)

Latent Variable	Survey Question	Figure 9.14		Figure 9.15	
		U	S	U	S
Support for the president	Approve of the way the president is handling his job	1	0.631	1	0.899
	Approve of the way the president is handling the economy	0.805 (0.043)	0.507	0.801 (0.036)	0.720
	Approve of the way the president is handling the situation in Iraq	1.117 (0.052)	0.704	0.772 (0.063)	0.694
Confidence in the war on terror	Think the government can win the war on terrorism	1	1.002		
	Think the government can protect the American people from terrorism	0.738 (0.123)	0.739		

Table A4 Continued

Latent Variable	Survey Question	Figure 9.14		Figure 9.15	
		U	S	U	S
Positive emotions about the war in Iraq	Feel hopeful about the war	1	0.714	1	0.786
	Proud of the war	1.188 (0.035)	0.849	1.129 (0.036)	0.887
	Enthusiastic about the war	1.325 (0.041)	0.947	1.170 (0.058)	0.919
Fear of terrorism	Nervous because of terrorism	1	0.865		
	Scared because of terrorism	1.137 (0.042)	0.983		
	Afraid because of terrorism	1.035 (0.047)	0.896		
Anger toward terrorists	Angry at terrorists	1	0.874	1	0.978
	Hostile to terrorists	1.015 (0.052)	0.887	0.718 (0.108)	0.702
	Disgusted by terrorists	0.941 (0.109	0.823	0.897 (0.141)	0.878
Anger toward Saddam Hussein	Angry at Saddam Hussein	1	0.862		
	Hostile to Saddam Hussein	1.065 (0.025)	0.918		
	Disgusted by Saddam Hussein	0.904 (0.028)	0.779		
National identification	Proud to be American			1	0.830
	Feel good when see the American flag flying			1.068 (0.071)	0.887

U = Unstandardized; S = Standardized.

Table A5 Coefficients from Logistic Regression Models of Change in President Job Approval, Based on TNSS (standard errors in parentheses)

	Wave1-to-Wave2	Wave1-to-Wave3
Change is "How much confidence in ability of govt. to win war on terrorism?"	−.361*** (.089)	−.336** (.099)
Change in "How angry do you feel when someone criticizes us?"	−.114 (.094)	−.220* (.109)
Change in "How good does it make you feel when you see the American flag flying?"	.221 (.156)	−.491** (.171)
Republican	−2.282*** (.331)	−2.320*** (.390)
Education	.187** (.057)	.197** (.069)
Age	.018* (.007)	.010 (.008)
Constant	−3.726*** (.711)	−3.421*** (.839)
Observations	690	505
Chi-Square	105.2(6)***	95.03(6)***

* $p < 0.05$, ** $p < 0.01$, *** $p < 0.001$ (two-tailed tests).

Notes

INTRODUCTION

1. Unless otherwise indicated, presidential approval ratings are based on Gallup Polls retrieved May 25, 2011, from the iPOLL Databank, The Roper Center for Public Opinion Research, University of Connecticut.
2. Several scholars have expanded the definition of "rally events" to include domestic events or events related to the president's health and life (Brace and Hinckley 1992; Lee 1977; Newman and Forcehimes 2010; Ostrom and Simon 1985).
3. In the aftermath of this incident, Eisenhower's job-approval rating remained just above 60 percent (based on data retrieved on May 21, 2020, from *The American Presidency Project*, https://www.presidency.ucsb.edu/statistics/data/presidential-job-approval).
4. *New York Times*, October 28, 1983, "Report to Nation," p. 1.
5. Following the invasion of Grenada, Reagan's public approval rating increased by only a few points, to 52 percent (based on data retrieved on May 21, 2020, from *The American Presidency Project*, https://www.presidency.ucsb.edu/statistics/data/presidential-job-approval).
6. For a similar finding from research on public reaction to wars in Britain, see Lai and Reiter (2005: 297).
7. Beijen, Otjes, and Kanne (2021) offer an additional reason why research on the rally-round-the-flag phenomenon should focus on the head of state's approval ratings. In a study on public opinion in the Netherlands during a March 2017 diplomatic crisis with Turkey, they found that even in the case of a coalition-government multiparty parliamentary system, the rally effect was limited to the public's view of the prime minister and not the vice prime minister. Based on this finding, they conclude that "when the public assesses foreign policy, it appears to be the case that responsibility mainly falls to the head of the government and not so much to other members of the government" (p. 19). Nevertheless, in response to more extreme events than the one examined by Beijen and coauthors, a rally effect may boost the public approval rating of an entire government.
8. See also my study of public opinion in Israel during the 2014 war with Hamas in Gaza, in which I show that Israelis from the ideological and political left were the group least likely to rally behind the leadership of Prime Minister Netanyahu (Feinstein 2018).
9. The assessment of public opinion during the 2021 war is based on unpublished results of survey research by the author of this book.
10. There may be additional conditions that affect the magnitude of rallies that are not considered in this brief discussion.

11. Baum and Potter (2015) presented a modified argument, which suggests that public opinion has the strongest impact on foreign policy in multiparty democracies. For a comprehensive discussion of the democratic constraint argument, see Gelpi (2017).
12. Except for some studies on emotions in national rituals (e.g., Skey 2006; Collins 2004, 2012).

Chapter 2

1. For a discussion of the increasing mistrust of politicians in the United States, see Adut (2018: chap. 4).
2. Other studies have taken this line of investigation a step further, pointing to characteristics of events such as the level of hostility, having a revisionist goal of imposing a new order in a foreign country or region, and whether the use of military force was a US initiative, as predictors of an increase in presidential job-approval ratings (e.g., Baker and Oneal 2001; Lian and Oneal 1993).
3. For a discussion of more integrative approaches to the rally-round-the-flag effect, which point to the role of the political elite, the media, and individual-level attributes, see Baker and Oneal (2001); Groeling and Baum (2008); Lian and Oneal (1993); and Oneal and Bryan (1995).
4. Another variant of this approach to the rally phenomenon considers the mass media an independent agent, which can mobilize popular consensus even when the political elite are divided (Baum and Groeling 2005; Groeling and Baum 2008; Iyengar and Simon 1994).
5. Chapman and Reiter (2004) also noted that the American public monitors the opinion of the United Nations Security Council to verify that presidents only go to war for genuinely defensive purposes.
6. Despite this difference, the rationalist and realist approaches to public opinion converge in the claim made by Gelpi and his coauthors that when important national interests are at stake, if people believe that a military action is likely to succeed, they will support the action even if it might lead to the loss of a substantial number of American lives (Gelpi, Feaver, and Reifler 2006, 2009). See also Herrmann, Tetlock, and Visser (1999).
7. More generally, studies have found that political opinions and behavior are not driven by egocentric concerns, but by sociotropic concerns (Joslyn and Haider-Markel 2007; Kinder and Kiewiet 1979) and the affective predispositions they evoke (Sears 2001).
8. For review of critical arguments about the mental capacity of individuals to assess threats to national security, see Cramer and Thrall (2009: 4–6).
9. This argument aligns with claims by scholars who apply the principles of constructivist theory in international relations research. They suggest that efforts to propagate a sense of security threat in the public are more likely to succeed when the leader emphasizes cultural differences between the home nation and its enemies (Cramer and Thrall 2009: 10; Kaufman 2001; Rousseau 2006; Rousseau and Garcia-Retamero 2009).

10. Scholars may have developed an explanation of the post–9/11 rally that highlights feelings rather than assessments, in part, because they themselves experienced strong emotions and observed others experiencing strong emotions in the days and weeks after the attacks. Further, this experience might have contributed to the broader "emotional turn" in social science (Berezin 2002: 33; Heaney 2011: 260). I speculate that this is true. In any case, the important point for this discussion is that these scholars shifted the focus to the ways that emotions motivate people to rally.

11. Nincic (1997) also suggested that presidents enjoy greater public support when they justify military initiatives as "protective interventions."

12. During wartime, media exposure and threat perception may not have a simple cause-and-effect relationship at the individual level, but rather may interact in the form of a "reinforcing spiral" (Slater 2007): the media propagates a sense of threat, and then worried individuals turn to the media to obtain more information about the crisis.

13. This situation is not unique to the United States. Even in Israel, where there is mandatory military service, during recent wars against Hamas in Gaza, most of the people who rallied behind the war and the prime minister neither participated in the fighting nor fell victim to Hamas's aggression (Feinstein 2018).

14. For the result of formal tests of the arguments discussed in this chapter, see the appendix to my article in *Social Science History* (Feinstein 2016a).

Chapter 3

1. *New York Times*, September 12, 2001, "Dispatches from a Day of Terror and Shock," p. A26.

2. *New York Times*, March 28, 2003, "Letters to the Editor," p. A16.

3. The photo, which was taken on February 23, 1945, at the end of a fierce battle against Japanese forces, has become an icon for American courage and perseverance.

4. September 11, 2001, Documentary Project, "Interview with Julie Dethrow, Logan, Utah, December 2, 2001." Retrieved on May 19, 2020, from https://www.loc.gov/item/afc911000160/.

5. On the role of humiliation in wars, see Lindner (2006). On recognition of enemies' identity and value as a mechanism of peacemaking, see Hicks (2011).

6. The foundation of Scheff's argument is Weber's (1946 [1922]: 249) claim that charismatic authority is born out of people's "distress and enthusiasm."

7. See Chapter 8 for a discussion of the Gulf War, which was an exception to this pattern.

8. This theoretical proposition is based on Theodore Kemper's (2011: chap. 13) status-power theory, which focuses on the confrontation between a group and an "other" and the perceived implications of this confrontation for the power and status that the ingroup has vis-à-vis the external other. Specifically, Kemper proposed that situations or actions that lead to a loss of power (or are perceived as such) elicit fear, while situations that lead to a loss of status (or are perceived as such) elicit anger.

9. Borrowing from the terminology of the appraisal theory of emotions, the term "positive emotions" is used here in reference to emotions that stem from a positive orientation toward a situation (e.g., joy) or toward the actual or expected ability to cope with a negative situation (e.g., pride, hope, confidence); by contrast, "negative emotions" stem from a negative orientation toward a situation and its causes (e.g., grief, fear, anger) or the lack of ability to cope with the situation (e.g., shame, embarrassment) (see Folkman 2008 for a review).

10. This theoretical proposition relies on Peter Burke's identity theory of emotions (Burke 1991; see also Stryker and Burke 2000), which suggests that during social interactions, actions that align with identity standards (i.e., how individuals believe they should act based on their identity) elicit pride, while actions that do not align with identity standards elicit shame.

11. The development of news reports is a fascinating issue that remains largely outside the scope of this discussion, which focuses on how news reports *impact* people's attitudes during rally periods (but see Baum and Potter 2008; Bennett and Paletz 1994: several chapters; Groeling and Baum 2008).

12. In some cases, specifically during the Korean and Vietnam Wars (Brewer 2011: 180; Casey 2008: chap. 1), US administrations made explicit attempts to use news channels to lead a low-key information campaign that maintained a sufficient level of public legitimacy for military interventions abroad but did not evoke strong affective reactions and war enthusiasm among the people.

13. For example, Craig LaMay (1991) reported that between December 1990 (the final run-up to the Gulf War) and February 1991 (the end of the war) television news stories devoted 83 percent of their airtime to the gulf crisis (1991: 47), and that between January 21 and February 3, 1991, the total news coverage on television networks' nightly broadcasts as well as in prominent newspapers and magazines grew to "130 percent of its normal volume, and 92.9 percent of this coverage was related to the events in the gulf" (1991: 46).

14. This shift is described as a transition from "cold cognition" to "hot cognition" in the terminology of cognitive science (Cerulo 2010).

15. Data retrieved on July 29, 2019, from *The American Presidency Project*, Santa Barbara, CA, https://www.presidency.ucsb.edu/statistics/data/presidential-job-approval.

16. The sociological point of view differs from the perspective of psychological texts, which tend to highlight the roots of enmity in the deepest elements of the human psyche (Rieber and Kelly 1991; e.g., Freud, Katz, and Riviere 1947).

17. Typically, an individual's membership in a "minimal group" is based on a single visual marker or a label that investigators randomly assign to participants. For example, investigators may tell some participants they are assigned to "the red group" and tell others they are assigned to "the blue group."

18. In a second study that analyzed original panel survey data collected in Israel, I showed that increased levels of national chauvinism among Jewish Israelis during Israel's war against the Hamas government in Gaza (in the summer of 2014) resulted in massive support for the war; at the same time, increased levels of identification with the national Jewish ingroup led a majority of Jewish Israelis to rally behind the leadership of

Prime Minister Netanyahu (Feinstein 2018). In addition, during the 2014 Gaza War (and in the Israeli-Palestinian conflict more generally; see Roccas, Klar, and Liviatan 2006), many Jewish Israelis exhibited a tendency to justify the home-nation's actions and deny any criticism of Israeli policies related to the conflict. Thus, through this pro-ingroup bias, they place the entire blame for the conflict and the high cost of the conflict in human lives and damage to property on the enemy (Feinstein 2018).

19. This proposition is certainly true for the enemies in the two studies mentioned in the previous note: Many Americans view the Iranian Islamic regime as having been an enemy since the Iranian Revolution in 1979. For most Israelis, the Hamas regime in Gaza is a long-standing nemesis; the Israeli-Palestinian conflict itself is a century old.

20. Along the same lines, Nigbur and Cinnirella (2007) proposed that relative to the general sense of national superiority vis-à-vis a broad category of unspecified "others" (the type of national chauvinism that is usually measured and discussed in survey-based studies of political attitudes during conflicts, including my own studies cited in this section), comparing the home nation to *specific* others "should . . . be associated with positive differentiation and generally more complimentary images of one's own group" (2007: 675). Thus, during conflict, increased general levels of national chauvinism and militancy may stem from comparing the home nation to the *specific enemy* in the conflict (rather than to a broad category of "others"). Smith-Lovin (2007) described one such national comparison (British–American) as follows: "The meaning of our category membership (e.g., what it means to be British) is influenced by the context to which we compare ourselves. [For example,] if the British compare themselves to Americans, traditionalism and reserve may be more salient" (2007: 110). Smith-Lovin's assertion implies that the perceived relationship between the home-nation (ingroup) and another nation (outgroup) may have "thick" content due to a history of engagement with the other group and interactions between the two groups.

21. Drawing analogies between current and historical events is also used as heuristic in foreign and military policymaking. For a critical discussion, see Khong (2020).

22. British political leaders also used an analogy to Nazi Germany during the 1956 Suez Crisis (Smith 2005: 79), and over the past several years, Israeli political leaders have frequently used it with reference to the Islamic Government of Iran, stressing the need to stop Iran's nuclear program.

23. On actual human sacrifice in ancient wars, see Ehrenreich (2011).

24. A Gallup Poll conducted in mid-January 2007 shows that, despite the recent execution of Saddam Hussein, about 62 percent of Republicans approved of the Iraq War but only 6 percent of Democrats and 24 percent of independent voters approved of the war (the percentages of Republican, Democrat, and independent voters who thought that the decision to go to war against Iraq was a mistake were 26, 80, and 49, respectively), and President Bush's job-approval rating was high among Republican voters (71 percent), low among independent voters (30 percent), and extremely low among Democrat voters (8 percent). Data were retrieved from the iPOLL Databank, The Roper Center for Public Opinion Research, University of Connecticut.

25. For an extended discussion of official war propaganda in the United States, see Brewer (2011).
26. *New York Times*, October 23, 1962, "Text of Kennedy's Address on Moves to Meet the Soviet Build-up in Cuba," p. 18.
27. *New York Times*, May 1, 1970, "Transcript of President's Address to the Nation on Military Action in Cambodia," p. 2.
28. These depictions were used in discourses about (respectively) the Philippines and World War I, World War II, Korea and Vietnam, and Iraq.
29. Further, by highlighting the ideological motivations of wars, war propaganda can obscure the material and political (in the sense of power seeking) interests behind these wars. Prior research has concluded that war propaganda has "served to camouflage any contradiction that might exist between America's pursuit of power and its principles. Indeed, propaganda projected the appealing notion that America's global ambitions and democratic traditions are one and the same" (Brewer 2011: 4).
30. See, for example, my discussion of the US public's differing reactions to the NATO intervention in Kosovo in 1999 (Feinstein 2017).

Chapter 4

1. A condensed version of Chapters 5–8 is included in an article published in the *Social Science History Journal* (Feinstein 2016a).
2. Further, unlike major jumps in presidential job-approval ratings (i.e., rallies around the flag), what appears to be a small increase in the president's approval ratings may actually reflect differences between the samples surveyed in public opinion polls (i.e., "sampling variability" in the jargon of quantitative research).
3. The database could not be extended to include events that occurred before 1950 because opinion polls had not yet been well developed and thus the data that earlier polls provide are incomplete and less reliable than data from later periods.
4. A longer, preliminary list of events was compiled from three sources: First, in their book on how public opinion polls affect presidential policies, Brace and Hinckley (1992: 185–87) provided a list of 106 events that took place between 1949 and 1988. Second, in a study of the relationship between the popularity of US presidents and their effectiveness in the legislative arena from 1953 to 1980, Ostrom and Simon (1985) developed a list of 85 "unanticipated events"—for instance, security crises, major diplomatic events, and events related to the personal life of the president. Third, Newman and Forcehimes (2010) attempted to create an exhaustive list of "rally events," while implementing new and arguably better selection criteria. Specifically, they added "centrality of media coverage" as a necessary condition for coding events as rally points. Newman and Forcehimes's coding effort produced a list of 120 events that occurred between 1953 and 2006. All three sources recorded both potential "positive" rally points—events that had the potential to increase presidential job-approval ratings—and potential "negative" rally

points—events that might have caused presidential job-approval ratings to decline (for instance, a sudden economic downturn). When compiling the list of candidate events for this analysis, I dropped all "negative" rally events and kept only events that could improve presidential job-approval ratings. To these, I added a handful of events based on two other prominent publications (Eichenberg 2005; Jentleson and Britton 1998). The resulting preliminary list of candidates contained 88 events. While I have been working on this book, several high-profile security events have happened; thus I extended the list of events analyzed in this study to include those more recent events.

5. The available data suggest that the Paris Peace Accord in January 1973, which ended the Vietnam War, and the Intermediate-Range Nuclear Forces Treaty with the Soviet Union, signed in December 1987, perhaps led to temporary increases in public approval of the president, but the evidence for rally effects is inconclusive. It is clear, however, that the impacts of these two events on public opinion were weaker than the impact of the events discussed in the following chapters.

6. In two instances—the 1961 Bay of Pigs invasion and the onset of the Afghanistan War in 2001—presidents were already very popular prior to the event; thus small increases in presidential job-approval ratings might have represented rally-round-the-flag effects. A third event, Operation Desert Fox (the American-British bombing campaign against Iraq in December 1998), was categorized as an ambiguous case because the effect of this military operation could not be disentangled from the effect of the House of Representatives' decision to impeach Clinton as a result of the Monica Lewinsky affair (December 19, 1998). All three ambiguous cases were initially excluded from the analysis, but to check for the possibility of selection bias they were later reintroduced into the analysis. The Afghanistan War meets the criteria for one of the pathways for the development of a rally-round-the-flag outcome (the pathway discussed in Chapter 5). The Bay of Pigs invasion, in contrast, does not fit the description of any of the pathways. Closer inspection of the data—which reveals that Kennedy's job-approval ratings had already begun to increase a few weeks prior to the invasion, perhaps because (in the context of the congressional election campaign) Kennedy seemed to have been taking a firmer line regarding communism—further increases the ambiguity of the case. In the case of Operation Desert Fox, it seems clearer that the event was not a rally point because the increase in the president's job-approval rating did not start with the attack in Iraq, but rather rose only after the decision to impeach Clinton.

7. The data used to classify events as one of these four types came from two sources: The Roper Center at the University of Connecticut and the American Presidency Project at the University of California in Santa Barbara. Both sources have compiled data sets from a variety of public opinion polls. To avoid measurement errors associated with differences in sampling design and the wording of questions, whenever possible, coding decisions were made by examining data collected by the *same* polling organization at different points in time. Furthermore, whenever possible, I first made coding decisions based on the data collected in Gallup polls and then looked at other polls for confirmation.

Chapter 5

1. Transcript of Kennedy's national address was retrieved on June 3, 2020, from https://www.jfklibrary.org/learn/about-jfk/historic-speeches/address-during-the-cuban-missile-crisis.

2. Photos of the missile sites taken by a U-2 spy plane were shown to Kennedy on October 16 (Garthoff 1989: 43), but the administration initially kept the issue secret from the public.

3. In addition, Kennedy stated that "jet bombers, capable of carrying nuclear weapons, are now being uncrated and assembled in Cuba, while the necessary air bases are being prepared," but in the public discourse that piece of information was obscured by the discussion about the missile problem.

4. Other factors contributing to Khrushchev's decision to deploy nuclear missiles in Cuba may have included a desire to cut defense spending by changing the course of the Cold War in a way that would make the deployment of large standing military forces redundant, his wish to use the missiles in Cuba as powerful leverage in his on-going effort to compel Western forces to move out of Berlin, and China's criticism of Moscow for not being decisive enough in its support for international communism (White 1995: chap. 3).

5. For details about the huge military, marine, and aerial force that was assembled in preparation for an attack against Cuba, see Gerthoff (1992: 45–46) and Brugioni (1991: chap. 15).

6. Throughout the crisis, reporters and editors willingly followed the White House's directive to exhibit patriotic restraint by not digging into government deliberations or revealing classified issues such as intelligence estimates of the enemy's strength and information about the deployment of US forces (George 2003: 98–102).

7. *Washington Post*, October 23, 1962, "Meeting the Cuban Crisis," p. A16. See also an editorial in the *New York Times* (October 23, 1962, p. 36). Even Republican newspapers such as the *New York Herald Tribune* expressed support for Kennedy's reaction (George 2003: 93).

8. For weeks prior to the crisis, Senator Kenneth B. Keating had warned that the Soviet Union had been deploying offensive missiles in Cuba (White 1995: chap.4).

9. The fact that several prominent leaders of the opposition party explicitly criticized Kennedy and his overall policy on Cuba and the Soviet Union, but a vast majority of US citizens nonetheless rallied behind Kennedy during the missile crisis, suggests that in contrast to the elite consensus thesis (discussed in Chapter 2), a consensus among the political elite is not a necessary condition for the emergence of a rally-round-the-flag effect.

10. *New York Times*, October 24, 1962, "Eisenhower Backs President in Crisis," p. 1.

11. *Washington Post*, April 17, 1962, "Cuban Holiday Marks Bay of Pigs Triumph," p. A12.

12. *New York Times* editors, April 18, 1961, "The Cuban Invasion," p. 36.

13. *New York Times*, October 5, 1962, "Citizens in 3 Areas Talk about Cuba; Most Want the U.S. to 'Do Something,'" p. 14.

14. *New York Times*, September 26, 1962, "Soviet Trawlers to Use New Port Planned in Cuba," p. 1; *New York Times*, September 26, 1962, "Castro's Russian 'Fishing' Port," p. 1.

15. Chalmers M. Roberts, "Part of Ransom Cash for Castro Is Expected to Come from CIA," *Washington Post, Times Herald*, October 11, 1962, p. A20.

16. George Gallup, "One American in Four Favors Invasion of Cuba at This Time," *Washington Post, Times Herald*, October 14, 1962, p. A11.

17. Other reasons included the belief that it was not yet time (but would be in the future) for a military attack against Cuba, and concerns about the possibility that military action against Cuba would escalate into a war with the Soviet Union.

18. *New York Times*, October 23, 1962, "Kennedy Cancels Campaign Talks," pp. 1, 18.

19. In addition, according to Robert Kennedy (1969: 26–27), after the missiles were exposed, the dominant feeling in the administration was one of "shocked incredulity"—they felt that Chairman Khrushchev had fooled them by repeatedly denying in the previous weeks that the Soviet Union was planning to install ground-to-ground missiles in Cuba, and that their own assessment process had failed because the US intelligence and officials in the administration had assured President Kennedy that the Soviet military buildup in Cuba did not include an installation of offensive weapons and that the Soviet Union did not intend to make Cuba a strategic base.

20. *New York Times*, October 23, 1962, "Text of Kennedy's Address on Moves to Meet the Soviet Build-up in Cuba," p. 18.

21. Further, it is possible that the estimated disapproval rating of Kennedy's policy included not only people who preferred a more peaceful approach through diplomacy, but also people who thought the policy was not tough enough because it did not include a military attack against Cuba (for examples of public expressions of the latter view, see Detzer 1979: 187).

22. Transcript of Kennedy's national address was retrieved on June 3, 2020, from https://www.jfklibrary.org/learn/about-jfk/historic-speeches/address-during-the-cuban-missile-crisis.

23. Barney Popkin, "Action Justified," Letter to the *New York Times*, October 25, 1962, p. 38.

24. The Monroe Doctrine is a US foreign policy doctrine introduced by President James Monroe in his annual address to Congress on December 2, 1823, in which he declared that the Old World and the New World were two separate systems, and that any attempt by European powers to expand their influence in the Western Hemisphere would be considered "dangerous to our peace and safety" and that any form of control or oppression of independent countries in the Western Hemisphere by a European power would be considered "[a] manifestation of an unfriendly disposition toward the United States." Since Monroe's speech, these principles have been central tenets of US foreign policy. (Excerpts from the presidential address to the Congress were retrieved on May 27, 2020, from https://www.ourdocuments.gov/doc.php?flash=false&doc=23&page=transcript.)

25. The symbolic importance of positioning Soviet missiles in Cuba is likely to have been the reason Khrushchev decided to do so in the first place. Karl Mueller and coauthors explained that "the presence of Soviet nuclear weapons off the coast of the United

States allowed Khrushchev to demonstrate a point about similar American weapons in Turkey. Now the Americans, Khrushchev believed, would learn how it felt to have a knife held close to their soft underbelly" (Mueller 2006: 174). Further, the authors noted that "in concrete terms, the missiles in Cuba did improve the nuclear balance for the Soviet Union, but not dramatically" (Mueller 2006: 174). Raymond Garthoff, who participated in the crisis deliberation as a staff-level adviser in the US State Department, offered a similar interpretation, maintaining that the Soviet missiles in Cuba could not restore the balance of power between the United States and the Soviet Union. Instead, the missiles were meant to be used as leverage to pressure the United States to remove its military bases near the Soviet Union (Garthoff 1989).

26. *The Washington Post*, "Meeting the Cuban Crisis," October 23, 1962, p. A16.

27. Frank C. Newamn, Letter to the *Washington Post*, October 26, 1962, p. 18.

28. *Time* magazine, November 2, 1962, "The U.S. Puts It on the Line," pp. 34–35.

29. The Editors of Encyclopaedia Britannica, 2018, "War on Drugs," *Encyclopædia Britannica*. Available at https://www.britannica.com/topic/war-on-drugs.

30. Seymour Hersh, *New York Times*, June 12, 1986, "Panama Strongman Said to Trade In Drugs...," p. A1.

31. Stephen Engelberg, "U.S. Official Express Concern over Charges against Panamanian," *New York Times*, June 13, 1986, p. A8.

32. John Herbers, "Panama General Accused by Helms," *New York Times*, June 23, 1986, p. A3.

33. Phil Gailey, "War on Narcotics Emerging as Issue in Fall Campaigns," *New York Times*, September 9, 1986, p. A1; William Safire, "The Drug Bandwagon," *New York Times*, September 11, 1986, p. A27; Linda Greenhouse, "Congress Approves Anti-Drug Bill as Senate Bars a Death Provision," *New York Times*, October 18, 1986, p. 1.

34. Bernard Weinraub, "White House Says Reagan Plans New Campaign against Drug Use," *New York Times*, July 19, 1986, p. A1; Bernard Weinraub, "Republicans Prod the White House to Move on Drugs," *New York Times*, August 8, 1986, p. A1; Joel Brinkley, "Competing for the Last Word on Drug Abuse," *New York Times*, August 7, 1986, p. A22; Jonathan Fuerbringer, "House Approves Use of Military to Fight Drugs," *New York Times*, September 12, 1986, p. A1.

35. R. W. Apple, Jr., "Drugs Dominating Florida Campaign," *New York Times*, October 5, 1986, p. 35.

36. Bernard Weinraub, "Reagan to Press Mexico on Drug Fight, Aide Says," *New York Times*, August 12, 1986, p. A10; Gerald M. Boyd, "Drug Talks Begun with Latin Lands," *New York Times*, September 26, 1986, p. A1; William Stockton, "13 Countries Plan to Fight Drugs," *New York Times*, October 11, 1986, p. 50.

37. Joel Brinkley, "U.S. Project Said to Curb Bolivian Drugs," *New York Times*, August 6, 1986, p. B4; Joel Brinkley, "U.S. Details Plan to Combat Drugs at Mexico Border," *New York Times*, August 14, 1986, p. A1.

38. Gerald M. Boyd, "Reagan Signs Anti-Drug Measure, Hopes for 'Drug-Free Generation,'" *New York Times*, October, 28, 1986, p. B19.

39. Gerald M. Boyd, "Reagans Advocate 'Crusade' on Drugs," *New York Times*, September 15, 1986, p. A1.

40. Remarks Announcing the Review of the National Security Council's Role in the Iran Arms and Contra Aid Controversy [November 25, 1986], retrieved on June 1, 2020, from https://www.reaganlibrary.gov/research/speeches/112586a.

41. For Meese's statement, see https://www.youtube.com/watch?v=ouxJiyhCl7U.

42. Data retrieved on July 29, 2019, from *The American Presidency Project* [online], Santa Barbara, CA, https://www.presidency.ucsb.edu/statistics/data/presidential-job-approval.

43. *New York Times*, November 19, 1987, "Iran-Contra Report Says President Bears 'Ultimate Responsibility' for Wrongdoing," p. A1.

44. Stephen Engelberg, "U.S. Aides Say Panama General Proposed Sabotage in Nicaragua," *New York Times*, November 19, 1987, p. A1.

45. Philip Shenon, "Noriega Indicted by U.S. for Links to Illegal Drugs," *New York Times*, February 6, 1988, p. 1.

46. Elaine Sciolino, "Reagan Asserts He Won't Retreat on Negotiations to Oust Noriega," *New York Times*, May 18, 1988, P. A1.

47. Ibid.

48. *New York Times*, May 18, 1988, "Transcript of President's News Conference on Foreign and Domestic Issues," P. A22.

49. These figures are based on the author's search of the *New York Times* archive.

50. Text of President George H. W. Bush's address to the nation on the National Drug Control Strategy, September 5, 1989. Retrieved on July 28, 2019, from *The American Presidency Project* [online], Santa Barbara, CA, https://www.presidency.ucsb.edu/documents/address-the-nation-the-national-drug-control-strategy.

51. *New York Times*, December 21, 1989, "A Transcript of Bush's Address on the Decision to Use Force in Panama," p. A19.

52. *New York Times*, December 20, 1989, "Ordered by Bush," p. 1.

53. *New York Times*, December 23, 1989, "For Military Families, Worry, Grief, and Pride," p. 14.

54. Gallup/Newsweek Poll, December 1989; Gordon Black/USA Today Poll, December 1989; ABC News Poll, December 1989. Data were retrieved May 22, 2011, from the iPOLL Databank, The Roper Center for Public Opinion Research, University of Connecticut. http://www.ropercenter.uconn.edu/data_access/ipoll/ipoll.html.

55. ABC News Poll, December 1989; Los Angeles Times Poll, December 1989. All data were retrieved May 22, 2011, from the iPOLL Databank, The Roper Center for Public Opinion Research, University of Connecticut. http://www.ropercenter.uconn.edu/data_access/ipoll/ipoll.html.

56. *New York Times*, December 28, 1989, "Letters to the Editor," p. A22.

57. See also James Risen, "Terror Acts by Baghdad Have Waned, U.S. Aides Say," *New York Times*, February 6, 2002, p. A10.

58. Relevant excerpts from Tenet's October 7, 2002, letter to the chairman of the Senate Intelligence Committee, Bob Graham, were reported in the news. See: *New York Times*, October 9, 2020, "C.I.A Letter to Senate on Baghdad's Intentions," p. A12.

59. *New York Times*, "Words of the C.I.A. and F.B.I. Chiefs: Dangers America Faces from al Qaeda," February 12, 2003, p. A18.

60. *New York Times*, March 18, 2003, "Bush's Speech on Iraq: 'Saddam Hussein and His Sons Must Leave,'" p. A14; *New York Times*, March 20, 2003, "Bush's Speech on the Start of the War," p. A20.
61. For further discussion of the opposition to the invasion of Iraq, see Chapter 9.
62. For a discussion of the cognitive biases that might have led Americans to believe that the government of Iraq had a secret plan for manufacturing nuclear weapons and that it supported anti-American terrorism, see Cramer and Thrall (2009: 5).
63. Interview with Phillipe Duhart (resident of Bakersfield at the time).
64. Gallup/CNN/USA Today Poll, March 2003. Retrieved August 31, 2011, from the iPOLL Databank, The Roper Center for Public Opinion Research, University of Connecticut. http://www.ropercenter.uconn.edu/data_access/ipoll/ipoll.html.
65. Princeton Survey Research Associates/Newsweek Poll, March 2003. Retrieved August 31, 2011, from the iPOLL Databank, The Roper Center for Public Opinion Research, University of Connecticut. http://www.ropercenter.uconn.edu/data_acc ess/ipoll/ipoll.html.
66. NBC News/Wall Street Journal Poll, March 2003. Retrieved August 31, 2011, from the iPOLL Databank, The Roper Center for Public Opinion Research, University of Connecticut. http://www.ropercenter.uconn.edu/data_access/ipoll/ipoll.html.
67. For a more detailed discussion of the misconceptions of the American public regarding Iraq see Kull, Ramsay, and Lewis (2003).
68. Gallup/CNN/USA Today Poll, March 2003. Retrieved August 31, 2011, from the iPOLL Databank, The Roper Center for Public Opinion Research, University of Connecticut. http://www.ropercenter.uconn.edu/data_access/ipoll/ipoll.html.
69. Ibid.
70. Ibid. For a full description of the trend in public attitudes about the invasion of Iraq prior to and during the war, see Feldman, Huddy, and Marcus (2015: chap. 3).
71. *New York Times*, "The War Begins." March 20, 2003, p. A32.
72. *Wall Street Journal*, "'The Hopes of Mankind,'" March 20, 2003, p. A18.
73. *New York Times*, March 28, 2003, "Letters to the Editor," p. A16.
74. *New York Times*, March 25, 2003, "Letters to the Editor," p. A16.
75. NBC News/Wall Street Journal Poll, March 2003; ABC News/Washington Post Poll, March 2003; CBS News/New York Times Poll, March 2003; CBS News Poll, March 2003; Gallup/CNN/USA Today Poll, March 2003. Data retrieved April 20, 2011, from the iPOLL Databank, The Roper Center for Public Opinion Research, University of Connecticut. http://www.ropercenter.uconn.edu/data_access/ipoll/ipoll.html.
76. Khmer Rouge (Red Khmer) was the popular name of the Communist Party in Cambodia, which took over the government in April 1975, a few weeks before the *Mayaguez* incident.
77. John T. Woolley and Gerhard Peters, *The American Presidency Project* [online], Santa Barbara, CA, https://www.presidency.ucsb.edu/documents/remarks-the-nation-following-recovery-the-ss-mayaguez.
78. The press, however, did report these aspects of the rescue operation. See for example, John W. Finney, "No Crew Aboard," *New York Times*, May 15, 1975, p. 89; Drew Middleton, "Heavy Resistance Surprised the Marines," *New York Times*, May 16, 1975, p. 14.

79. The failed rescue operation in the Iran hostage crisis (on April 24, 1980) shows that heroic rescue operations do not become rally points when they are not successful.

80. Indeed, that era included other incidents of American ships penetrating the declared territorial waters of foreign countries (e.g., several incidents that occurred during the fishery disputes with Ecuador), but none of these led to the use of military power by the United States. These counterexamples show that the specific context of the *Mayaguez* incident was consequential for Ford's decision to order a military rescue operation. Johan Greene argued that the White House viewed the hostage situation as an opportunity to prove the nation's military power and Ford's power as a president (1995:144). When President Ford ordered the rescue operation, he might also have been thinking of a second incident: the *Pueblo* incident of 1968 in which the Democratic People's Republic of Korea (DPRK) captured a US intelligence ship (Khong 2020: 5). The ship did not fight the seizure and was released only after the United States formally admitted to and apologized for spying on the DPRK.

81. Harris Survey, May 1975. Retrieved March 17, 2011, from the iPOLL Databank, The Roper Center for Public Opinion Research, University of Connecticut. http://www.ropercenter.uconn.edu/data_access/ipoll/ipoll.html.

82. *Los Angeles Times*, May 20, 1975, "Letter to the Times," p. C6.

83. *Washington Post*, May 19, 1975, "Letters to the Editor," p. A23.

84. *Los Angeles Times*, May 20, 1975, "Letter to the Times," p. C6.

85. One final military engagement, the invasion of Lebanon in 1958, did not produce a rally-round-the-flag effect. This conflict involved neither presidential nationalist rhetoric nor the opportunity to reclaim national honor, and therefore is a much less interesting case. I describe the case in the Appendix.

86. *New York Times*, April 29, 1965, "Presidential Text," p. 14.

87. *New York Times*, May 3, 1965, "Text of Johnson's Address on Moves in the Conflict in the Dominican Republic," p. 10.

88. Ferguson (1973). See also Brands (1987) and Felten (1999).

89. Figures based on Gallup Polls. Data retrieved September 2, 2011, from the iPOLL Databank, The Roper Center for Public Opinion Research, University of Connecticut. http://www.ropercenter.uconn.edu/data_access/ipoll/ipoll.html.

90. The 1971 invasion of Laos was another major escalation of the Vietnam War, but it did not involve sending American ground forces, and thus did not become a major public issue in the United States.

91. *New York Times*, May 1, 1970, "Transcript of President's Address to the Nation on Military Action in Cambodia," p. 2.

92. Harris Survey, May, 1970. Retrieved August 26, 2011, from the iPOLL Databank, The Roper Center for Public Opinion Research, University of Connecticut. http://www.ropercenter.uconn.edu/data_access/ipoll/ipoll.html.

93. The approval ratings of the operations are based on a Harris Survey conducted in May 1970. Presidential job-approval ratings are based on Gallup Polls conducted in May and June 1970. Data retrieved August 26, 2011, from the iPOLL Databank, The Roper Center for Public Opinion Research, University of Connecticut. http://www.ropercenter.uconn.edu/data_access/ipoll/ipoll.html.

94. JEWEL is an acronym for Joint Endeavor for Welfare, Education, and Liberation.
95. *New York Times*, October 28, 1983, "Report to Nation," p. 1.
96. Ibid., p. 10.
97. Ibid., p. 1.
98. A CBS/Washington Post poll reported that following Reagan's national address, 65 percent of respondents approved of the invasion of Grenada, and the approval rating increased to 71 percent in the first week of November. However, it is likely that the actual ratings were somewhat lower, as indicated by estimates provided by Gallup/Newsweek and CBS News/New York Times polls for the same period, which were 5–6 points lower. See the following note for more on what seems to be an over-estimation trend in the CBS News/Washington Post poll.
99. There are considerable differences between the presidential job-approval ratings reported by the ABC News/Washington Post Poll and other polls. The ABC News/Washington Post Poll reported that president's job-approval rating was 54 percent before Reagan's national address on Grenada and the Beirut barracks bombing, and that it increased to 63 percent after these events. In contrast, the Gallup/Newsweek and CBS News/New York Times poll reports approval ratings of 49 percent before the address, and the CBS News/New York Times Gallup polls report approval ratings of only 48 percent and 53 percent following the address (ABC News/Washington Post Poll, October 1983; ABC News/Washington Post Poll, November 1983; CBS News/New York Times Poll, October 1983; Gallup Poll, October 1983; Gallup Poll (AIPO), October 1983. Data retrieved August 18, 2011, from the iPOLL Databank, The Roper Center for Public Opinion Research, University of Connecticut. http://www.ropercenter.uconn.edu/data_access/ipoll/ipoll.html.

    Even using the higher estimates from the CBS News/Washington Post Poll, the invasion of Grenada would be coded as a borderline rally point.
100. Critical views of this sort were expressed in many letters to the press, see for example: *Los Angeles Times*, October 28, 1983, "Letters to the Times," p. C6 (letter by Bruce A. Clark); *Los Angeles Times*, November 4, 1983, "Letters to the Times," p. F6 (letter by Jim Porter); *New York Times*, November 6, 1983, "A Failed 'Hidden Agenda' on the Americas," p. E20 (by Roy V. Jackson).
101. *Los Angeles Times*, November 11, 1983, "Letters to the Times," p. F6.
102. *New York Times*, October 30, 1983, "Letter to the Editor," p. E18.
103. *Los Angeles Times*, November 8, 1983, "'Moral Cost' of Grenada," p. C6.

Chapter 6

1. The text of Monroe's first inaugural address was retrieved from the website of *The American Presidency Project*, https://www.presidency.ucsb.edu/documents/inaugural-address-23.
2. The Editors of Encyclopaedia Britannica, "Iran Hostage Crisis." See also Farber (2009) and Bowden (2007).

3. An earlier attempt to seize the embassy occurred on February 14, 1979. The embassy was surrounded by underground guerrilla forces and taken over for a few hours until the Iranian government intervened and ended the seizure (although one Marine was held hostage for six days).

4. Peter L. Hahn, "How Jimmy Carter Lost Iran," *Washington Post*, October 22, 2017, https://www.washingtonpost.com/news/made-by-history/wp/2017/10/22/how-jimmy-carter-lost-iran/.

5. *Washington Post*, November 6, 1979, "Recklessness in Iran," p. A20.

6. Joseph Kraft, "Soft on Iran," *Washington Post*, November 6, 1979, p. A21.

7. *New York Times*, November 9, 1979, "The Stakes in Iran," p. A34.

8. *Washington Post*, November 10, 1979, "Letters to the Editor," p. 22.

9. –Terence Smith, "Carter, Denouncing Terror, Warns Iran on Hostages' Safety; Says Blackmail Won't Work Addressing A.F.L-C.I.O., He Holds Teheran Accountable for 62 Americans' Well-Being," *New York Times*, November 16, 1979, https://www.presidency.ucsb.edu/documents/american-federation-labor-and-congress-industrial-organizations-remarks-the-13th.

10. Ibid., p. A16.

11. See, for example, *New York Times*, November 21, 1979, "U.S. Warns It Has 'Other Remedies' if Diplomacy Fails on Hostages; Carrier Force Head toward Iran," p. 1; *New York Times*, November 29, 1979, "Transcript of the President's News Conference on the Crisis over the Hostages in Iran," p. A20.

12. Gallup Poll data, retrieved May 25, 2011 from the iPOLL Databank, The Roper Center for Public Opinion Research, University of Connecticut. http://www.ropercenter.uconn.edu/data_access/ipoll/ipoll.html.

13. Carter's low levels of public support were due to the nation's struggling economy (especially the growing unemployment rate and rising oil prices, which began after the 1973 Arab–Israeli War and intensified in the aftermath of the Iranian Revolution); his perceived naïveté among many politicians and laypeople in light of his emphasis on morality and universalism in foreign affairs; the political right's harsh criticism of his foreign policy as too soft (especially with respect to the Soviet Union) (Smith 1986); and disappointment among large segments of the political left (especially labor organizations, feminists, and black Americans) regarding his domestic policies, which they criticized as too conservative or making progress too slowly (Glad 1980: 437–38).

14. *New York Times*, November 16, 1979, "Transcript of President's Speech to the A.F.L-C.I.O.," p. A16.

15. Gallup Poll data, retrieved May 25, 2011, from the iPOLL Databank, The Roper Center for Public Opinion Research, University of Connecticut.

16. CNN Editorial Research, "September 11, 2001: Background and Timeline of the Attacks" (March 27, 2015). Retrieved September 23, 2020, from https://edition.cnn.com/2013/07/27/us/september-11-anniversary-fast-facts.

17. 9/11 Commission Report (2004), National Commission on Terrorist Attacks upon the United States. United States Government Publishing Office.

18. Brad Plumer, "Nine Facts about Terrorism in the United States since 9/11," *Washington Post*, September 11, 2013. Retrieved from www.washingtonpost.com/news/wonk/wp/2013/09/11/nine-facts-about-terrorism-in-the-united-states-since-911.

19. Bin Laden denied this accusation. Three years later, on October 30, 2004, in an 18-minute recorded address to the American people that was broadcast on the Qatar-based international al-Jazeera TV network, bin Laden admitted that he was responsible for the September 11 attacks (BBC News, "Excerpts: Bin Laden video": http://news.bbc.co.uk/2/hi/middle_east/3966817.stm.

20. *New York Times*, September 12, 2001, "Dispatches from a Day of Terror and Shock," p. A26.

21. Elisabeth Bumiller and David E. Sanger, "A Day of Terror: The President; a Somber Bush Says Terrorism Cannot Prevail," *New York Times*, September 12, p. A1.

22. CNN Editorial Research, "1993 World Trade Center Bombing Fast Facts." Retrieved September 23, 2020, from https://edition.cnn.com/2013/11/05/us/1993-world-trade-center-bombing-fast-facts/index.html.

23. Following his arrest in 1995, Ramzi Yousef, one of the main conspirators, confessed that the group's plan was to topple one of the towers in the hope that it would fall on the other tower and topple it as well, which would have killed an enormous number of people; however, that intent was not publicly known in the immediate aftermath of the attack (J. Gilmore Childers, Henry J. DePippo, "Terrorists in America: Five Years after the World Trade Center," February 24, 1998. Hearing before the US Senate Judiciary Committee, Subcommittee on Technology, Terrorism, and Government Information. Retrieved April 26, 2020, from https://web.archive.org/web/20071227065444/http://judiciary.senate.gov/oldsite/childers.htm).

24. *New York Times*, February 28, 1993, "Impact Expanding," p. 34.

25. An estimate provided by a CBS/NYT public opinion poll.

26. An estimate provided by a Gallup/CNN/USA opinion poll.

27. Years later, al-Zawahiri became the leader of al-Qaeda after the death of Osama bin Laden.

28. *New York Times*, August 8, 1998, "Clinton Pledges Hunt for Those Responsible," p. A8.

29. *New York Times*, August 21, 1998, "Clinton's Words: 'There Will Be No Sanctuary for Terrorists,'" p. A12.

30. Gallup Poll, August 1998. Retrieved Sep-1-2011 from the iPOLL Databank, The Roper Center for Public Opinion Research, University of Connecticut. http://www.ropercenter.uconn.edu/data_access/ipoll/ipoll.html.

31. It is reasonable to expect that sending ground troops to "clear out" terrorist sanctuaries might have resulted in a stronger rally effect; however, there is no way to test this hypothesis.

32. Further, in the absence of a rally effect, about a third of the public believed that one of the reasons Clinton decided to order the strike was to shift public attention away from the Monica Lewinsky scandal Gallup Poll, August 1998; ABC News Poll, August 1998; Pew News Interest Index Poll, August 1998; Los Angeles Times Poll, August 1998. Data retrieved September 1, 2011, from the iPOLL Databank, The Roper Center for Public Opinion Research, University of Connecticut. http://www.ropercenter.uconn.edu/data_access/ipoll/ipoll.html.

33. *New York Times*, January 31, 1988, "Tet Offensive: Turning Point in Vietnam War." Retrieved September 23, 2020, from https://www.nytimes.com/1988/01/31/world/tet-offensive-turning-point-in-vietnam-war.html.

34. *New York Times*, October 25, 1983, "Transcript of President Reagan's News Conference on the Attack in Beirut," p. A10.

35. *New York Times*, October 28, 1983, "Transcript of Address by President on Lebanon and Grenada," p. A10.

36. There is an intriguing caveat to this initial assessment—the fact that sitting presidents did not use nationalist rhetoric when discussing attacks on US military targets raises the possibility of a reverse rally process: perhaps administrations choose not to accentuate successful attacks against US military targets because such attacks make the military look weak and incapable of protecting even its own forces. In other words, whereas attacks on civilians are considered an illegitimate method of war and thus can be used to propagate nationalist sentiment, attacks on military installations are an expected part of armed conflict and military missions, and thus when these attacks succeed the government may choose to minimize them to reduce public criticism.

Chapter 7

1. Retrieved on June 21, 2020, from https://www.reaganlibrary.gov/archives/speech/inaugural-address-1981.

2. The final weeks of the 1984 presidential election campaign saw a steady increase in Reagan's job-ojapproval ratings, which reached about 63 percent following his second inauguration but then quickly dropped back to the low 50s.

3. I do not discuss the three attacks on US embassies (two in Lebanon and one in Kuwait) in this chapter, but the fact that none became a rally-point aligns with the chapter's main argument that rallies emerge only if the president's rhetoric has a nationalist tone and points to a clear enemy as the target of military retaliation. Reagan's reaction to each of these attacks was relatively mellow, did not convey a nationalist message, and did not point to a clear enemy.

4. Sources provide different estimates of the number of Americans on board, ranging from 82 to 135.

5. The hijackers' other demands were "the release of two Shia Muslims held by Spanish authorities for shooting a Libyan diplomat, the release of seventeen Shia Muslim imprisoned in Kuwait for a series of six bombing attacks in December 1983, an end to Arab world oil and arms transactions with the United States, a removal of US navy ships from the Lebanese coast prior to the hostages' release, and a pledge that the United States and Israel would not retaliate once the situation was resolved" (Winkler 2006: 66).

6. –*Los Angeles Times*, June 19, 1985, "'Rescue Us and We Die,' Pilot Warns from Cockpit," p. 1. Neither the *New York Times* nor the *Washington Post* reported this incident, perhaps because their editors did not want to be accused of helping the terrorists spread their message or placing pressure on the American public and decision-makers.

7. Ibid.

8. *Washington Post*, June 19, 1985, "Transcript of President Reagan's News Conference," p. A16.
9. On Amal and the Shi'a in Lebanon, see Norton and Binder (1987).
10. *Los Angeles Times*, June 19, 1985, "Reagan: No Negotiations with Shia Muslim Captors," pp. 1, 13.
11. Data were retrieved August 18, 2011, from *The American Presidency Project*, University of California, Santa Barbara, http://www.presidency.ucsb.edu/data/pop ularity.php?pres=40&sort=time&direct=DESC&Submit=DISPLAY.
12. According to Jonathan Bearman (1986: 288), sources within the administration confirmed that the raid was intended to kill Qaddafi. Moreover, according to Dennis Piszkiewicz (2003: 66), "President Reagan's address contained a few paragraphs that were never made public. They were to be read if U.S. sources could confirm that Qaddafi had been killed in the raid."
13. Time/Yankelovich Clancy Shulman Poll, April 1986. Retrieved August 18, 2011, from the iPOLL Databank, The Roper Center for Public Opinion Research, University of Connecticut. http://www.ropercenter.uconn.edu/data_access/ipoll/ipoll.html.

Chapter 8

1. Cited in Kalb, Peters, and Woolley (2006: 70).
2. Data retrieved September 23, 2009, from the Roper Center for Public Opinion Research, https://ropercenter.cornell.edu/presidential-approval/.
3. Technically, President Truman ordered the US air and sea forces to assist South Korea on June 26, 1950, one day before the UN Security Council passed Resolution 83, which recommended that member states provide military assistance to South Korea (Fisher 1995).
4. *Washington Post*, July 9, 1950, "Letters to the Editor," p. B4.
5. *Washington Post*, July 4, 1950, "Letters to the Editor," p. 8.
6. *New York Times*, July 1, 1950, "Letters to the Times," p. 9.
7. Estimate was retrieved August 18, 2011, from *The American Presidency Project*, University of California, Santa Barbara, http://www.presidency.ucsb.edu/data/pop ularity.php?pres=33&sort=time&direct=DESC&Submit=DISPLAY.
8. Congressional Research Service, "American War and Military Operations Casualties: Lists and Statistics" (p. 2). Retrieved July 19, 2021, from https://fas.org/sgp/crs/natsec/RL32492.pdf.
9. Harry S. Truman, Statement by the President on the Violation of the 38th Parallel in Korea. Online by Gerhard Peters and John T. Woolley. Retrieved July 19, 2021, from *The American Presidency Project*, https://www.presidency.ucsb.edu/node/230840.
10. Harry S. Truman, Statement by the President on the Situation in Korea. Online by Gerhard Peters and John T. Woolley. Retrieved July 19, 2021, from *The American Presidency Project*, https://www.presidency.ucsb.edu/node/230845.

11. John T. Woolley and Gerhard Peters, *The American Presidency Project*, Santa Barbara, CA, http://www.presidency.ucsb.edu/ws/?pid=13544 (retrieved August 10, 2011). See also Brewer (2011: 149).

12. John T. Woolley and Gerhard Peters, *The American Presidency Project*, Santa Barbara, CA, http://www.presidency.ucsb.edu/ws/?pid=13544.

13. The UN Security Council passed several additional resolutions shortly after the passage of Resolution 660: On August 8, 1990, Resolution 661 authorized the imposition of economic sanctions on Iraq. On August 25, Resolution 665 authorized a naval blockade of Iraq to enforce the economic sanctions. On November 29, Resolution 678 issued an ultimatum for Iraq to withdraw its forces from Kuwait by January 15, and empowered member states to use "all necessary means" to enforce this resolution.

14. Several researchers have developed interesting analyses of Bush's determination to intervene. John Mueller (1994: 51–52) argued that as the crisis in the Persian Gulf unfolded, Bush, who until then was known for being a politician who preferred compromise over confrontation, had gradually developed a conviction that standing against Iraq could save the world from serious future troubles. As evidence, Mueller pointed to Bush's frequent comparison of the situation in the Persian Gulf to the rise of the Nazi regime in Germany. Others have suggested that Bush's main concerns were the damage that the Iraqi conquest of Kuwait (which held almost 10 percent of the world's oil reserves) would inflict on the West's economy, and the balance of power in the Middle East (Lewis 2018: 327). A more critical reading of Bush's strategy might suggest that his true concern was not so much saving the world, the West, or the Middle East, but rather protecting the oil interests of the United States (and arguably the interests of the oil industry his family was part of) by preventing Iraq from becoming the overlord of the world's oil supply (Gardner 2010; Kellner 1992). Other possible motivations for the decision to use military power against Iraq include the desire to prove that the United States was the only world superpower after the collapse of the Soviet Union or to justify the maintenance of an enormous security budget even though the Cold War was over, the wish to distract the public from an economic crisis at home and from Bush's other failed domestic policies, and Bush's personal desire to overcome his image as a "wimp" (Kellner 1992).

15. R. W. Apple, Jr., "U.S. Says Its Troops in the Gulf Could Reach 100,000 in Months," *New York Times*. August 11, 1990, p. 1.

16. Retrieved July 19, 2021, from the American Rhetoric Online Speech Bank, https://www.americanrhetoric.com/speeches/georgehwbushkuwaitinvasion.htm.

17. *Washington Post*, August 8, 1990, "To Rescue Kuwait," p. A20.

18. Thomas L. Friedman. "No Compromise on Kuwait, Bush Says," *New York Times*, October 24, 1990, p. A10.

19. Years later, this analogy was used again, especially by neoconservative politicians, to justify the invasion of Iraq in 2003 (Brewer 2011: 5; Zulaika 2009).

20. Gallup/Newsweek Polls, November 1990, December 1990, January 1991. Retrieved September 3, 2011, from the iPOLL Databank, The Roper Center for Public Opinion Research, University of Connecticut, http://www.ropercenter.uconn.edu/data_access/ipoll/ipoll.html.

21. Los Angeles Times Poll, January 1991. Retrieved August 6, 2011, from the iPOLL Databank, The Roper Center for Public Opinion Research, University of Connecticut, http://www.ropercenter.uconn.edu/data_access/ipoll/ipoll.html.

22. *Wall Street Journal*, January 19, 1991, "Letters to the Editor," p. A9.

23. *Wall Street Journal*, January 25, 1991, "Letters to the Editor," p. A13.

24. Transcript of George H. W. Bush's remarks to the American Legislative Exchange Council, retrieved on June 26, 2018, from *The American Presidency Project*, Santa Barbara, CA, http://www.presidency.ucsb.edu/ws/?pid=19351.

25. A counterfactual test of this interpretation would entail speculating about how the public would have reacted had Bush launched a military attack against Iraq without the support of the international community. Under such circumstances, it is likely that a significant portion of the US public would have opposed the war, because rather than inciting nationalist emotions of pride, confidence, and hope, going to war to save a foreign country would have resurrected memories of Vietnam.

26. *New York Times*, December 5, 1992, "Transcript of President's Address on Somalia," p. 4.

27. CBS News/New York Times Poll, December 1992. Retrieved March 19, 2011, from the iPOLL Databank, The Roper Center for Public Opinion Research, University of Connecticut, http://www.ropercenter.uconn.edu/data_access/ipoll/ipoll.html. For review of public opinion on the intervention in Somalia, see Klarevas (2000).

28. Interestingly, public opinion polls show that shortly before the military operation in Haiti was supposed to begin, about 55 percent of Americans approved of the way President Clinton was handling the situation in Haiti. However, soon after an agreement was reached, the support rate declined by about 10 percent (ABC News Poll, September 1994; CBS News/New York Times Poll, September 1994; Washington Post Poll, September 1994; PSRA/Newsweek Poll, September 1994. All data retrieved March 19, 2011, from the iPOLL Databank, The Roper Center for Public Opinion Research, University of Connecticut, http://www.ropercenter.uconn.edu/data_access/ipoll/ipoll.html). These findings suggest that reaching an agreement that prevented the United States from demonstrating its supreme military power eroded public support for Clinton's policy, even though the political objective of restoring democracy in Haiti was achieved.

Chapter 9

1. *New York Times*, September 12, 2001, "Dispatches from a Day of Terror and Shock," p. A26.

2. *New York Times*, March 28, 2003, "Letters to the Editor," p. A16.

3. Gallup/CNN/USA Today Poll # 2003–19: US at War, March 22–23, 2003.

4. The research design accounts for the significant differences between data sources: the Gallup poll and the first round of TNSS contain only a few questions about individuals' emotions. Thus, in the first stage of the analysis these data are analyzed using conventional regressions. In the second stage, structural equations are estimated

to analyze the second and third rounds of TNSS data because they contain sets of questions about emotions, thus allowing for robust estimation of their effects. The final stage utilizes longitudinal data from TNSS, which due to data limitations cannot reveal much about emotional changes but do expose a shift in national identification during the decline of the rally effect of the September 11 attacks.

5. The statistical models included only control variables that were statistically significant in a preliminary analysis; however, re-running the analysis with the omitted non-significant control variables did not change the results.

6. Gallup, CNN, and USA Today 2001 (September).

7. CBS News and New York Times 2001 (September).

8. CBS News, and New York Times 2001 (September); Gallup 2001 (September); Gallup, CNN, and USA Today 2001 (September).

9. In a preliminary step, confirmatory factor analysis (CFA) via Stata was used to check whether the data support the anticipated latent factors. The results confirmed my expectations about the latent factors and their indicators. I used EQS to estimate structural equation models.

   All but three of the variables used in this step of the analysis follow the conventional form of public opinion scales with four degrees of response. The three variables that measure respondents' approval/disapproval of the way the president was handling his job, the economy, and the situation in Iraq are binary variables, coded "1" for "approve" and "0" for "disapprove." These variables serve as indicators in the dependent latent variable, "support for the president."

10. Models were estimated using the arbitrary distribution generalized least squares (AGLS) method and the Lee-Poon-Bentler technique of estimating correlations among ordinal variables. Each of the variables had only a few missing observations, but because list-wise deletion would have resulted in the loss of about half of the cases, pair-wise deletion was used. All models were re-estimated using the maximum-likelihood method with the Jamshidian-Bentler EM-type missing data procedure. The differences in the estimates produced by the two methods are minimal.

11. Because only a few of the relevant questions asked in Wave 1 were asked in a consistent format in the later waves, any evidence offered in this section is rather partial.

12. Only about one percent of respondents moved from disapproval to approval of the president's work.

13. For the same reason, two control variables—income and gender—were also dropped from the model.

14. As an additional test, I estimated fixed-effects models (results not shown). All findings were similar to those reported in Figure 9.16, with one exception: the coefficient for anger toward those who criticized the United States was not statistically significant.

15. House and Senate votes on a bill authorizing the president to use military power against Iraq (which was passed in 2002) highlighted the controversial character of the invasion of Iraq: 39 percent of Democratic congresspeople and 58 percent of Democratic senators supported the bill, compared to 97 percent of Republican

congresspeople and 98 percent of Republican senators (Jacobson 2010: 590). By contrast, on September 18, 2001, a bill authorizing military action in Afghanistan or against any countries, groups, or individuals involved in terrorist activities directed at the United States passed with almost unanimous support among members of both parties (420–1 in the House and 98–0 in the Senate).

16. For a discussion of this division within American nationalism, see Lieven (2004).

17. Elisabeth Bumiller and David E. Sanger, "A Day of Terror: The President; a Somber Bush Says Terrorism Cannot Prevail," *New York Times*, September 12, p. A1.

18. Data on the presidential approval rating were retrieved from *The American Presidency Project* [online], Santa Barbara, CA, https://www.presidency.ucsb.edu/statistics/data/presidential-job-approval.

19. Indeed, as Brewer noted, official narratives of a conflict can provoke contention rather than unifying the nation precisely because they draw on the idea of a chosen people with a global mission (Brewer 2011: 9).

20. This chapter is adapted from "Applying Sociological Theories of Emotions to the Study of Mass Politics: The Rally-Round-the-Flag Phenomenon in the United States as a Test Case," which was published in *Sociological Quarterly* (Feinstein 2020).

CONCLUSION

1. See also Tim Johnston's February 13, 2008, article, "Australia Says 'Sorry' to Aborigines for Mistreatment," *New York Times*, retrieved from http://www.nytimes.com/2008/02/13/world/asia/13aborigine.html.

2. Figures are based on Newspoll data retrieved in June 2015 from http://polling.newspoll.com.au/cgi-bin/polling//display_poll_data.pl?mode=trend&page=continue_results&question_id=2420&url_caller=trend.

3. Rudd's predecessor, John Howard, had refused to issue an official apology to the Aboriginal people despite growing public demand for the government to acknowledge this dark period in Australia's history (Rule and Rice 2015; Wilkie 1997; Reed 2006). Howard justified his reluctance by claiming that current Australians were not responsible for the wrongdoings of the past (Auguste 2010), and the wrongs of one particular period should not make Australians regret their grand national history (Short 2012: 298).

Appendix

1. *Washington Post*, July 16, 1958, "President's Statement on Action in Lebanon," p. A6.

2. Other supporting conditions for a rally were also absent in the case of the intervention in Lebanon, especially a widespread feeling of national humiliation or a call from the United Nations for the United States to intervene in Lebanon.

3. Data for the figures were retrieved on July 6, 2021, from *The American Presidency Project*, https://www.presidency.ucsb.edu/statistics/data/presidential-job-approval. In addition to raw poll estimates, Appendix Figures A1–A13 show moving averages to overcome occasional sampling errors and ensure that what seems to be a significant shift in public opinion represents a true shift.

References

Aday, Sean. 2010. "Leading the Charge: Media, Elites, and the Use of Emotion in Stimulating Rally Effects in Wartime." *Journal of Communication* 60(3): 440–65.

Adolphs, Ralph, and Daniel Tranel. 1999. "Preferences for Visual Stimuli Following Amygdala Damage." *Journal of Cognitive Neuroscience* 11(6): 610–16.

Adut, Ari. 2018. *Reign of Appearances: The Misery and Splendor of the Public Sphere.* Cambridge, UK: Cambridge University Press.

Alexander, Jeffrey C. 2004. "From the Depths of Despair: Performance, Counterperformance, and 'September 11.'" *Sociological Theory* 22(1): 88–105.

Alin, Erika G. 1994. *The United States and the 1958 Lebanon Crisis: American Intervention in the Middle East.* Lanham, MD: University Press of America.

Althaus, Scott L. 2008. "Free Falls, High Dives, and the Future of Democratic Accountability." In *The Politics of News: The News of Politics*, edited by Doris Graber, Denis McQuail, and Pippa Noris, 161–89. Washington, DC: Congressional Quarterly Press.

Aminzade, Ronald R., and Doug McAdam. 2001. "Emotions and Contentious Politics." In *Silence and Voice in the Study of Contentious Politics*, edited by Ronald R. Aminzade, Jack A. Goldstone, Doug McAdam, Elizabeth J. Perry, William H. Sewell Jr, Sidney Tarrow, and Charles Tilly, 14–50. Cambridge, UK: Cambridge University Press.

Anderson, Benedict R. 1991. *Imagined Communities: Reflections on the Origin and Spread of Nationalism*, revised and extended edition. London; New York: Verso.

Antonsich, Marco. 2016. "The 'Everyday' of Banal Nationalism: Ordinary People's Views on Italy and Italian." *Political Geography* 54: 32–42.

Auguste, Isabelle. 2010. "Rethinking the Nation: Apology, Treaty and Reconciliation in Australia." *National Identities* 12(4): 425–36.

Baekgaard, Martin, Julian Christensen, Jonas Krogh Madsen, and Kim Sass Mikkelsen. 2020. "Rallying around the Flag in Times of Covid-19: Societal Lockdown and Trust in Democratic Institutions." *Journal of Behavioral Public Administration* 3(2): 1–12.

Baker, W. D., and J. R. Oneal. 2001. "Patriotism or Opinion Leadership? The Nature and Origins of the 'Rally 'round the Flag' Effect." *Journal of Conflict Resolution* 45(5): 661–87.

Bar-Tal, Daniel. 2013. *Intractable Conflicts: Socio-Psychological Foundations and Dynamics.* Cambridge, UK: Cambridge University Press.

Barta, Tony. 2008. "Sorry, and Not Sorry, in Australia: How the Apology to the Stolen Generations Buried a History of Genocide." *Journal of Genocide Research* 10(2): 201–14.

Baum, Matthew A. 2002. "The Constituent Foundations of the Rally-Round-the-Flag Phenomenon." *International Studies Quarterly* 46(2): 263–98.

Baum, Matthew A. 2004. "How Public Opinion Constrains the Use of Force: The Case of Operation Restore Hope." *Presidential Studies Quarterly* 34(2): 187–226.

Baum, Matthew A., and Tim Groeling. 2005. "What Gets Covered?: How Media Coverage of Elite Debated Drives the Rally-'round-the-Flag Phenomenon, 1979–1998." in *In the Public Domain: Presidents and the Challanges of Public Leadership*, edited by L. C. Han and D. Heith, 49–72. Albany: State University of New York Press.

Baum, Matthew, and Tim J. Groeling. 2010. *War Stories: The Causes and Consequences of Public Views of War*. Princeton, NJ: Princeton University Press.

Baum, Matthew A., and Philip B. K. Potter. 2008. "The Relationships between Mass Media, Public Opinion, and Foreign Policy: Toward a Theoretical Synthesis." *Annual Review of Political Science* 11: 39–65.

Baum, Matthew A., and Philip B. K. Potter. 2015. *War and Democratic Constraint*. Princeton, NJ: Princeton University Press.

Baylouny, Anne Marie. 2009. "US Foreign Policy in Lebanon." Faculty and Researcher Publications. Calhoun: Institutional Archive of the Naval Postgraduate School.

Beamish, Thomas D., Harvey Molotch, and Richard Flacks. 1995. "Who Supports the Troops? Vietnam, the Gulf War, and the Making of Collective Memory." *Social Problems* 42(3): 344–60.

Bearman, Jonathan. 1986. *Qadhafi's Libya*. London: Zed Books.

Bechara, Antoine, Antonio R. Damasio, Hanna Damasio, and Steven W. Anderson. 1994. "Insensitivity to Future Consequences Following Damage to Human Prefrontal Cortex." *Cognition* 50(1–3): 7–15.

Bechara, Antoine, Hanna Damasio, and Antonio R. Damasio. 2000. "Emotion, Decision Making and the Orbitofrontal Cortex." *Cerebral Cortex* 10(3): 295–307.

Beijen, Marijne, Simon Otjes, and Peter Kanne. 2021. "Rally 'round the Prime Minister: A Study into the Effects of a Diplomatic Conflict on Public Opinion under Coalition Government." *Acta Politica*: 1–22. (Online first)Benford, Robert D., and David A. Snow. 2000. "Framing Processes and Social Movements: An Overview and Assessment." *Annual Review of Sociology* 26: 611–39.

Bennett, W. Lance. 1990. "Toward a Theory of Press-State." *Journal of Communication* 40(2): 103–27.

Bennett, W. Lance. 1994. "The News about Foreign Policy." In *Taken by Storm: The Media, Public Opinion, and US Foreign Policy in the Gulf War*, edited by W. L. Bennett and D. L. Paletz, 12–42. Chicago and London: University of Chicago Press.

Bennett, W. L., and David L. Paletz, eds. 1994. *Taken by Storm: The Media, Public Opinion, and Us Foreign Policy in the Gulf War*. Chicago and London: University of Chicago Press.

Berezin, Mabel. 2002. "Secure States: Toward a Political Sociology of Emotions." In *Emotions and Sociology*, edited by J. Barbalet, 33–52. Oxford: Blackwell.

Berinsky, Adam J. 2007. "Assuming the Costs of War: Events, Elites, and American Public Support for Military Conflict." *The Journal of Politics* 69(04): 975–97.

Berinsky, Adam J. 2009. *In Time of War: Understanding American Public Opinion from World War II to Iraq*. Chicago and London: University of Chicago Press.

Billig, Michael. 1995. *Banal Nationalism*. London: Sage.

Blais, André, Damien Bol, Marco Giani, and Peter Loewen. 2020. "Covid-19 Lockdowns Have Increased Support for Incumbent Parties and Trust in Government." *British Politics and Policy at LSE*. http://eprints.lse.ac.uk/104895/.

Blinder, Scott B. 2007. "Going Public, Going to Baghdad: Presidential Agenda-Setting and the Electoral Connection in Congress." In *The Polarized Presidency of George W. Bush*, edited by George C. Edwards III and Desmond King, 325–50. Oxford: Oxford University Press.

Bliss, Stacy L., Eun Jong Oh, and Robert L. Williams. 2007. "Militarism and Sociopolitical Perspectives among College Students in the U.S. and South Korea." *Peace and Conflict* 13(2): 175–99.

Bonikowski, Bart. 2013. "Varieties of Popular Nationalism in Modern Democracies: An Inductive Approach to Comparative Research on Political Culture." Weatherhead Center for International Affairs, Cambridge.

Bonikowski, Bart. 2016. "Nationalism in Settled Times." *Annual Review of Sociology* 42: 427–49.

Bonikowski, Bart, and Paul DiMaggio. 2016. "Varieties of American Popular Nationalism." *American Sociological Review* 81(5): 949–80.

Bonikowski, Bart, Yuval Feinstein, and Sean Bock. 2021. "The Partisan Sorting of 'America': How Nationalist Cleavages Shaped the 2016 US Presidential Election." *American Journal of Sociology* 127(2): 492–561.

Bowden, Mark. 2007. *Guests of the Ayatollah: The Iran Hostage Crisis: The First Battle in America's War with Militant Islam.* New York: Grove/Atlantic.

Brace, Paul, and Barbara Hinckley. 1992. *Follow the Leader: Opinion Polls and the Modern Presidents.* New York: BasicBooks.

Brands, H. W., Jr. 1987. "Decisions on American Armed Intervention: Lebanon, Dominican Republic, and Grenada." *Political Science Quarterly* 102(4): 607–24.

Brecher, Michael, and Jonathan Wilkenfeld. 1997. *A Study of Crisis.* Ann Arbor: The University of Michigan Press.

Brewer, Susan A. 2011. *Why America Fights: Patriotism and War Propaganda from the Philippines to Iraq.* Oxford: Oxford University Press.

Brody, Richard A. 1991. *Assessing the President: The Media, Elite Opinion, and Public Support.* Stanford, CA: Stanford University Press.

Brody, Richard A. 1994. "Crisis, War, and Public Opinion." In *Taken by Storm: The Media, Public Opinion, and U.S. Foreign Policy in the Gulf War,* edited by L. W. Bennett and D. L. Paletz, 210–27. Chicago and London: University of Chicago Press.

Brody, Richard A. 2002. "The American People and President Bush." *The Forum* 1(1): Article 5.

Brubaker, R. 2004. "In the Name of the Nation: Reflections on Nationalism and Patriotism." *Citizenship Studies* 8: 115–27.

Brubaker, Rogers. 2006. *Nationalist Politics and Everyday Ethnicity in a Transylvanian Town.* Princeton, NJ: Princeton University Press.

Brugioni, Dino A. 1991. *Eyeball to Eyeball: The Inside Story of the Cuban Missile Crisis.* New York: Random House.

Burgess, Stephen F. 2002. "Operation Restore Hope: Somalia and the Frontiers of the New World Order." In *From Cold War to New World Order: The Foreign Policy of George H. W. Bush,* edited by M. Bose and R. Perotti, 259–73. Westport, CT: Greenwood Press.

Burke, Peter J. 1991. "Identity Processes and Social Stress." *American Sociological Review* 56(6): 836–49.

Busch, Andrew. 2001. *Ronald Reagan and the Politics of Freedom.* Lanham, MD: Rowman & Littlefield.

Byrne, Malcolm. 2014. *Iran-Contra: Reagan's Scandal and the Unchecked Abuse of Presidential Power.* Lawrence, Kansas: University Press of Kansas.

Bytzek, Evelyn. 2011. "Questioning the Obvious: Political Events and Public Opinion on the Government's Standing in Germany 1977–2003." *International Journal of Public Opinion Research* 23(4): 406–36.

Cainkar, Louis A. 2009. *Homeland Insecurity: The Arab American and Muslim American Experience after 9/11.* New York: Russell Sage Foundation.

Cannon, Lou. 1991. *President Reagan: The Role of a Lifetime.* New York: Simon & Schuster.

Carey, James W. 2002. "American Journalism on, before, and after September 11." In *Journalism after September 11*, edited by Barbie Zelizer and Stuart Allan, 71–90. New York and London: Routledge.

Casey, Steven. 2001. *Cautious Crusade: Franklin D. Roosevelt, American Public Opinion, and the War against Nazi Germany*. Oxford: Oxford University Press.

Casey, Steven. 2008. *Selling the Korean War: Propaganda, Politics, and Public Opinion in the United States, 1950–1953*. Oxford and New York: Oxford University Press.

Cerulo, Karen A. 2010. "Mining the Intersections of Cognitive Sociology and Neuroscience." *Poetics* 38(2): 115–32.

Chanley, Virginia A. 2002. "Trust in Government in the Aftermath of 9/11: Determinants and Consequences." *Political Psychology* 23(3): 469–83.

Chapman, Terrence L., and Dan Reiter. 2004. "The United Nations Security Council and the Rally 'round the Flag Effect." *Journal of Conflict Resolution* 48(6): 886–909.

Clore, Gerald L., Karen Gasper, and Erika Garvin. 2000. "Affect as Information." In *Handbook of Affect and Social Cognition*, edited by J. P. Ford, 121–45. Mahwah, NJ: Lawrence Erlbaum Associates.

Collins, Randall. 2004. "Rituals of Solidarity and Security in the Wake of Terrorist Attack." *Sociological Theory* 22(1): 53–87.

Collins, Randall. 2012. "Time-Bubbles of Nationalism: Dynamics of Solidarity Ritual in Lived Time." *Nations and Nationalism* 18(3): 383–97.

Cramer, Jane K., and A. Trevor Thrall. 2009. "Introduction: Understanding Threat Inflation." In *American Foreign Policy and the Politics of Fear: Threat Inflation since 9/11*, edited by A. Trevor Thrall and Jane K. Cramer, 19–33. New York: Routledge.

Crowson, H. Michael. 2009. "Nationalism, Internationalism, and Perceived UN Irrelevance: Mediators of Relationships between Authoritarianism and Support for Military Aggression as Part of the War on Terror." *Journal of Applied Social Psychology* 39(5): 1137–62.

Cumings, Bruce. 1994. *War and Television*. London and New York: Verso.

Dayan, Daniel, and Elihu Katz. 1992. *Media Events*. Cambridge, MA: Harvard University Press.

Denich, Bette. 1994. "Dismembering Yugoslavia: Nationalist Ideologies and the Symbolic Revival of Genocide." *American Ethnologist* 21(2): 367–90.

Detzer, David. 1979. *The Brink: Cuban Missile Crisis, 1962*. New York: Crowell.

Diamond, Larry. 2015. "Facing up to the Democratic Recession." *Journal of Democracy* 26(1): 141–55.

Dockrill, Saki. 1996. *Eisenhower's New-Look National Security Policy, 1953–61*. New York: St. Martin's Press.

Donnelly, Jack. 2000. *Realism and International Relations*. Cambridge, UK: Cambridge University Press.

Dorman, William A., and Steven Livingston. 1994. "News and Historical Content: The Establishing Phase of the Persian Gulf Policy Debate." In *Taken by Storm: The Media, Public Opinion, and Us Foreign Policy in the Gulf War*, edited by W. L. Bennett and D. L. Paletz, 63–81. Chicago and London: University of Chicago Press.

Druckman, James N. 2001. "The Implications of Framing Effects for Citizen Competence." *Political Behavior* 23(3): 225–56.

Druckman, James N., and Rose McDermott. 2008. "Emotion and the Framing of Risky Choice." *Political Behavior* 30(3): 297–321.

Edwards, George C., and Tami Swenson. 1997. "Who Rallies? The Anatomy of a Rally Event." *The Journal of Politics* 59(1): 200–12.

Ehrenreich, Barbara. 2011. *Blood Rites: Origins and History of the Passions of War.* London, UK: Granta Books.

Eichenberg, Richard C. 2005. "Victory Has Many Friends: US Public Opinion and the Use of Military Force, 1981–2005." *International Security* 30(1): 140–77.

Eichenberg, Richard C., Richard J. Stoll, and Matthew Lebo. 2006. "War President: The Approval Ratings of George W. Bush." *Journal of Conflict Resolution* 50(6): 783–808.

Elwood, William N. 1994. *Rhetoric in the War on Drugs: The Triumphs and Tragedies of Public Relations.* Westport, CT: Praeger.

Emirbayer, Mustafa, and Chad A. Goldberg. 2005. "Pragmatism, Bourdieu, and Collective Emotions in Contentious Politics." *Theory and Society* 34(5–6): 469–518.

Entman, Robert M. 2003. "Cascading Activation: Contesting the White House's Frame after 9/11." *Political Communication* 20(4): 415–32.

Entman, Robert M., and Benjamin I. Page. 1994. "The News before the Storm: The Iraq War Debate and the Limits to Media Independence." In *The Gulf War, the Media, and US Foreign Policy*, edited by Tom Mayer and Edward S. Greenberg, 82–101. Chicago: University of Chicago Press.

Erlich, Aaron, and Calvin Garner. 2021. "Subgroup Differences in Implicit Associations and Explicit Attitudes during Wartime." *International Studies Quarterly* 65(2): 528–41.

Esaiasson, Peter, Jacob Sohlberg, Marina Ghersetti, and Bengt Johansson. 2020. "How the Coronavirus Crisis Affects Citizen Trust in Institutions and in Unknown Others: Evidence from 'the Swedish Experiment.'" *European Journal of Political Research* 60: 748–60.

Falleti, Tulia G., and James Mahoney. 2015. "The Comparative Sequential Method." *Advances in Comparative-Historical Analysis*, edited by James Mahoney and Kathleen Thelen, 211–39. Cambridge, UK: Cambridge University Press.

Farber, David. 2009. *Taken Hostage: The Iran Hostage Crisis and America's First Encounter with Radical Islam.* Princeton, NJ: Princeton University Press.

Fearon, James D. 1994. "Domestic Political Audiences and the Escalation of International Disputes." *American Political Science Review* 88(3): 577–92.

Feinstein, Yuval. 2016a. "Rallying around the President: When and Why Do Americans Close Ranks behind Their Presidents during International Crisis and War?" *Social Science History* 40(2): 305–38.

Feinstein, Yuval. 2016b. "Pulling the Trigger: How Threats to the Nation Increase Support for Military Action via the Generation of Hubris." *Sociological Science* 3: 317–34.

Feinstein, Yuval. 2017. "The Rise and Decline of 'Gender Gaps' in Support for Military Action: United States, 1986–2011." *Politics & Gender* 13(4): 618–55.

Feinstein, Yuval. 2018. "One Flag, Two Rallies: Mechanisms of Public Opinion in Israel during the 2014 Gaza War." *Social Science Research* 69: 65–82.

Feinstein, Yuval, and Uri Ben-Eliezer. 2019. "Failed Peace and the Decline in Liberalism in Israel: A Spiral Model." *Mediterranean Politics* 24(5): 568–91.

Feinstein, Yuval, and Bart Bonikowski. 2021. "Nationalist Narratives and Anti-Immigrant Attitudes: Exceptionalism and Collective Victimhood in Contemporary Israel." *Journal of Ethnic and Migration Studies* 47(3): 741–61.

Feinstein, Yuval. 2020. "Applying Sociological Theories of Emotions to the Study of Mass Politics: The Rally-round-the-Flag Phenomenon in the United States as a Test Case." *The Sociological Quarterly* 61(3): 422–47.

Feinstein, Yuval. 2021. "Potent but Precarious: When, How, and Why National Identities Have Strong Impact on Attitude Formation in Response to Events."

Feldman, Stanley, Leonie Huddy, and George E Marcus. 2015. *Going to War in Iraq: When Citizens and the Press Matter.* Chicago: University of Chicago Press.

Felten, Peter. 1999. "Yankee, Go Home and Take Me with You: Lyndon Johnson and the Dominican Republic." In *The Foreign Policies of Lyndon Johnson: Beyond Vietnam*, edited by H. W. Brands, 98–144. College Station: Texas A&M University Press.

Ferguson, Yale H. 1973. "Review: The Dominican Intervention of 1965: Recent Interpretations." *International Organization* 27(4): 517–48.

Fine, Gary A. 2002. "Thinking about Evil: Adolf Hitler and the Dilemma of the Social Construction of Reputation." In *Culture in Mind: Toward a Sociology of Culture and Cognition*, edited by Karen A. Cerulo, 227–37. New York: Routledge.

Finlayson, Alan. 1998. "Psychology, Psychoanalysis and Theories of Nationalism." *Nations and Nationalism* 4(2): 145–62.

Firestone, Juanita M., and Richard J. Harris. 2006. "Support and Opposition for Invading Iraq: Did the President's Speech Make a Difference?" *International Journal of Public Administration* 29(10): 895–909.

Fisher, Louis. 1995. *Presidential War Power.* Lawrence: University Press of Kansas.

Flam, Helena, and Debra King. 2007. *Emotions and Social Movements.* London and New York: Routledge.

Flamm, Michael W. 2009. "The Reagan Presidency and Foreign Policy: Controversies and Legacies." In *Debating the Reagan Presidency*, edited by J. E. Flamm and W. Michael, 101–81. Lanham, MD: Rowman & Littlefield.

Folkman, Susan. 2008. "The Case for Positive Emotions in the Stress Process." *Anxiety, Stress, and Coping* 21(1): 3–14.

Fox, Jon E., and Cynthia Miller-Idriss. 2008. "Everyday Nationhood." *Ethnicities* 8(4): 536–63.

Fousek, John. 2000. *To Lead the Free World: American Nationalism and the Cultural Roots of the Cold War.* Chapel Hill: University of North Carolina Press.

Freud, Sigmund, Sander Katz, and Joan Riviere. 1947. *Freud: On War, Sex and Neurosis.* New York: Arts & Science Press.

Gadarian, Shana Kushner. 2010. "The Politics of Threat: How Terrorism News Shapes Foreign Policy Attitudes." *The Journal of Politics* 72(2): 469–83.

Gardner, Lloyd. 2010. "The Ministry of Fear: Selling the Gulf Wars." In *Selling War in a Media Age: The Presidency and Public Opinion in the American Century*, edited by K. Osgood and A. K. Frank, 224–49. Gainesville: University Press of Florida.

Garthoff, Raymond L. 1989. *Reflections on the Cuban Missile Crisis.* Washington, DC: Brookings Institution.

Garthoff, Raymond L. 1992. "The Cuban Missile Crisis: An Overview." In *The Cuban Missile Crisis Revisited*, edited by James A. Nathan, 41–53. New York: Palgrave Macmillan.

Gartner, Scott S., and Gary M. Segura. 2000. "Race, Casualties, and Opinion in the Vietnam War." *Journal of Politics* 62(1): 115–46.

Gelpi, Christopher. 2017. "Democracies in Conflict: The Role of Public Opinion, Political Parties, and the Press in Shaping Security Policy." *Journal of Conflict Resolution* 61(9): 1925–49.

Gelpi, Christopher, Peter D. Feaver, and Jason Reifler. 2006. "Success Matters: Casualty Sensitivity and the War in Iraq." *International Security* 30(3): 7–46.

Gelpi, Christopher, Peter Feaver, and Jason Aaron Reifler. 2009. *Paying the Human Costs of War: American Public Opinion and Casualties in Military Conflicts*. Princeton, NJ: Princeton University Press.

Georgarakis, George N. 2017. "Unlocking the Rally-round-the-Flag Effect Conundrum: Affective and symbolic factors in a multidimensional understanding of the French public trust under terrorist threat." Master Thesis. Paris, France: Institut d'Études Politiques de Paris.

George, Alice L. 2003. *Awaiting Armageddon: How Americans Faced the Cuban Missile Crisis*. Chapel Hill: University of North Carolina Press.

Gershkoff, Amy, and Shana Kushner. 2005. "Shaping Public Opinion: The 9/11-Iraq Connection in the Bush Administration's Rhetoric." *Perspectives on Politics* 3(3): 525–37.

Giddens, Anthony. 1991. *Modernity and Self-Identity: Self and Society in the Late Modern Age*. Stanford, CA: Stanford University Press.

Girard, Philippe R. 2004. *Clinton in Haiti: The 1994 U.S. Invasion of Haiti*. New York: Palgrave Macmillan.

Glad, Betty. 1980. *Jimmy Carter, in Search of the Great White House*. New York: W. W. Norton.

Goldfinch, Shaun, Ross Taplin, and Robin Gauld. 2021. "Trust in Government Increased during the Covid-19 Pandemic in Australia and New Zealand." *Australian Journal of Public Administration* 80(1): 3–11.

Goodwin, Jeff, James M. Jasper, and Francesca Polletta. 2004. "Emotional Dimensions of Social Movements." In *The Blackwell Companion to Social Movements*, edited by David A. Snow, Sarah A. Soule, and Hanspeter Kriesi, 413–32. Oxford: Blackwell.

Greene, John Robert. 1995. *The Presidency of Gerald R. Ford*. Lawrence: University Press of Kansas.

Greenfeld, Liah. 2006. *Nationalism and the Mind: Essays on Modern Culture*. Oxford: Oneworld.

Gries, Peter. 2014. *The Politics of American Foreign Policy: How Ideology Divides Liberals and Conservatives over Foreign Affairs*. Stanford, CA: Stanford University Press.

Groeling, Tim, and Matthew A. Baum. 2008. "Crossing the Water's Edge: Elite Rhetoric, Media Coverage, and the Rally-round-the-Flag Phenomenon." *Journal of Politics* 70(4): 1065–85.

Gross, Kimberly, Paul R. Brewer, and Sean Aday. 2009. "Confidence in Government and Emotional Responses to Terrorism after September 11, 2001." *American Politics Research* 37(1): 107–28.

Hale, Henry E. 2018. "How Crimea Pays: Media, Rallying 'round the Flag, and Authoritarian Support." *Comparative Politics* 50(3): 369–91.

Hallin, Daniel C., and Todd Gitlin. 1994. "The Gulf War as Popular Culture and Television Drama." In *Taken by Storm: The Media, Public Opinion, and US Foreign Policy in the Gulf War*, edited by W. L. Bennett and D. L. Paletz, 149–63. Chicago and London: University of Chicago Press.

Hamanaka, Shingo. 2021. "'Rallying round the Flag Effect' in Israel's First Covid-19 Wave." *Israel Affairs* 27(4): 675–90.

Hayes, Carlton J. H. 1926. *Essays on Nationalism*. New York: Macmillan.

Heaney, Jonathan G. 2011. "Emotions and Power: Reconciling Conceptual Twins." *Journal of Political Power* 4(2): 259–77.

Hendrickson, Ryan C. 2002. *The Clinton Wars: The Constitution, Congress, and War Powers*. Nashville, TN: Vanderbilt University Press.

Herman, Joost. 2006. "The Dutch Drive for Humanitarianism: Inner Origins and Development of the Gidsland Tradition and Its External Effects." *International Journal* 61(4): 859–74.

Herrmann, R. K., P. Isernia, and P. Segatti. 2009. "Attachment to the Nation and International Relations: Dimensions of Identity and Their Relationship to War and Peace." *Political Psychology* 30(5): 721–54.

Herrmann, Richard K., Philip E. Tetlock, and Penny S. Visser. 1999. "Mass Public Decisions to Go to War: A Cognitive-Interactionist Framework." *The American Political Science Review* 93(3): 553–73.

Hersh, Seymour M. 2003. "Selective Intelligence." *The New Yorker*, May 4. https://www.newyorker.com/magazine/2003/05/12/selective-intelligence.

Hetherington, Marc J., and Michael Nelson. 2003. "Anatomy of Rally Effect: George W. Bush and the War on Terrorism." *Political Science and Politics* 36(1): 37–42.

Hicks, Donna. 2011. *Dignity: The Essential Role It Plays in Resolving Conflict.* New Haven, CT: Yale University Press.

Hilsman, Roger. 1996. *The Cuban Missile Crisis: The Struggle over Policy.* Westport, CT: Praeger.

Hinckley, Ronald H. 1988. "Public Attitudes toward Key Foreign Policy Events." *The Journal of Conflict Resolution* 32(2): 295–318.

Hirsch, John L., and Robert B. Oakley. 1995. *Somalia and Operation Restore Hope: Reflections on Peacemaking and Peacekeeping.* Washington, DC: United States Institute of Peace Press.

Holsti, Ole. 1998. "Public Opinion and the U.S. Foreign Policy after the Cold War." In *After the End: Making U.S. Foreign Policy in the Post-Cold War World*, edited by J. M. Scott, 138–69. Durham, NC, and London: Duke University Press.

Horowitz, Donald L. 1985. *Ethnic Groups in Conflict.* Berkeley: University of California Press.

Huddy, L. 2001. "From Social to Political Identity: A Critical Examination of Social Identity Theory." *Political Psychology* 22(1): 127–56.

Huddy, Leonie, Stanley Feldman, Charles Taber, and Gallya Lahav. 2005. "Threat, Anxiety, and Support of Antiterrorism Policies." *American Journal of Political Science* 49(3): 593–608.

Huddy, Leonie, Stanley Feldman, and Erik Cassese. 2007. "On the Distinct Political Effects of Anxiety and Anger." In *The Affect Effect: Dynamics of Emotions in Political Thinking and Behavior*, edited by R. W. Neuman, G. E. Marcus, A. N. Crigler, and M. MacKuen, 202–30. Chicago: University of Chicago Press.

Hutcheson, John, David Domke, Andre Billeaudeaux, and Philip Garland. 2004. "U.S. National Identity, Political Elites, and a Patriotic Press Following September 11." *Political Communication* 21: 27–50.

Iyengar, Shanto, and Adam Simon. 1994. "News Coverage of the Gulf Crisis and Public Opinion: A Study of Agenda-Setting, Priming, and Framing." In *Taken by the Storm: The Media, Public Opinion, and U.S. Foreign Policy in the Gulf War*, edited by L. W. Bennett and D. L. Paletz, 167–85. Chicago and London: University of Chicago Press.

Jacobson, Gary C. 2007. *A Divider, Not a Uniter: George W. Bush and the American People.* New York: Pearson Longman.

Jacobson, Gary C. 2010. "A Tale of Two Wars: Public Opinion on the U.S. Military Interventions in Afghanistan and Iraq." *Presidential Studies Quarterly* 40(4): 585–610.

Jasper, James M. 1998. "The Emotions of Protest: Affective and Reactive Emotions in and around Social Movements." *Sociological Forum* 13(3): 397–424.

Jentleson, Bruce W. 1992. "The Pretty Prudent Public: Post Post-Vietnam American Opinion on the Use of Military Force." *International Studies Quarterly* 36(1): 49–74.

Jentleson, Bruce W., and Rebecca L. Britton. 1998. "Still Pretty Prudent: Post-Cold War American Public Opinion on the Use of Military Force." *The Journal of Conflict Resolution* 42(4): 395–417.

Jervis, Robert. 1980. "The Impact of the Korean War on the Cold War." *Journal of Conflict Resolution* 24(4): 563–92.

Johnson, Dominic D. P. 2004. *Overconfidence and War: The Havoc and Glory of Positive Illusions*. Cambridge, MA: Harvard University Press.

Joslyn, Mark R., and Donald P. Haider-Markel. 2007. "Sociotropic Concerns and Support for Counterterrorism Policies." *Social Science Quarterly* 88(2): 306–19.

Kahneman, Daniel, and Jonathan Renshon. 2009. "Hawkish Biases." In *American Foreign Policy and the Politics of Fear: Threat Inflation since 9/11*, edited by T. A. Thrall and J. K. Cramer, 97–114. London and New York: Routledge.

Kahaneman, Daniel, and Amos Tversky. 1979. "Prospect Theory: An Analysis of Decision under Risk." *Econometrica* 47(2): 363–91.

Kalb, Deborah, Gerhard Peters, and John T. Woolley. 2006. *State of the Union: Presidential Rhetoric from Woodrow Wilson to George W. Bush*. Washington, DC: CQ Press.

Kalin, Michael, and Nicholas Sambanis. 2018. "How to Think about Social Identity." *Annual Review of Political Science* 21: 239–57.

Kam, Cindy D., and Jennifer M. Ramos. 2008. "Joining and Leaving the Rally: Understanding the Surge and Decline in Presidential Approval Following 9/11." *Public Opinion Quarterly* 72(4): 619–50.

Katz, Elihu, Jay G. Blumler, and Michael Gurevitch. 1973. "Uses and Gratifications Research." *Public Opinion Quarterly* 37(4): 509–23.

Katz, Elihu, and Tamar Liebes. 2007. "'No More Peace!': How Disaster, Terror and War Have Upstaged Media Events." *International Journal of Communication* 1: 157–66.

Kaufman, Stuart J. 2001. *Modern Hatreds: The Symbolic Politics of Ethnic War*. Ithaca, NY: Cornell University Press.

Kaufmann, Chaim. 2004. "Threat Inflation and the Failure of the Marketplace of Ideas: The Selling of the Iraq War." *International Security* 29(1): 5–48.

Kellner, Douglas. 1992. *The Persian Gulf TV War*. Boulder, CO: Westview Press.

Kemper, Theodore D. 2002. "Predicting Emotions in Groups: Some Lessons from September 11." In *Emotions and Sociology*, edited by J. Barbalet, 53–68. Oxford: Blackwell.

Kemper, Theodore. D. 2011. *Status, Power and Ritual Interaction: A Relational Reading of Durkheim, Goffman and Collins*. Farnham, Surrey, England: Ashgate Pub.

Kennedy, Robert F. 1969. *Thirteen Days: A Memoir of the Cuban Missile Crisis*. New York: W. W. Norton.

Kertzer, Joshua D., and Ryan Brutger. 2016. "Decomposing Audience Costs: Bringing the Audience Back into Audience Cost Theory." *American Journal of Political Science* 60(1): 234–49.

Kertzer, Joshua D., and Thomas Zeitzoff. 2017. "A Bottom-up Theory of Public Opinion about Foreign Policy." *American Journal of Political Science* 61(3): 543–58.

Khong, Yuen Foong. 2020. *Analogies at War*. Princeton, NJ: Princeton University Press.

Kinder, Donald R., and D. Roderick Kiewiet. 1979. "Economic Discontent and Political Behavior: The Role of Personal Grievances and Collective Economic Judgments in Congressional Voting." *American Journal of Political Science* 23(3): 495–527.

Klarevas, Louis J. 2000. "Trends: The United States Peace Operation in Somalia." *The Public Opinion Quarterly* 64(4): 523–40.

Kohn, Hans. 1944. *The Idea of Nationalism: A Study in Its Origins and Background.* New York: Macmillan.

Kohut, Andrew, and Robert C. Toth. 1994. "Arms and the People." *Foreign Affairs* 73(6): 47–61.

Kohut, Andrew, and Robert C. Toth. 1996. "Managing Conflict in the Post-Cold War World: A Public Perspective." Aspen, CO: Aspen Institute.

Kosterman, Rick, and Seymour Feshbach. 1989. "Toward a Measure of Patriotic and Nationalistic Attitudes." *Political Psychology* 10(2): 257–74.

Krebs, Ronald R., and Jennifer K. Lobasz. 2007. "Fixing the Meaning of 9/11: Hegemony, Coercion, and the Road to War in Iraq." *Security Studies* 16(3): 409–51.

Krebs, Ronald R., and Jennifer Lobasz. 2009. "The Sound of Silence: Rhetorical Coercion, Democratic Acquiescence, and the Iraq War." In *American Foreign Policy and the Politics of Fear: Threat Inflation since 9/11*, edited by T. A. Thrall and J. K. Cramer, 135–52. New York: Routledge.

Kull, Steven, and Clay Ramsey. 2001. "The Myth of the Reactive Public: American Public Attitudes on Military Fatalities in the Post-Cold War Period." In *Public Opinion and the International Use of Force*, edited by P. Everets and P. Isneria, 205–28. London: Routledge.

Kull, Steven, Clay Ramsay, and Evan Lewis. 2003. "Misperceptions, the Media, and the Iraq War." *Political Science Quarterly* 118(4): 569–98.

Kulyk, Volodymyr. 2016. "National Identity in Ukraine: Impact of Euromaidan and the War." *Europe-Asia Studies* 68(4): 588–608.

Lai, Brian, and Dan Reiter. 2005. "Rally 'round the Union Jack? Public Opinion and the Use of Force in the United Kingdom, 1948–2001." *International Studies Quarterly* 49(2): 255–72.

LaMay, Craig Llewellyn. 1991. "By the Numbers II: Measuring the Coverage: The Press and the Persian Gulf Conflict." In *The Media at War: The Press and the Persian Gulf Conflict: A Report of the Gannett Foundation*, edited by Everette E. Dennis and the Gannet Foundation, 41–50. New York: Gannett Foundation Gannett Foundation Media Center.

Lambert, Alan J., Laura D. Scherer, John Paul Schott, Kristina R. Olson, Rick K. Andrews, Thomas C. O'Brien, and Alison R. Zisser. 2010. "Rally Effects, Threat, and Attitude Change: An Integrative Approach to Understanding the Role of Emotion." *Journal of Personality and Social Psychology* 98(6): 886–903.

Lang, Gladys Engel, and Kurt Lang. 1994. "The Press as Prologue: Media Coverage of Saddam's Iraq, 1979–1990." In *Taken by Storm: The Media, Public Opinion, and US Foreign Policy in the Gulf War*, edited by W. L. Bennett and D. L. Paletz, 43–62. Chicago and London: University of Chicago Press.

Lanoue, David J., and Barbara Headrick. 1998. "Short-Term Political Events and British Government Popularity: Direct and Indirect Effects." *Polity* 30(3): 417–33.

Larson, Eric V. 1996. "Ends and Means in the Democratic Conversation: Understanding the Role of Casualties in Support for the U.S. Military Operations." RAND: Doctoral dissertation. https://www.rand.org/content/dam/rand/pubs/rgs_dissertations/2006/RGSD124.pdf.

Larson, Eric V., and Bogdan Savych. 2005. *American Public Support for U.S. Military Operations from Mogadishu to Baghdad*. Santa Monica, CA: RAND.

Lebow, Richard Ned. 1992. "The Traditional and Revisionist Interpretations Reevaluated: Why Was Cuba a Crisis?" In *The Cuban Missile Crisis Revisited*, edited by J. A. Nathan, 161–86. New York: Palgrave Macmillan.

Lebow, Richard Ned. 2008. *A Cultural Theory of International Relations*. Cambridge, UK; New York: Cambridge University Press.

LeDoux, Joseph E. 1996. *The Emotional Brain: The Mysterious Underpinnings of Emotional Life*. New York: Simon & Schuster.

Lee, Jong R. 1977. "Rallying around the Flag: Foreign Policy Events and Presidential Popularity." *Presidential Studies Quarterly* 7(4): 252–56.

Lehrer, Jonah. 2009. *How We Decide*. Boston: Houghton Mifflin Harcourt.

Lerner, Jennifer S., and Dacher Keltner. 2001. "Fear, Anger, and Risk." *Journal of Personality and Social Psychology* 81(1): 146–59.

Lerner, Jennifer S., Roxana M. Gonzalez, Deborah A. Small, and Baruch Fischhoff. 2003. "Effects of Fear and Anger on Perceived Risks of Terrorism: A National Field Experiment." *Psychological Science* 14(2): 144–50.

LeShan, Lawrence L. 1992. *The Psychology of War: Comprehending Its Mystique and Its Madness*. Chicago: Noble Press.

Levy, Jack S. 2012. "Coercive Threats, Audience Costs, and Case Studies." *Security Studies* 21(3): 383–90.

Lewis, Adrian R. 2018. *The American Culture of War: A History of US Military Force from World War II to Operation Enduring Freedom*. New York and London: Routledge.

Li, Qiong, and Marilynn B. Brewer. 2004. "What Does It Mean to Be an American? Patriotism, Nationalism, and American Identity after 9/11." *Political Psychology* 25(5): 727–39.

Lian, Bradley, and John R. Oneal. 1993. "Presidents, the Use of Military Force, and Public Opinion." *The Journal of Conflict Resolution* 37(2): 277–300.

Lieven, Anatol. 2004. *America Right or Wrong: An Anatomy of American Nationalism*. New York: Oxford University Press.

Lindner, Evelin. 2006. *Making Enemies: Humiliation and International Conflict*. Westport, CT: Praeger.

Lippmann, Walter. 1922. *Public Opinion*. New York: Harcourt, Brace.

Little, Douglas. 1996. "His Finest Hour? Eisenhower, Lebanon, and the 1958 Middle East Crisis." *Diplomatic History* 20(1): 27–54.

Livingstone, Neil C. 1988. "The Raid on Libya and the Use of Force in Combating Terrorism." In *Beyond the Iran Contra Crisis: The Shape of U.S. Anti-Terrorism Policy in the Post-Reagan Era*, edited by N. C. Livingstone and T. E. Arnold, 65–84. Lexington, MA: Lexingon Books.

Lorell, Mark A., Charles Kelley, Deborah R. Hensler, Rand Corporation, and United States Air Force. 1985. *Casualties, Public Opinion, and Presidential Policy during the Vietnam War*. Santa Monica, CA: RAND.

MacArthur, John R. 1992. *Second Front: Censorship and Propaganda in the Gulf War*. New York: Hill and Wang.

Mahoney, James. 2003. "Strategies of Causal Assessment in Comparative Historical Analysis." In *Comparative Historical Analysis in the Social Sciences*, edited by J. Mahoney and D. Rueschemeyer, 337–72. Cambridge, UK: Cambridge University Press.

Mahoney, James, and Dietrich Rueschemeyer. 2003. "Comparative Historical Analysis: Achievements and Agendas." In *Comparative Historical Analysis in the Social*

Sciences, edited by J. Mahoney and D. Rueschemeyer, 3–38. Cambridge, UK: Cambridge University Press.

Manheim, Jarol B. 1994. "Strategic Public Diplomacy: Managing Kuwait's Image during the Gulf Conflict." In *Taken by Storm: The Media, Public Opinion, and US Foreign Policy in the Gulf War*, edited by W. L. Bennett and D. L. Paletz, 131–48. Chicago and London: University of Chicago Press.

Mann, Michael. 1987. "The Roots and Contradictions of Modern Militarism." *New Left Review* 162: 35–50.

Marcus, G. E. 2000. "Emotions in Politics." *Annual Review of Political Science* 3: 221–50.

Marcus, George E., W. Russell Neuman, and Michael MacKuen. 2000. *Affective Intelligence and Political Judgment*. Chicago: University of Chicago Press.

Mayer, Jane. 2009. *The Dark Side: The Inside Story of How the War on Terror Turned into a War on American Ideals*. New York: Anchor Books.

McCartney, Paul T. 2004. "American Nationalism and US Foreign Policy from September 11 to the Iraq War." *Political Science Quarterly* 119(3): 399–423.

McCleary, D. F., and R. L. Williams. 2009. "Sociopolitical and Personality Correlates of Militarism in Democratic Societies." *Peace and Conflict* 15(2): 161–87.

McLaughlin, Neil. 1996. "Nazism, Nationalism, and the Sociology of Emotions: Escape from Freedom Revisited." *Sociological Theory* 14(3): 241–61.

Meacham, Jon. 2019. *The Soul of America: The Battle for Our Better Angels*. New York: Random House.

Mearsheimer, John J. 1990. "Back to the Future: Instability in Europe after the Cold War." *International Security* 15: 5–56.

Mercer, Jonathan. 2005. "Rationality and Psychology in International Politics." *International Organization* 59(1): 77–106.

Mercer, Jonathan. 2010. "Emotional Beliefs." *International Organization* 64(1): 1–31.

Merriman, Peter, and Rhys Jones. 2017. "Nations, Materialities and Affects." *Progress in Human Geography* 41(5): 600–17.

Miller, Joanne M. 2007. "Examining the Mediators of Agenda Setting: A New Experimental Paradigm Reveals the Role of Emotions." *Political Psychology* 28(6): 689–717.

Morrow, Lance. 2001. "The Case for Rage and Retribution." *Time*: 48.

Mouffe, Chantal. 1993. *The Return of the Political*. London and New York: Verso.

Mueller, John E. 1970. "Presidential Popularity from Truman to Johnson." *The American Political Science Review* 64(1): 18–34.

Mueller, John E. 1973. *War, Presidents, and Public Opinion*. New York: Wiley.

Mueller, John E. 1994. *Policy and Opinion in the Gulf War*. Chicago: University of Chicago Press.

Mueller, Karl P. 2006. *Striking First: Preemptive and Preventive Attack in U.S. National Security Policy*. Santa Monica, CA: RAND Project Air Force.

Mummendey, Amélie, Bernd Simon, Carsten Dietze, Melanie Grünert, Gabi Haeger, Sabine Kessler, Stephan Lettgen, and Stefanie Schäferhoff. 1992. "Categorization Is Not Enough: Intergroup Discrimination in Negative Outcome Allocation." *Journal of Experimental Social Psychology* 28(2): 125–44.

Mutz, Diana C. 1998. *Impersonal Influence: How Perceptions of Mass Collectivities Affect Political Attitudes*. Cambridge, UK. Cambridge University Press.

Nacos, Brigitte Lebens. 1990. *The Press, Presidents, and Crises*. New York: Columbia University Press.

Neiger, Motti, and Karni Rimmer-Tsory. 2013. "The War That Wasn't on the News: 'In-Group Nationalism' and 'Out-Group Nationalism' in Newspaper Supplements." *Journalism* 14(6): 721–36.

Neuman, W. Russell, George E. Marcus, Michael MacKuen, and Ann N. Crigler. 2007. *The Affect Effect: Dynamics of Emotion in Political Thinking and Behavior*. Chicago: University of Chicago Press.

Newman, Brian, and Andrew Forcehimes. 2010. "'Rally round the Flag' Events for Presidential Approval Research." *Electoral Studies* 29(1): 144–54.

Newton, Kenneth. 2020. "Government Communications, Political Trust and Compliant Social Behaviour: The Politics of Covid-19 in Britain." *The Political Quarterly* 91(3): 502–13.

Nigbur, Dennis, and Marco Cinnirella. 2007. "National Identification, Type and Specificity of Comparison and Their Effects on Descriptions of National Character." *European Journal of Social Psychology* 37(4): 672–91.

Nincic, Miroslav. 1997. "Loss Aversion and the Domestic Context of Military Intervention." *Political Research Quarterly* 50(1): 97–120.

Norpoth, Helmut. 1987. "The Falklands War and Government Popularity in Britain: Rally without Consequence or Surge without Decline?" *Electoral Studies* 6(1): 3–16.

Norton, Augustus R., and Leonard Binder. 1987. *Amal and the Shi'a: Struggle for the Soul of Lebanon*. Austin, Texas: University of Texas Press.

Oberschall, A. 2000. "The Manipulation of Ethnicity: From Ethnic Cooperation to Violence and War in Yugoslavia." *Ethnic and Racial Studies* 23(6): 982–1001.

Oneal, John R., and Anna Lillian Bryan. 1995. "The Rally 'round the Flag Effect in U.S. Foreign Policy Crises, 1950–1985." *Political Behavior* 17(4): 379–401.

Ostrom, Charles W., Jr., and Dennis M. Simon. 1985. "Promise and Performance: A Dynamic Model of Presidential Popularity." *The American Political Science Review* 79(2): 334–58.

Page, Benjamin I., and Robert Y. Shapiro. 1992. *The Rational Public: Fifty Years of Trends in Americans' Policy Preferences*. Chicago: University of Chicago Press.

Parker, Suzzane L. 1995. "Toward an Understanding of 'Rally' Effects: Public Opinion in the Persian Gulf War." *Public Opinion Quarterly* 59: 526–46.

Perrin, Andrew J., and Sondra J. Smolek. 2009. "Who Trusts? Race, Gender, and the September 11 Rally Effect among Young Adults." *Social Science Research* 38(1): 134–45.

Peters, Ellen, Daniel Västfjäll, Tommy Gärling, and Paul Slovic. 2006. "Affect and Decision Making: A 'Hot' Topic." *Journal of Behavioral Decision Making* 19(2): 79–85.

Petersen, Roger Dale. 2002. *Understanding Ethnic Violence: Fear, Hatred, and Resentment in Twentieth-Century Eastern Europe*. Cambridge UK, and New York: Cambridge University Press.

Pfiffner, James. 2004. "Did President Bush Mislead the Country in His Arguments for War with Iraq?" *Presidential Studies Quarterly* 34(1): 25–46.

Piszkiewicz, Dennis. 2003. *Terrorism's War with America: A History*. Westport, CT: Praeger.

Polsby, Nelson W. 1964. *Congress and the Presidency*. Englewood Cliffs, NJ: Prentice-Hall.

Price, Vincent, Lilach Nir, and Joseph N. Cappella. 2005. "Framing Public Discussion of Gay Civil Unions." *Public Opinion Quarterly* 69(2): 179–212.

PRWatch, The Center for Media Democracy. 2011. "How PR Sold the War in the Persian Gulf." https://www.prwatch.org/node/25/print.

Quek, Kai. 2017. "Type II Audience Costs." *The Journal of Politics* 79(4): 1438–43.

Radway, Laurence I. 2002. "George Bush, Mass Nationalism, and the Gulf War." In *From Cold War to New World Order: The Foreign Policy of George H. W. Bush*, edited by M. Bose and R. Perotti, 465–82. Wesport, CT: Greenwood Press.

Ragin, Charles C. 1987. *The Comparative Method: Moving beyond Qualitative and Quantitative Strategies*. Berkeley: University of California Press.

Rahn, Wendy M., Brian Kroeger, and Cynthia M. Kite. 1996. "A Framework for the Study of Public Mood." *Political Psychology* 17(1): 29–58.

Rampton, Sheldon, and John C. Stauber. 2003. *Weapons of Mass Deception: The Uses of Propaganda in Bush's War on Iraq*. New York: Jeremy P. Tarcher/Penguin.

Rasenberger, Jim. 2012. *The Brilliant Disaster: JFK, Castro, and America's Doomed Invasion of Cuba's Bay of Pigs*. New York: Simon and Schuster.

Rasinski, Kenneth A., Jennifer Berktold, Tom W. Smith, and Bethany L. Albertson. 2002. "America Recovers: A Follow-up to a National Study of Public Response to the September 11th Terrorist Attacks." Chicago: University of Chicago: National Organization for Research (NORC). https://www.norc.org/PDFs/publications/Rasinskik_America_Recovers_2002.pdf.

Reed, Jan. 2006. *Appreciative Inquiry: Research for Change*. Thousand Oaks, CA: Sage Publications.

Reeskens, Tim, and Quita Muis. 2020. "A New Democratic Norm (Al)?: Political Legitimacy Amidst the Covid-19 Pandemic." In *The New Common: How the Covid-19 Pandemic Is Transforming Society*, edited by Emile Aarts, Hein Fleuren, Margariet Sitskoorn, and Ton Wilthagen, 189–94. Springer International Publishing.

Rieber, Robert W., and Robert J. Kelly. 1991. "Substance and Shadow: Images of the Enemy." In *The Psychology of War and Peace: The Image of the Enemy*, edited by R. W. Rieber, 3–39. New York and London: Plenum Press.

Rielly, John E. 1979. "American Public-Opinion and United-States Foreign-Policy." *Atlantic Community Quarterly* 17(2): 227–38.

Roccas, Sonia, Yechiel Klar, and Ido Liviatan. 2006. "The Paradox of Group-Based Guilt: Modes of National Identification, Conflict Vehemence, and Reactions to the in-Group's Moral Violations." *Journal of Personality and Social Psychology* 91(4): 698.

Roshwald, Aviel. 2006. *The Endurance of Nationalism: Ancient Roots and Modern Dilemmas*. Cambridge, UK: Cambridge University Press.

Ross, Andrew A. G. 2013. *Mixed Emotions: Beyond Fear and Hatred in International Conflict*. Chicago: University of Chicago Press.

Rottinghaus, B. 2009. "Strategic Leaders: Determining Successful Presidential Opinion Leadership Tactics through Public Appeals." *Political Communication* 26(3): 296–316.

Rousseau, David L. 2006. *Identifying Threats and Threatening Identities: The Social Construction of Realism and Liberalism*. Stanford, CA: Stanford University Press.

Rousseau, David L., and Rocio Garcia-Retamero. 2009. "Estimating Threats: The Impact and Interaction of Identity and Power." In *American Foreign Policy and the Politics of Fear: Threat Inflation since 9/11*, edited by T. A. Thrall and J. K. Cramer, 72–96. New York: Routledge.

Rowe, John Carlos. 1991. "The 'Vietnam Effect' in the Persian Gulf War." *Cultural Critique* (19): 121–39.

Rule, John, and Elizabeth Rice. 2015. "Bringing Them Home: Scorecard Report." Canberra: National Sorry Day Committee.

Russel, Alec, and Jack Fairweather. 2003. "We Got Him." In *The Telegraph*, December 15. https://www.telegraph.co.uk/news/worldnews/middleeast/iraq/1449512/We-got-him.html.

Russett, Bruce M. 1990. *Controlling the Sword: The Democratic Governance of National Security*. Cambridge, MA: Harvard University Press.

Saunders, Harold H. 1985. "Diplomacy and Pressure, November 1979–May 1980." In *American Hostages in Iran: The Conduct of a Crisis*, edited by W. Christopher, H. H. Saunders, G. Sick, R. Carswell, Richard J. Davis, Jr., J. Hoffman, and R. B. Owen, 72–143. New Haven, CT, and London: Yale University Press.

Schechter, Danny. 2004. "Selling the Iraq War: The Media Management Strategies We Never Saw." In *War, Media, and Propaganda*, edited by Y. R. Kamalipour and N. Snow, 25–32. Lanham, MD: Rowman & Littlefield.

Scheff, Thomas J. 1990. *Microsociology: Discourse, Emotion, and Social Structure*. Chicago: University of Chicago Press.

Scheufele, Dietram A., Matthew C. Nisbet, and Ronald E. Ostman. 2005. "September 11: News Coverage, Public Opinion, and Support for Civil Liberties." *Mass Communication and Society* 8(3): 197.

Schildkraut, Deborah J. 2002. "The More Things Change . . . American Identity and Mass and Elite Responses to 9/11." *Political Psychology* 23(3): 511–35.

Schubert, James N., Patrick A. Stewart, and Margaret Ann Curran. 2002. "A Defining Presidential Moment: 9/11 and the Rally Effect." *Political Psychology* 23(3): 559–83.

Schultz, Kenneth A. 2001. "Looking for Audience Costs." *Journal of Conflict Resolution* 45(1): 32–60.

Schumacher, Edward. 1986. "The United States and Libya." *Foreign Affairs* 65(2): 329–48.

Schwarz, Benjamin C. 1994. *Casualties, Public Opinion and US Military Intervention: Implications for US Regional Deterrence Strategies*. Santa Monica, CA: RAND.

Schwarz, Norbert, and Gerald L. Clore. 2003. "Mood as Information: 20 Years Later." *Psychological Inquiry* 14(3–4): 296–303.

Scranton, Margaret E. 1991. *The Noriega Years: U.S.-Panamanian Relations, 1981–1990*. Boulder, CO: L. Rienner.

Sears, David O. 2001. "The Role of Affect in Symbolic Politics." In *Citizens and Politics*, edited by J. H. Kuklinski, 14–40. Cambridge, UK, and New York: Cambridge University Press.

Sewell, William H., Jr. 1992. "A Theory of Structure: Duality, Agency, and Transformation." *American Journal of Sociology* 98(1): 1–29.

Sharafutdinova, Gulnaz. 2020. "Public Opinion Formation and Group Identity: The Politics of National Identity Salience in Post-Crimea Russia." *Problems of Post-Communism*: 1–13.

Shaw, Donald L., and Shannon E. Martin. 1993. "The Natural, and Inevitable, Phases of War Reporting: Historical Shadows, New Communication in the Persian Gulf." In *The Media and the Persian Gulf War*, edited by R. E. Denton, Jr., 43–69. Westport, CT: Praeger.

Shearman, Peter. 1985. "The Soviet Union and Grenada under the New Jewel Movement." *International Affairs (Royal Institute of International Affairs 1944-)* 61(4): 661–73.

Short, Damien. 2012. "When Sorry Isn't Good Enough: Official Remembrance and Reconciliation in Australia." *Memory Studies* 5(3): 293–304.

Sick, Gary. 2018. "The United States in the Persian Gulf: From Twin Pillars to Dual Containment." In *The Middle East and the United States*, edited by David W. Lesch and Mark L. Haas, 237–52. New York: Routledge.

Simon, Jeffrey D. 2001. *The Terrorist Trap: America's Experience with Terrorism*. Bloomington: Indiana University Press.

Simons, Geoffrey L. 1993. *Libya: The Struggle for Survival.* New York: St. Martin's Press.

Skey, Michael. 2006. "'Carnivals of Surplus Emotion? Towards an Understanding of the Significance of Ecstatic Nationalism in a Globalising World." *Studies in Ethnicity and Nationalism* 6(2): 143–61.

Skitka, Linda J., Christopher W. Bauman, Nicholas P. Aramovich, and G. Scott Morgan. 2006. "Confrontational and Preventative Policy Responses to Terrorism: Anger Wants a Fight and Fear Wants 'Them' to Go Away." *Basic & Applied Social Psychology* 28(4): 375–84.

Skocpol, Theda. 1984. *Vision and Method in Historical Sociology.* Cambridge, UK, and New York: Cambridge University Press.

Slater, Michael D. 2007. "Reinforcing Spirals: The Mutual Influence of Media Selectivity and Media Effects and Their Impact on Individual Behavior and Social Identity." *Communication Theory* 17(3): 281–303.

Slovic, Paul, Melissa L. Finucane, Ellen Peters, and Donald G. MacGregor. 2007. "The Affect Heuristic." *European Journal of Operational Research* 177(3): 1333–52.

Smith, Anthony D. 1992. "Chosen Peoples: Why Ethnic-Groups Survive." *Ethnic and Racial Studies* 15(3): 436–56.

Smith, Gaddis. 1986. *Morality, Reason, and Power: American Diplomacy in the Carter Years.* New York: Hill and Wang.

Smith, Philip. 2005. *Why War?: The Cultural Logic of Iraq, the Gulf War, and Suez.* Chicago: University of Chicago Press.

Smith, Rogers M. 1997. *Civic Ideals: Conflicting Visions of Citizenship in U.S. History.* New Haven, CT: Yale University Press.

Smith, Tom W. 2003. "Trends: The Cuban Missile Crisis and US Public Opinion." *Public Opinion Quarterly* 67(2): 265–93.

Smith, Tom W., and Seokho Kim. 2006. "National Pride in Comparative Perspective: 1995/96 and 2003/04." *International Journal of Public Opinion Research* 18(1): 127–36.

Smith, Tom W., Kenneth A. Rasinski, and Marianna Toce. 2001. "America Rebounds: A National Study of Public Response to the September 11th Terrorist Attacks." Chicago: University of Chicago; National Organization for Research (NORC).

Smith-Lovin, Lynn. 2007. "The Strength of Weak Identities: Social Structural Sources of Self, Situation and Emotional Experience." *Social Psychology Quarterly* 70(2): 106–24.

Snyder, Jack, and Erica D. Borghard. 2011. "The Cost of Empty Threats: A Penny, Not a Pound." *American Political Science Review* 105(3): 437–56.

Sofaer, Abraham D. 2003. "Iran-Contra: Ethical Conduct and Public Policy." *Houston Law Review* 40: 1081.

St. John, Ronald Bruce. 2002. *Libya and the United States: Two Centuries of Strife.* Philadelphia: University of Pennsylvania Press.

Stern, Sheldon M. 2003. *Averting "the Final Failure": John F. Kennedy and the Secret Cuban Missile Crisis Meetings.* Stanford, CA: Stanford University Press.

Stinchcombe, Arthur L. 1978. *Theoretical Methods in Social History.* New York: Academic Press.

Stivers, William. 1987. "Eisenhower and the Middle East." In *Reevaluation Eisenhower: American Foreign Policy in the 1950s,* edited by R. A. Melanson and D. Mayers, 192–219. Urbana and Chicago: University of Illinois Press.

Stryker, Sheldon, and Peter J. Burke. 2000. "The Past, Present, and Future of an Identity Theory." *Social Psychology Quarterly* 63: 284–97.

Swidler, Ann. 1986. "Culture in Action: Symbols and Strategies." *American Sociological Review* 51(2): 273–86.

Taber, Charles S. 2003. "Information Processing and Public Opinion." In *Oxford Handbook of Political Psychology*, edited by D. O. Sears, L. Huddy, and R. Jervis, 433–76. New York: Oxford University Press.

Tajfel, Henri, and John C. Turner. 1986. "The Social Identity Theory of Intergroup Behaviour." In *Psychology of Intergroup Relations*, edited by S. Worchel and W. G. Austin, 7–24. Chicago: Nelson-Hall.

Tambiah, Stanley. 1996. *Leveling Crowds. Ethnonationalist Conflicts and Collective Violence in South Asia*. Berkeley: University of California Press.

Taylor, John. 1992. "Touched with Glory: Heroes and Human Interest in the News." In *Framing the Falklands War: Nationhood, Culture and Identity*, edited by James Aulich, 13–32. Milton Keynes, England: Open University Press.

Tenet, George. 2007. *At the Center of the Storm: My Years at the CIA*, edited by B. Harlow. New York: HarperCollins.

Theiler, Tobias. 2018. "The Microfoundations of Diversionary Conflict." *Security Studies* 27(2): 318–43.

Thelen, Kathleen, and James Mahoney. 2015. "Comparative-Historical Analysis in Contemporary Political Science." *Advances in Comparative-Historical Analysis* 3: 36.

Thrall, A. Trevor, and Jane K. Cramer. 2009. *American Foreign Policy and the Politics of Fear: Threat Inflation since 9/11*. New York: Routledge.

Tiryakian, Edward A. 2004. "Durkheim, Solidarity, and September 11." In *The Cambridge Companion to Durkheim*, edited by J. C. Alexander and P. Smith, 305–21. Cambridge, UK: Cambridge University Press.

Tomz, Michael. 2007. "Domestic Audience Costs in International Relations: An Experimental Approach." *International Organization* 61(4): 821–40.

Tsfati, Yariv, and Lilach Nir. 2017. "Frames and Reasoning: Two Pathways from Selective Exposure to Affective Polarization." *International Journal of Communication* 11: 22.

Tversky, Amos, and Daniel Kahneman. 1981. "The Framing of Decisions and the Psychology of Choice." *Science* 211(4481): 453–58.

van Dooremalen, Thijs. 2021. "How Happenings Do (Not) Turn into Events: A Typology and an Application to the Case of 9/11 in the American and Dutch Public Spheres 72(3)." *The British Journal of Sociology*: 725–41.

Van Evera, Stephen. 1994. "Hypotheses on Nationalism and War." *International Security* 18(4): 5–39.

Voeten, Erik, and Paul R. Brewer. 2006. "Public Opinion, the War in Iraq, and Presidential Accountability." *Journal of Conflict Resolution* 50(6): 809–30.

Waltz, Kenneth N. 1967. "Electoral Punishment and Foreign Policy Crises." In *Domestic Sources of Foreign Policy*, edited by J. N. Rosenau, 263–94. New York: Free Press.

Way, Baldwin, and Roger Masters. 1996. "Political Attitudes: Interactions of Cognition and Affect." *Motivation and Emotion* 20(3): 205–36.

Weber, Max. 1946 [1922]. "Foundation and Instability of Charismatic Authority." In *From Max Weber: Essays in Sociology*, edited by H. H. Gerth and C. W. Mills, 248–52. New York: Oxford University Press.

Weber, Max. 1978. *Economy and Society: An Outline of Interpretive Sociology*. Berkeley: University of California Press.

Weimann, Gabriel. 1987. "Media Events: The Case of International Terrorism." *Journal of Broadcasting & Electronic Media* 31(1): 21–39.

Weldes, Jutta. 1999. *Constructing National Interests: The United States and the Cuban Missile Crisis*. Minneapolis: University of Minnesota Press.

Western, Jon W. 2005. *Selling Intervention and War: The Presidency, the Media, and the American Public*. Baltimore, MD: Johns Hopkins University Press.

White, Mark. 1995. *The Cuban Missile Crisis*. New York: New York University Press.

Wilkie, Meredith. 1997. *Bringing Them Home: Report of the National Inquiry into the Separation of Aboriginal and Torres Strait Islander Children from Their Families*: Sydney, Australia. Human Rights and Equal Opportunity Commission.

Willer, Robb. 2004. "The Effects of Government-Issued Terror Warnings on Presidential Approval Ratings." *Current Research in Social Psychology* 10(1): 1–12.

Winkler, Carol. 2006. *In the Name of Terrorism: Presidents on Political Violence in the Post-World War II Era*. Albany: State University of New York Press.

Wroe, Ann. 1991. *Lives, Lies and the Iran-Contra Affair*. London: Tauris.

Xiaoming, Zhang. 2002. "China, the Soviet Union, and the Korean War: From an Abortive Air War Plan to a Wartime Relationship." *Journal of Conflict Studies* XXII(1): 73–88.

Yam, Kai Chi, Joshua Conrad Jackson, Christopher M. Barnes, Jenson Lau, Xin Qin, and Hin Yeung Lee. 2020. "The Rise of Covid-19 Cases Is Associated with Support for World Leaders." *Proceedings of the National Academy of Sciences* 117(41): 25429–33.

Young, Marilyn B. 2010. "Hard Sell: The Korean War." In *Selling War in a Media Age*, edited by K. Osgood and A. K. Frank, 113–39. Gainesville: University Press of Florida.

Yudina, Anna. 2015. "The Rally 'round the Flag Effect in Russia: How an International Crisis Turns Regime Opponents into Regime Supporters." Master of Arts, Russian, East European, and Eurasian Studies, University of North Carolina at Chapel Hill.

Zakaria, Fareed. 2007. *The Future of Freedom: Illiberal Democracy at Home and Abroad*, revised edition. New York: W. W. Norton.

Zaller, John. 1991. "Information, Values, and Opinion." *American Political Science Review* 85(4): 1215–37.

Zaller, John. 1992. *The Nature and Origins of Mass Opinion*. Cambridge, UK, and New York: Cambridge University Press.

Zaller, John. 1994a. "Strategic Politicians, Public Opinion, and the Gulf Crisis." In *Taken by Storm: The Media, Public Opinion, and US Foreign Policy in the Gulf War*, edited by L. W. Bennett and D. L. Paletz, 250–74. Chicago and London: University of Chicago Press.

Zaller, John. 1994b. "Elite Leadership of Mass Opinion." In *Taken by Storm: The Media, Public Opinion, and US Foreign Policy in the Gulf War*, edited by L. W. Bennett and D. L. Paletz, 186–209. Chicago and London: University of Chicago Press.

Zhang, Shu Guang. 1995. *Mao's Military Romanticism: China and the Korean War, 1950–1953*. Lawrence: University Press of Kansas.

Zimmer, Oliver. 2003. "Boundary Mechanisms and Symbolic Resources: Towards a Process-Oriented Approach to National Identity." *Nations and Nationalism* 9(2): 173–93.

Zulaika, Joseba. 2009. *Terrorism: The Self-Fulfilling Prophecy*. Chicago and London: University of Chicago Press.

Index

Abu Nidal Organization, 141
Achille Lauro hijacking (1985), 137
Aday, Sean, 106
Adut, Ari, 29–30
Afghanistan, 128, 131–32, 210. *See also*
    Afghanistan War (2001-2021)
Afghanistan War (2001-2021)
    Iraq War and, 184
    national honor and, 173–75
    rally-round-the-flag effect and, 3, 144,
        165, 173, 176, 206, 211
    US public opinion about terrorist
        threats and, 173–75
Albania, 131
Al Qaeda, 101–3, 127–28
Amal Militia (Lebanon), 138–39
anger, 35–36, 176–81, 215
anxiety, 164, 174–79, 213
al-Assad, Hafez, 138, 141
Australia, 194, 196

Balkan wars (1990s), 59
Batista, Fulgencio, 86
Bay of Pigs invasion (Cuba, 1961)
    Central Intelligence Agency and, 87, 89
    Cuban Missile Crisis and, 76
    media coverage of, 87–88
    national humiliation and, 49, 76, 88
    national prestige and, 44
    ransoming of prisoners following, 89
    US public opinion regarding, 88
Beirut Marine barracks attacks (1983),
    117, 134–35, 137, 203, 209
Beirut US Embassy attacks (1983-84), 137
Berinsky, Adam, 27
Berlin nightclub bombing (1986), 141
Berri, Nabih, 139–40
Bin Laden, Osama
    Kenya and Tanzania embassy bombings
        (1998) and, 132
    killing of, 61, 207

September 11 terrorist attacks, 127–28
    as US enemy, 60, 128
    US hunt (2001-11) for, 101, 183
Bishop, Maurice, 116
Bonikowski, Bart, 106–7
Bosch, Juan, 112
Bremer, Paul, 55–56
Brewer, Paul R., 106
Brewer, Susan, 32, 66, 156
Bush, George H.W.
    approval ratings of, 3, 12, 64, 78–79, 99,
        145, 152, 154, 161, 204, 210
    Gulf War and, 3, 12, 15, 59, 64, 145, 147,
        152–60, 204, 210
    New World Order doctrine and, 67, 161
    Panama invasion and, 3, 12, 36, 78, 99–
        100, 111, 204, 210
    Pan Am Flight 103 terrorist attack
        and, 140
    presidential rhetoric of, 59, 67, 99, 111,
        145, 152–53, 156, 161
    Somalia intervention and, 160–61, 204, 210
    on the "Vietnam Syndrome," 159
    war on drugs and, 99
Bush, George W.
    Afghanistan War and, 3, 165, 173, 176,
        206, 211
    approval ratings of, 3, 11–12, 27, 40, 56,
        79, 101, 104, 107, 165–67, 170–73,
        176–84, 186, 206, 210–14
    Bin Laden and, 101
    Iraq War and, 3, 11–12, 34–35, 55–56,
        64, 101–4, 107, 111, 165–67, 170–72,
        176–84, 206, 211
    presidential rhetoric of, 35, 101, 103–4,
        111, 127–29, 186
    September 11 terrorist attacks and, 3,
        11–12, 27, 39–40, 127–29, 165, 173,
        176, 182, 186, 206, 211
    War on Terror and, 11, 128, 165, 173,
        178, 183, 195

Cambodia
    Mayaguez incident and, 110–11
    US invasion (1970) of, 65, 83, 113–15,
        200, 209
Capehart, Homer E., 87
Carter, Jimmy
    approval ratings of, 12, 79, 124, 126,
        202, 209
    Iran hostage crisis and, 12, 123–26, 128,
        133, 202
    presidential rhetoric and, 123–26, 128,
        133
    Shah of Iran and, 122
Cassese, Erik, 91, 177
Castro, Fidel
    Bay of Pigs invasion and, 87–88
    Cuban Missile Crisis and, 90
    Operation Mongoose targeting, 87
    as US enemy, 60, 87, 89, 113, 117
    war on drugs and, 97
Cédras, Raoul, 161
Central Intelligence Agency (CIA)
    Bay of Pigs invasion and, 87, 89
    Dominican Republic invasion (1965)
        and, 113
    drug trafficking and, 96
    Egyptian Islamic Jihad and, 131
    Iran-Contra Affair and, 95–96
    Iraq War and, 101–3
    kidnapping of Beirut station chief
        (1984) and, 137
    Nicaraguan civil war and, 118
    Noriega regime in Panama and, 100
    Operation Mongoose (Cuba) and, 87
Chamberlain, Mary, 147
Charlie Hebdo attacks (Paris, 2015), 192
Cheney, Dick, 102
China, 134, 150–51
Clinton, Bill
    approval ratings of, 131–32, 205, 210
    Haiti intervention (1994) and, 161, 205,
        210
    Kenya and Tanzania embassy bombings
        and, 132, 205
    Lewinsky affair and, 132
    presidential rhetoric of, 130–32
    World Trade Center attack (1993) and,
        130–31, 205, 210
Coard, Bernard, 116

Cohen, Stanley E., 100
Cold War. *See also* Soviet Union
    Cuban Missile Crisis and, 84–89
    Domino Theory and, 149
    Gulf War and, 146–47, 152
    Korean War and, 146–50
    Lebanon intervention (1958) and, 197
    Truman Doctrine and, 148
    U-2 incident and, 5
    US-Soviet air engagements (1953), 76,
        209
Colombia, 97
    confidence, 170–71, 174–75, 178, 212
Congress
    Cuban Missile Crisis and, 85
    election (1986) and, 94–95
    Gulf War and, 15
    Iran-Contra Affair and, 97
    Mayaguez incident and, 110
    Noriega regime in Panama and, 97
    as opinion leaders, 24, 29, 36
    Patriot Act and, 16
    presidential oversight function of, 14
    rally-round-the-flag effect and, 11, 15
    September 11 terrorist attacks and, 186
    Truman Doctrine and, 148
    World War II and, 151
COVID-19 pandemic, 194–95
Cowden, Roland E., 38, 127, 163
Crimea War (2014), 192–93
crisis
    Cuban Missile Crisis (1962) and, 3, 49,
        64, 76, 83–86, 89–93, 111, 200, 209
    Iran hostage crisis (1979-81) and, 12,
        123–26, 128, 133, 202
Cuba. *See also* Cuban Missile Crisis (1962)
    Bay of Pigs invasion and, 44, 49, 76,
        87–90, 118, 200, 209
    Grenada and, 116–17
    US invasion of Dominican Republic
        (1965) and, 112–13
Cuban Missile Crisis (1962)
    anti-communism explanations
        regarding, 32, 93
    Bay of Pigs invasion and, 76
    Cuba's fears of US invasion and, 84
    emotional responses to, 90–91
    Executive Committee of the National
        Security Council (ExComm) and, 89

media coverage of, 85, 92–93
Monroe Doctrine and, 49, 92
national honor and, 19, 89–90
national humiliation and, 86, 146
national prestige and, 146
national security perceptions during,
   90–91
presidential rhetoric and, 64, 84, 90–91,
   111
proposed US airstrike on Cuba and,
   89–90
rally-round-the-flag effect and, 3, 49,
   76, 79, 83, 86, 90, 111, 119, 146, 200,
   209
removal of missiles from Cuba at end
   of, 93
Soviet Union and, 84–91, 116
United Nations and, 84
US naval blockade of Cuba and, 49,
   84–85, 89–92
US nuclear missiles in Turkey and, 84, 93
US superpower status and, 86, 89, 90, 92

Daniels, Harry, 147
Democratic People's Republic of Korea
   (DPRK). *See* North Korea
Democrats
   Cuban Missile Crisis and, 85, 89
   Gulf War and, 154
   Iraq War and, 11, 30, 34, 103, 183, 185
   September 11 attacks and, 39
Dethrow, Julie, 38–40
DiMaggio, Paul, 106–7
Dodd, Christopher, 154
Dominican Republic, 79, 83, 112–13, 200,
   209
Dukakis, Michael, 154

Egyptian Islamic Jihad, 131
Ehrenreich, Barbara, 62
Eisenhower, Dwight
   approval ratings of, 5, 199, 209
   Cuban Missile Crisis and, 85–86
   Lebanon intervention and, 68, 197, 199,
     209
   U-2 incident and, 5, 199, 209
El Salvador, 118, 137
emotions
   anger and, 35–36, 176–81, 215

anxiety and, 164, 174–79, 213
confidence, 170–71, 174–75, 178, 212
Cuban Missile Crisis and, 90–91
fear, 170–71, 177–78, 212, 215
hatred, 59, 105, 180
hope, 164, 177–78, 185, 210, 215
Iraq War and, 91, 164, 166, 170–73,
   176–81, 185, 212
national honor and, 6–7, 12–13, 19,
   34, 36, 39–41, 45, 47–48, 50, 81–82,
   104–6, 108, 111, 121–22, 132, 135,
   144, 163–64, 175–76, 181, 186, 191,
   194, 196, 213
national humiliation, 7, 13, 35, 45, 47–
   48, 50, 68, 76, 81, 101, 103, 107, 112,
   127, 132, 144, 146
rage and, 14, 58, 105, 135, 144, 180–81
rally-round-the-flag effect and, 35–36,
   47–51, 163–64, 170–76, 182
sadness, 170–71, 212
September 11 terrorist attacks and, 39,
   48–50, 91, 102, 163–64, 175–76, 180,
   186, 213–14
social movement mobilization and, 17
enemies
   Ayatolla Khomeini, 60, 122–23, 141
   Bin Laden and, 60, 128
   Castro and, 60, 87, 89, 113, 117
   Hussein and, 59, 63–64, 113, 117, 155–58,
     177–79
   Muammar Qaddafi, 60, 141
   Noriega and, 60, 94, 96, 100, 113, 117
   presidential rhetoric and, 63–64
   rally-round-the-flag effect and, 7, 40,
     55–62, 81, 104–5, 112, 117, 128, 139,
     141–42, 150, 152, 159–62, 177

fear, 170–71, 177–78, 212, 215
Feaver, Peter, 26–27
Feldman, Stanley, 30, 91, 177
Feschbach, Seymour, 65–66
Fisher, Louis, 110
Ford, Gerald, 36, 108–11, 201, 209
Formosa (Taiwan), 149
France, 4, 149, 192

Gardner, Martha and Michael, 38, 107, 163
Gay, Vance B., 109–10
Gaza War (2014), 12, 193

Gaza War (2021), 12
Gehr, Harmon M., 118
Gelpi, Peter D., 26–27
Germany, 4, 192
gratification effect, 30–31
Great Britain, 4, 62, 192
Greece, 148
Greece, Mike, 158
Greenfeld, Liah, 41–43
Grenada invasion (1983)
  anti-communism explanations
    regarding, 32, 117
  Beirut barracks bombing and, 117, 134
  Cuba and, 116–17
  international condemnations of, 118
  Iran hostage crisis and, 117, 119
  national prestige and, 116, 118
  presidential rhetoric and, 116–17
  rally-round-the-flag effect's absence
    following, 5, 74, 83, 116–19, 134, 137,
    203, 209
  Revolutionary Military Council and,
    116
  Soviet Union and, 116–17, 134
  St. George's School of Medicine students
    and, 116–17
  Vietnam Syndrome and, 116, 119
Gross, Kimberly, 106
Gulf War (1991)
  Cold War and, 146–47, 152
  Congressional authorization of, 15
  decision to deploy US troops and, 15
  Hill and Knowlton public relations firm
    and, 156–57
  Hussein and, 59, 63–64, 153, 155–59
  Korean War compared to, 146–47, 152,
    159
  media coverage of, 53, 154–59
  national honor and, 152–53, 158
  national prestige and, 147, 154, 158–59
  presidential rhetoric during, 59, 66, 145,
    152–53, 156
  rally-round-the-flag effect and, 3, 12,
    19–20, 36, 64, 74, 79, 145–47, 152,
    154, 158–59, 162, 192, 204, 210
  Saudi Arabia and, 153
  United Nations and, 146–47, 152–53,
    156, 160

  US domestic opposition to, 36
  US hostages in Iraq (1990) and, 157
  US military successes in, 12
  US superpower status as "leader of the
    free world" and, 19–20, 145–46, 152,
    158
  Vietnam Syndrome and, 145, 152, 159
  World War II compared to, 59, 153, 156

Hainan Island incident (2001), 134
Haiti, 109, 160–62, 205, 210
Hamas, 12
  hatred, 59, 105, 180
Hayes, Carlton, 65
Helms, Jesse, 94
Hezbollah, 95, 138–40
Hill and Knowlton public relations firm,
  156–57
Hitler, Adolph, 59, 148, 155–56
honor. See national honor
  hope, 164, 177–78, 185, 210, 215
Huddy, Leonie, 30, 91, 177
humiliation. See national humiliation
Hussein, Saddam
  chemical weapons used in Iran-Iraq
    War by, 155
  execution of, 60–61
  Gulf War and, 59, 63–64, 153, 155–59
  Hitler compared to, 59, 155–56
  Iraq War and, 55–56, 59, 63, 101, 103–4,
    106, 177–79
  terrorist organizations and, 101, 141
  as US enemy, 59, 63–64, 113, 117, 155–59,
    177–79
  US forces' capture (2003) of, 55–56, 211

Intrater, Samuel, 123–24
Iran, anti-American terrorism sponsored
  by, 141–42
Iran-Contra affair (1986)
  arms sales to Iran and, 95
  Central Intelligence Agency and, 95–96
  hostage releases in Lebanon and, 95
  illegal funding of Contra rebels in
    Nicaragua and, 96
  media coverage of, 96–97
  Noriega and, 97, 100
  Reagan and, 96–97

Iran hostage crisis (1979-81)
  civilians as target of, 121–22, 129–30, 135–36
  media coverage of, 123
  national honor and, 19, 124–25
  national humiliation and, 117, 119, 123–24, 139, 157
  national prestige and, 123
  presidential rhetoric and, 122–26, 128, 133
  rally-round-the-flag effect and, 36, 79, 121–24, 126, 128, 133, 135–36, 202, 209
  Reagan inauguration at the end of, 137
  United Nations and, 126
  US immigration restrictions against Iran and, 125–26
  US military deaths in rescue attempt (1980) and, 122, 209
  US oil embargo against Iran and, 124–26
Iran-Iraq War (1980s), 155
Iraq War (2003-12)
  Al Qaeda and, 101–2
  "Axis of Evil" and, 35, 101, 184
  casualty levels in, 26–27, 167, 169, 171–72, 211
  Central Intelligence Agency and, 101–3
  Democrats and, 11, 30, 34, 103, 183, 185
  emotional responses to, 91, 164, 166, 170–73, 176–81, 185, 212
  Hussein's capture (2003) and, 55–56, 211
  Hussein's execution (2006) and, 60–61
  Hussein's role as enemy in, 63
  media coverage of, 53, 102–4, 184
  national honor and, 35, 101, 104, 106–7, 177, 186, 212
  political polarization and, 55, 187
  presidential rhetoric and, 101, 103–4, 111
  public opinion regarding terrorism in the United States and, 167, 169, 171–72, 211
  rally-round-the-flag effect and, 3, 11–12, 20, 26–27, 35–36, 55–56, 61, 64, 79, 83, 101, 103–4, 106–8, 111, 119–20, 144, 165–73, 176, 180, 186–87, 206, 211

Republicans and, 11, 61, 183, 185
  September 11 terrorist attacks and, 101–7
  United Nations and, 184
  US domestic opposition to, 11, 30, 36, 103
  US military success during initial phases of, 167–68, 171–72, 182, 211
  War on Terror and, 55–56, 104, 107, 185, 195
  weapons of mass destruction and, 64, 101–4, 106, 184
Israel
  Gaza War (2014) and, 12, 193
  Gaza War (2021) and, 12
  Hezbollah and, 138–39
  Iran-Contra Affair and, 96
  rally-round-the-flag effect in, 4, 12, 192–93
  United States and, 130, 140
Iwo Jima, battle (1945) of, 39, 50

Jackson, Jesse, 154
Jacobson, Gary, 183
Jentleson, Bruce W., 28
Jezarian, Gregory, 107
Johnson, Lyndon, 79, 112–13, 200, 209

Kennedy, John F.
  approval ratings of, 3, 49, 79, 87, 90, 200, 209
  Bay of Pigs invasion and, 87–88, 90, 200, 209
  Cuban Missile Crisis and, 3, 49, 64, 76, 83–86, 89–93, 111, 200, 209
  presidential rhetoric of, 64, 84, 90–91, 111
  Republican criticism of, 85–87
Kennedy, Robert, 89–90
Kenya, US embassy bombing (1998) in, 121, 129–33, 205, 210
Khmer Rouge, 108
Khobar Towers bombing (Saudi Arabia, 1996), 134, 205, 210
Khomeini, Ayatollah, 60, 122–23, 141
Khrushchev, Nikita, 5, 84, 86, 93
Kim Il Sung, 150
Kohn, Hans, 65

Korean War
China and, 150
Cold War and, 146–50
Domino Theory and, 149
Gulf War compared to, 146–47, 152, 159
media coverage of, 150
national prestige and, 147
nuclear weapons and, 149
presidential rhetoric and, 148–50
rally-round-the-flag effect's absence in, 74, 147, 151, 162
Soviet Union and, 147–48, 150–51
United Nations and, 146–47, 149, 160
US death toll in, 149
US public opinion regarding, 147
World War II and, 151
Koslowski, Joseph, 118
Kosovo War (1999), 66, 205, 210
Kosterman, Rick, 65–66
Kraft, Joseph, 123
Kuwait
Gulf War and, 15, 59, 64, 146, 152, 155–58
Iraq's invasion (1990) of, 151, 153, 156, 160
media coverage of, 156–57
US embassy bombing (1983) in, 137

La Belle discotheque bombing (Berlin, 1986), 141
Lebanon
Amal Militia and, 138–39
Beirut Marine barracks attacks (1983) in, 117, 134, 137, 203, 209
Beirut US Embassy attacks (1983-84) in, 137
Hezbollah and, 95, 138–40
Palestine Liberation Organization and, 140
US hostages (1984-85) held in, 136–40
US intervention (1958) in, 68, 109, 197, 199
Lewis, Adrian, 148–49
Liberation Army, 130
Libya bombing (1986)
Libya's support for anti-American terrorism and, 141–42
Qaddafi's survival following, 143

rally-round-the-flag effect's absence following, 142–44, 210
Reagan approval ratings and, 80, 136–37, 142–43, 203, 210
Lockerbie terrorist attack (1988). See Pan Am Flight 103 terrorist attack (1988)

Mann, Michael, 33–34
Marcus, George E., 30
Mayaguez incident (1975)
Congress and, 110
national honor and, 19, 83, 108–11
national prestige and, 83, 108–11
presidential rhetoric and, 68, 83, 108, 110–11
rally-round-the-flag effect and, 10, 36, 68, 79, 83, 108–11, 119, 192, 201, 209
US military personnel killed in, 108
Vietnam War and, 108–11
media coverage
agenda-setting and, 28, 52
Bay of Pigs invasion and, 87–88
Cuban Missile Crisis and, 85, 92–93
framing effects and, 28, 52, 54
gratification effect and, 30–31
Gulf War and, 53, 154–59
Iran-Contra Affair and, 96–97
Iran hostage crisis and, 123
Iraq War and, 53, 102–4, 184
Korean War and, 150
"media events" and, 52–55, 85, 144
Noriega and, 98
political polarization and, 55
priming effects and, 28, 52
public awareness and, 52
rally-round-the-flag effect and, 7, 11–13, 40, 51–55, 183, 192
September 11 attacks and, 53–54, 127, 186, 214
US invasion of Dominican Republic (1965) and, 113
Meese, Ed, 96
Mill, John Stuart, 75
Monroe, James, 121
Monroe Doctrine, 49, 92
Morrow, Lance, 105
Mouffe, Chantal, 60
Mueller, John, 3–5, 8, 17–18

national honor
    definition of, 42
    Gulf War (1991) and, 152–53, 158
    initial stages of war and, 61
    Iran hostage crisis and, 19, 124–25
    Iraq War and, 35, 101, 104, 106–7, 177,
        186, 212
    Mayaguez incident and, 19, 83, 108–11
    national exceptionalism and, 65–67, 106
    Panama invasion and, 19, 98, 100
    rally-round-the-flag effect and, 6–7,
        12–13, 34, 36, 40–41, 45, 47–48, 50,
        81–82, 104–5, 108, 111, 121–22, 132,
        135, 144, 164, 175, 181, 186, 191, 194,
        196
    September 11 terrorist attacks and, 19,
        39–40, 104–6, 163, 176, 186, 213
    Vietnam War and, 19, 39–40, 104–6,
        163, 176, 186, 213
    War on Terror and, 35, 174–75
    Weber and, 41
national humiliation
    attacks against civilian targets and, 45,
        82
    Bay of Pigs invasion and, 49, 76, 88
    Cuban Missile Crisis (1962) and, 86, 146
    Iran hostage crisis (1979-81) and, 117,
        119, 123–24, 139, 157
    military defeats and, 45
    prospect theory and, 46
    rally-round-the-flag effect and, 7, 13,
        45, 47–48, 50, 68, 76, 81, 112, 132, 144
    retaliation and, 43, 50, 82
    September 11 terrorist attacks and, 35,
        101, 103, 107, 127, 146
    Vietnam War and, 27, 45, 108–11, 114,
        116, 119, 145, 152, 159
    war on drugs and, 98–99
nationalism
    cultural exceptionalism and, 43
    "dark side" of, 18
    illiberal nationalism and, 196
    Jacksonian nationalism and, 185
    Jeffersonian nationalism and, 185
    national exceptionalism and, 65–68
    political polarization and, 195–96
    rally-round-the-flag affect and, 17–18,
        175–76, 180–82, 184–85, 213–14

    solidarity and, 44
    symbolic value and, 41–42
national prestige
    Bay of Pigs invasion and, 44
    Beirut barracks attack (1983) and, 134
    Cuban Missile Crisis and, 146
    definition of, 42–43
    Grenada invasion and, 116, 118
    Gulf War (1991) and, 147, 154, 158–59
    Iran hostage crisis and, 123
    Korean War and, 147
    "leader of the free world" claims and,
        46, 50–51, 82
    Mayaguez incident (1975) and, 83,
        108–11
    national security challenges and, 44
    rally-round-the-flag effect and, 7, 34,
        42–43, 45, 47–48, 50, 63, 81–82, 111,
        121, 135, 144–46, 181, 191, 196
    relational aspects of, 43
    US invasion of Dominican Republic
        (1965), 112–13
    World War II and, 146
Netanyahu, Benjamin, 12, 193
Netherlands, 42
Nicaragua, 96–97
Nixon, Richard
    approval ratings of, 115–16, 201, 209
    Cambodia invasion (1970) and, 65,
        113–15, 201, 209
    war on drugs and, 94
Nolthenius, Bob, 110
Noriega, Manuel
    Central Intelligence Agency and, 100
    Iran-Contra Affair and, 97, 100
    media coverage of, 98
    as US enemy, 60, 94, 96, 100, 113, 117
    US invasion of Panama and, 99–100
    war on drugs and, 94, 97–100
North, Oliver, 97–98
North Atlantic treaty Organization
    (NATO), 66
North Korea, 133, 148–51, 159

Obama, Barack, 61, 207, 211
Odierno, Raymond, 56
Operation Desert Storm (1991). *See* Gulf
    War (1991)

Operation Mongoose (Cuba), 87
Operation Restore Hope (Somalia, 1992), 160, 204, 210
Operation Uphold Democracy (Haiti, 1994), 160–61, 205
Otto, Julie, 99–100

Paddock, Jo Ann R., 158
Palestinian Liberation Organization (PLO), 140
Panama invasion (1989)
    Iran-Contra Affair and, 94
    national honor and, 19, 98, 100
    presidential rhetoric and, 111
    rally-round-the-flag effect and, 3, 12, 36, 74, 78–79, 83, 94, 98–100, 111, 119, 204, 210
    US military successes in, 99, 145
    war on drugs and, 94, 99–100
Pan Am Flight 103 terrorist attack (1988), 136–37, 140–141, 203, 210
Patriot Act (2001), 16
Pearl Harbor attack (1941), 16, 27, 49, 105, 127, 180
Pentagon terrorist attack (2001), 102, 127, 130
Philippines, 149
Poindexter, John M., 97
Powell, Colin, 102
presidential rhetoric
    Bush (George H.W.) and, 59, 67, 99, 111, 145, 152–53, 156, 161
    Bush (George W.) and, 35, 101, 103–4, 111, 127–29, 186
    Cambodia invasion (1970) and, 65, 114–15
    Carter and, 123–26, 128, 133
    civilizational rhetoric and, 66
    Clinton and, 130–32
    Cuban Missile Crisis and, 64, 84, 90–91, 111
    enemy construction and, 63–64
    framing and, 68–69
    Grenada invasion (1983) and, 116–17
    Gulf War and, 59, 66, 145, 152–53, 156
    Iraq War (2003-12) and, 101, 103–4, 111
    Kennedy and, 64, 84, 90–91, 111
    Korean War and, 148–50

Mayaguez incident and, 68, 83, 108, 110–11
nation-affirming rhetoric and, 64–66, 68, 81, 108, 133, 135
national exceptionalism and, 65–68
New World Order doctrine and, 67
Panama invasion and, 111
rally-round-the-flag effect and, 7, 13, 63–69, 110–12, 119, 122, 126, 128–29, 133, 139
Reagan and, 12, 117, 134–36, 139, 141
September 11 attacks and, 122, 127–28, 186
Truman and, 148–52
US embassy bombings in Africa (1997) and, 131–32
Vietnam War and, 117
war on drugs and, 99
World Trade Center attack (1993) and, 130–31
prospect theory, 45–46

Qaddafi, Muammar, 141–43

Rafsanjani, Hashemi, 139
rage, 14, 58, 105, 135, 144, 180–81
rally-round-the-flag effect
    Afghanistan War and, 3, 144, 165, 173, 176, 206, 211
    aggressive war making policies and, 14–15
    attacks on US civilians and, 76, 81, 121–22, 129–33, 135–36, 139
    attacks on US military personnel and, 133–35
    audience cost and, 12, 62
    Australia and, 194, 196
    civil liberties restrictions and, 15–16
    COVID-19 pandemic and, 194–95
    Cuban Missile Crisis and, 3, 49, 76, 79, 83, 86, 90, 111, 119, 146, 200, 209
    definition and measurement of, 8–9, 77–81
    elite consensus and, 11–13, 24–25, 28–31, 36, 186–87
    emotions and, 35–36, 47–51, 163–64, 170–76, 182
    enemies and, 7, 40, 55–62, 81, 104–5, 112, 117, 128, 139, 141–42, 150, 152, 159–62, 177

event-level mechanisms and, 7, 10–13, 108, 110

Germany and, 4, 192

Gulf War and, 3, 12, 19–20, 36, 64, 74, 79, 145–47, 152, 154, 158–59, 162, 192, 204, 210

individual-level mechanisms and, 6–7, 20, 47

Iran hostage crisis and, 36, 79, 121–24, 126, 128, 133, 135–36, 202, 209

Iraq War and, 3, 11–12, 20, 26–27, 35–36, 55–56, 61, 64, 79, 83, 101, 103–4, 106–8, 111, 119–20, 144, 165–73, 176, 180, 186–87, 206, 211

Israel and, 4, 12, 192–93

manipulation of threat approach and, 24–25, 33–35

Mayaguez incident and, 10, 36, 68, 79, 83, 108–11, 119, 192, 201, 209

media coverage and, 7, 11–13, 40, 51–55, 183, 192

multivariate explanations of, 74–76

national honor and, 6–7, 12–13, 34, 36, 40–41, 45, 47–48, 50, 81–82, 104–5, 108, 111, 121–22, 132, 135, 144, 164, 175, 181, 186, 191, 194, 196

national humiliation and, 7, 13, 45, 47–48, 50, 68, 76, 81, 112, 132, 144

nationalism and, 17–18, 175–76, 180–82, 184–85, 213–14

national prestige and, 7, 34, 42–43, 45, 47–48, 50, 63, 81–82, 111, 121, 135, 144–46, 181, 191, 196

necessary conditions and, 10–13, 62, 191

negative cases and, 5–6, 19, 36, 74, 83, 111–20, 129–35, 139–44, 160–62

optimism bias and, 14

origins of the term, 3

partisan identity and, 10, 181–82, 212

policymaking options expanded by, 13–14, 195

political awareness levels and, 9–10

political polarization and, 187, 196

presidential rhetoric and, 7, 13, 63–69, 110–12, 119, 122, 126, 128–29, 133, 139

rationalist approach and, 17, 24–31, 41, 143, 167, 172, 183

realist approach and, 24–25, 31–34, 104, 110, 118

security-concerned public approach and, 24–25, 32–33

September 11 terrorist attacks and, 3, 10–12, 20, 27, 33, 36, 38–40, 48–50, 79, 105–6, 121–22, 127–29, 133, 135–36, 146, 163, 165–66, 173, 176, 180, 182, 184, 186–87, 192, 206, 211, 213–14

small increases in presidential approval compared to, 73–74, 77, 79

sufficient conditions and, 6–8, 13, 76

support for US troops and, 120

United Kingdom and, 4, 192

United Nations authorization and, 160–61

US military action as an analytical variable and, 76

US status as "leader of the free world" and, 145–46

variation in magnitude of, 192

variation in national cultures and, 193–94

War on Terror and, 11, 165, 184

World War II and, 27, 50, 146, 148, 151

Randolph, Philip, 147–48

rationalism

bounded rationality and, 26

casualty levels and, 26–27

cost-benefit analysis and, 24–26, 167

elite consensus argument and, 24–25, 28–31, 36

initial phases of war and, 26–28

negative cases and, 36

partisanship and, 183

rational public approach and, 26, 143, 171–72

Reagan, Nancy, 95

Reagan, Ronald

approval ratings of, 5, 70, 96, 117, 136–37, 142–43, 203, 209–10

Beirut barracks attack and, 134–35, 203, 209

Congressional elections (1986) and, 94

Grenada invasion and, 5, 116–19, 134, 137, 209

inaugural address (1981) of, 136

Reagan, Ronald (*cont.*)
  Iran-Contra Affair and, 96–97
  Kuwait embassy bombing (1983) and, 137
  Libya bombing (1986) and, 80, 136–37, 141–43, 203, 210
  Panama and, 94, 97–98
  Pan Am Flight 103 terrorist attack and, 136–37, 140–141, 203, 210
  presidential rhetoric of, 12, 117, 134–36, 139, 141
  TWA Flight 847 hijacking and, 136, 138–41, 203, 209
  war on drugs and, 94–96, 98, 100
realism
  manipulation of threat approach and, 24–25, 33–35
  national security emphasis in, 24–25, 32–33, 41, 104, 110, 118
  security-concerned public approach and, 24–25, 32–33, 36
  state competition and, 31
Reifler, Jason, 26–27
Republicans
  Cuban Missile Crisis and, 85–87
  elections (1986) and, 94–95
  Iraq War and, 11, 61, 183, 185
  war on drugs and, 94
Rice, Condoleezza, 103
Rome airport attack (1985), 137, 141
Roosevelt, Franklin D., 27, 146, 151
Root, George Fredrick, 3
Ross, Andrew A., 179–80
Rudd, Kevin, 194, 196
Russia, 4, 192–93

al-Sabah, Saud Nasir, 157
  sadness, 170–71, 212
Sandinistas, 96–97
San Salvador terrorist attack (1985), 137
Saudi Arabia, 134, 153, 155, 210
Saunders, Harold, 124
Scheff, Thomas, 47
Schultz, George, 143
Schultz, Kenneth, 62
September 11 terrorist attacks (2001)
  Al Qaeda as perpetrator of, 127–28
  anti-Arab and anti-Muslim attacks following, 16

  civilians as target of, 121–22, 130, 133, 135–36
  death toll in, 127
  elite consensus following, 11, 186–87
  emotional responses to, 39, 48–50, 91, 102, 163–64, 175–76, 180, 186, 213–14
  Iraq War and, 101–7
  media coverage of, 53–54, 127, 186, 214
  national honor and, 19, 39–40, 104–6, 163, 176, 186, 213
  national humiliation and, 35, 101, 103, 107, 127, 146
  national prestige and, 146
  national security explanations regarding, 33
  Pearl Harbor attack compared to, 49, 105, 127, 180
  Pentagon terrorist attack and, 102, 127, 130
  presidential rhetoric and, 122, 127–28, 186
  rally-round-the-flag effect following, 3, 10–12, 20, 27, 33, 36, 38–40, 48–50, 79, 105–6, 121–22, 127–29, 133, 135–36, 146, 163, 165–66, 173, 176, 180, 182, 184, 186–87, 192, 206, 211, 213–14
  United Flight 93 attack and, 49, 129
  War on Terror and, 11, 195
  World Trade Center attack and, 38–39, 102, 126–27, 130
Shah of Iran (Mohammad Reza Pahlavi), 122
Shelton, Rollin, 118
Simon, Jeffrey, 143
Smith, Michael C., 124
Smith, Tom, 90–91
social identity theory, 57
Somalia, 160–62, 204, 210
South Korea, 148–50
Soviet Union. *See also* Cold War
  collapse (1991) of, 146
  Cuban Missile Crisis and, 84–91, 116
  Grenada and, 117, 134
  Korean War and, 147–48, 150–51
  Truman Doctrine and, 148
  U-2 incident (1960) and, 5

US air force engagements (1953) with, 76, 209
Stalin, Joseph, 148
Stethem, Robert Dean, 138–39
Sudan, US bombing (1998) of, 131–32, 210
Switzerland, 42

Taiwan, 149
Tanzania, US embassy bombing (1998) in, 121, 129–33, 205, 210
Tenet, George T., 102–3
terrorism. *See also* War on Terror; *specific attacks and organizations*
  Hussein and, 101, 141
  Iran's sponsorship of, 141–42
  US public opinion regarding threat from, 167, 169, 171–75, 211
Tet Offensive (1968), 133–34, 200, 209
Truman, Harry S.
  approval ratings of, 148, 151, 198, 209
  Korean War and, 147–52, 159, 198, 209
  nuclear weapons and, 149
  presidential rhetoric and, 148–52
  Truman Doctrine and, 148, 151
  World War II and, 148
Trump, Donald, 208, 211
Turkey, 84, 93, 148
Turner, Richard, 100
TWA Flight 847 hijacking (1985), 136, 138–41, 203, 209

U-2 incident (1960), 5, 199, 209
Ukraine, 193
United Flight 93 terrorist attack (2001), 49, 129
United Kingdom, 4, 62, 192
United Nations
  appeals to US leadership by, 7, 46, 76, 81–82, 161
  Cuban Missile Crisis and, 84
  Gulf War and, 146–47, 152–53, 156, 160
  Iran hostage crisis and, 126
  Iraq War and, 102, 184
  Korean War and, 146–47, 149, 160
  Operation Restore Hope (Somalia, 1992) and, 160
  Operation Uphold Democracy (Haiti, 1994) and, 160–61

Security Council of, 82, 84, 126, 142, 147, 152, 160–61
United States
  as "leader of the free world," 7, 44, 46, 50–51, 66, 70, 76, 81–82, 86, 113, 145–48, 152, 158
  UN appeals to, 7, 46, 76, 81–82, 161
US House of Representatives and US Senate. *See* Congress
USS Pueblo attack (1968), 133, 200, 209

Vienna airport attack (1985), 137, 141
Vietnam War
  Cambodia invasion (1970) and, 65, 83, 113–14
  national honor and, 114–15
  national humiliation and "Vietnam Syndrome" following, 27, 45, 108–11, 114, 116, 119, 145, 152, 159
  presidential rhetoric and, 117
  Tet Offensive and, 133–34, 200, 209
  US domestic opposition to, 120
  US withdrawal from South Vietnam (1975) and, 109
  Vietnamization strategy in, 114

War on Terror
  Bin Laden's killing and, 61
  civil liberties restrictions in United States and, 16
  declaration (2001) of, 128
  grand conflict rhetoric and, 66
  Iraq War and, 55–56, 104, 107, 185, 195
  national honor and, 35, 174–75
  political polarization and, 195–96
  rally-round-the-flag effect and, 11, 165, 184
  September 11 terrorist attacks and, 11, 195
  US perceptions about terrorist threats and, 173–75, 177–79, 182–83
Weber, Max, 41, 45
Willer, Robb, 104
Wilson, Woodrow, 67, 145
Windle, Jeffrey, 109
World Trade Center attack (1993), 121, 129–31, 133, 210
World Trade Center attack (2001), 38–39, 102, 126–27, 129–30

World War II
  Balkan front in, 59
  Gulf War compared to, 59, 153, 156
  Iwo Jima, battle (1945) of, 39, 50
  Japanese American internment during, 16
  media coverage and, 151
  Pearl Harbor attack (1941) and, 16, 27,
    49, 105, 127, 180

rally-round-the-flag effect and, 27, 50,
    146, 148, 151
  Roosevelt and, 151
  Truman and, 148
  US death toll in, 151
  US national prestige and, 146

al-Zawahiri, Ayman, 131